THE APPRECIATIVE INQUIRY SUMMIT

D0356954

THE
APPRECIATIVE
INQUIRY SUMMIT

A PRACTITIONER'S GUIDE FOR LEADING LARGE-GROUP CHANGE

James D. Ludema
Diana Whitney
Bernard J. Mohr
Thomas J. Griffin

BK®

BERRETT-KOEHLER PUBLISHERS, INC.
San Francisco

Berrett-Koehler Publishers, Inc.
235 Montgomery Street, Suite 650
San Francisco, CA 94104-2916
Tel: (415)288-0260   Fax: (415) 362-2512   www.bkconnection.com

Ordering Information
Quantity sales. Special discounts are available on quantity purchases by corporations, associations, and others. For details, contact the "Special Sales Department" at the Berrett-Koehler address above.
Individual sales. Berrett-Koehler publications are available through most bookstores. They can also be ordered direct from Berrett-Koehler: Tel: (800) 929-2929; Fax: (802) 864-7626; www.bkconnection.com
Orders for college textbook/course adoption use. Please contact Berrett-Koehler: Tel: (800) 929-2929; Fax: (802) 864-7626.
Orders by U.S. trade bookstores and wholesalers. Please contact Publishers Group West, 1700 Fourth Street, Berkeley, CA 94710. Tel: (510) 528-1444; Fax (510) 528-3444.

Berrett-Koehler and the BK logo are registered trademarks of Berrett-Koehler Publishers, Inc. Printed in the United States of America

Berrett-Koehler books are printed on long-lasting acid-free paper. When it is available, we choose paper that has been manufactured by environmentally responsible processes. These may include using trees grown in sustainable forests, incorporating recycled paper, minimizing chlorine in bleaching, or recycling the energy produced at the paper mill.

Project Manager: Susie Yates, Publication Services, Inc.
Supervising Editor: Dave Mason, Publication Services, Inc.
Design: Kelly J. Applegate, Publication Services, Inc.
Layout: Michael Tarleton, Publication Services, Inc.

Library of Congress Cataloging-in-Publication Data
The Appreciative Inquiry Summit: a practitioner's guide for leading large-group change/ by James D. Ludema. . . [et al.].
    p. cm.
Includes bibliographical references and index.
ISBN 1-57675-248-8
    I. Organizational change—Handbooks, manuals, etc. 2. Management—Employee participation—Handbooks, manuals, etc. 3. Organizational effectiveness—Handbooks, manuals, etc. I. Ludema, James D., 1957-

HD58.8.A729 2003
658.4'02—dc21

                                              2003045221

First Edition
      08 07 06 05 04 03   10 9 8 7 6 5 4 3 2 1

CONTENTS

FOREWORD

David L. Cooperrider

Excuse my overflowing excitement for this book.

Just recently I was part of an extraordinary Appreciative Inquiry (AI) Summit—exactly the kind this book is all about—with the one of the largest trucking companies in the United States. It was a whole-system strategic planning meeting—not just with the top ten executives of the company, but with over 300 truck drivers, dock workers, senior executives, teamsters, managers, and customers coming together across all boundaries to co-create their business plan. A *Forbes* business writer surprised Roadway by asking if she could participate in the three-day event. The "AI Summit" would engage and involve every kind of stakeholder at the Winston-Salem, North Carolina, terminal and she, Joanne Gordon, had never seen anything like it. We explained to Joanne how Roadway was doing something nobody else in the industry was doing, and how Roadway had already successfully piloted AI Summits at 5 of their 300 terminals around the country. It was part of their "Breakthrough Leadership Program" designed by the Weatherhead School of Management at Case Western Reserve University.

Prior to the summit the *Forbes* journalist was quite convinced that the session was going to be some kind of large-group "cheer-leading" or "therapy" session—not the real thing of joint business planning. She even talked about it that way. So she arrived at the summit asking tough, skeptical questions. Here are the opening lines in the feature story she later wrote: "Teamsters and managers writing business plans together? This is how James Staley hopes to save Roadway Express from Consolidated Freightways' fate. It was a scene not often seen in the history of labor-management relations."

As the article unfolded, the reporter's skepticism began to soften. She even sounded shocked at the level of business capability and passion demonstrated, for example, by the dock workers and drivers. It was clearly hard for this writer to let go of preconceptions (for example, how can a large group of hundreds come together to do the real business planning?), but, fortunately, she was involved firsthand. She then wrote descriptively about what she saw:

> A team of short-haul drivers came up with 12 cost-cutting and revenue-generating ideas. One of the most ambitious: Have each of the 32 drivers in Winston-Salem deliver just one more customer order each hour. Using management data, the drivers calculated the 288 additional daily shipments, at average revenue of $212 each and with a 6% margin, would generate just about $1 million a year of operating profit.

Still cautious, she offered her view that improvements of this kind were "unlikely." But the gloomy prediction was soon shattered. At its analyst meeting several months later, Roadway Corporation reported that revenues for the sixteen weeks constituting the company's fourth quarter were $1,074,110,000—up 25.7 percent compared with revenues of $854,640,000 for the same period the previous year.

The company reported fourth-quarter income from continuing operations of $25,923,000, or $1.37 per share (diluted), compared with $13,477,000, or $0.72 per share (diluted), from the year before. Operating ratios improved significantly, and according to later analysis, the employee-driven improvements translated into $17 million in additional revenue for the year and $7 million annual profit. This exciting breakthrough was a result of the combined efforts across all 300 terminals of the 27,000-employee system. But here is the telling fact: Of the top 5 terminals leading the company in gains, all were sites that had worked as organizational effectiveness sites using appreciative inquiry, and 3 of the 5 had conducted large-scale AI Summits, just like the kind this book talks about. Although this story is still in its early phases, the emerging impact appears enormous.

The AI Summit is the most business relevant, powerful, and humanly significant way of bringing people together I have ever been part of, and this book, for the first time, outlines in the most practical way how to design, guide, and lead an AI Summit. Everything you need is right here: the stories, the models, the design templates, the guidelines, and the key concepts. Most important, however, this volume conveys a special spirit. The time is right, say Jim Ludema, Diana Whitney, Bernard Mohr, and Tom Griffin, for celebrating what human beings are capable of achieving together and for advancing a "positive revolution in change."

Part of my overflowing excitement for this book comes from years of knowing and collaborating with each of the authors. Not only are they individually first-rate human beings, but they live what they write about and have put their ideas to the test in large and small corporations, in communities, and with international organizations working on global issues of environmental sustainability, peace, and human health. As I look back on high-point moments in my professional life, many of them have been with the very authors of this volume.

With Jim Ludema, I had the very privileged place of serving as his dissertation chairman when he built his seminal theory about the power of hope, inspiration, and joy to energize extraordinary performance in people and in organizations. With Diana Whitney, there were high-wire moments of daring creativity with GTE and with the worldwide effort to help lift up something akin to a UN among the world's diverse religions—the United Religions Initiative.

With Bernard Mohr, there were the weeks we spent together creating and re-creating the successful large-group designs for the First International Conference on Appreciative Inquiry, held in Baltimore. It was held just weeks after 9/11 and helped give birth to a worldwide appreciative inquiry searching for exemplar stories of "Business as an Agent of World Benefit." With Tom Griffin, there is my deep admiration for his pioneering work with appreciative inquiry at U.S. Cellular and for his groundbreaking dissertation research at Benedictine University on the role of wholeness in large-group processes.

So I know it firsthand: This book has a special strength and integrity to it. It emerges through the combined talents of four people who many would agree are among the best in the rapidly growing field of appreciative, strength-based approaches to inquiry and change.

Jim, Diana, Bernard, and Tom have written a wonderfully clear book that should soon be in the libraries of anyone interested not only in appreciative inquiry but in any kind of strategic change. As the story of Roadway Express and many others shared in this volume demonstrate, the AI Summit can have a tremendous impact. But more than that, at least for me, it is a method that consistently brings out the very best in human beings and continuously expands my sense of hope. When people experience the *wholeness* of the systems they live and work in—when we have the courage and trust to bring together people at every level to connect to the "positive core" of their past, present, and future capacities combined—something magical happens.

This book can help your business. The AI Summit is not difficult. All it takes is a belief in collective human capacity and a desire to challenge conventional patterns of change that continue to fragment and isolate us from one another. As the authors attest, the AI Summit—bringing hundreds of people together interactively for three to five days—requires at least a little dose of courage.

A CEO I recently worked with at first rolled his eyes at the idea of a 500-person organizational summit. But he explored the idea further by talking to other leaders who had experience with the approach. Six months later the company did its first AI Summit and his comment to me at the end, with a twinkle in his eye, was: "I don't know what all the fuss was about."

Enjoy this book. Let it help you reduce "the fuss." And then experience how appreciation, inquiry, and the power of wholeness combine to bring out the best in organizational and interhuman capacity.

David L. Cooperrider
Weatherhead School of Management
Case Western Reserve University
Cleveland, Ohio
January 2003

PREFACE

Every once in a while a client or a colleague will ask a question that surprises us. This happened a couple years ago when Gina Hinrichs, an internal OD consultant at John Deere Harvester Works, came to us with the following story. "I've used appreciative inquiry for years with individuals and teams, and I've seen impressive results. But now I want to take it to the level of the whole system. Our new Business Unit Leader for header manufacturing, Andy Gianulis, wants to boost our competitiveness by reducing costs, improving quality, and speeding up new product cycle time. And he wants to do it *immediately*. My question is: What would an Appreciative Inquiry Summit process look like if it were perfectly designed to produce fast bottom-line business results in a large unionized manufacturing plant?"

Wow, what a question! Over the years, we had used the Appreciative Inquiry Summit (AI Summit) approach with many organizations in a variety of applications, but nothing quite like this. The plant had been in operation for over seventy years. Many employees had been working together for more than twenty years. Processes were highly routinized and patterns of relationship were deeply engrained. Was it really reasonable to expect this plant to produce significant, lasting change in the mere three to five days of a typical AI Summit? How would we involve everyone? How would we come to agreement on a clear purpose and task? How would we create conditions of cooperation and trust? How would we get our arms around the enormous complexity of designing, manufacturing, and marketing the precisely engineered header products?[1] It was an exciting but daunting challenge!

Nevertheless, with the full and courageous support of Andy, the union leaders, and John Munn of Product Engineering, and along with Gina and a group of her highly skilled "process pros," we took the whole system (wage employees, management, customers, suppliers, dealers, and representatives from corporate—about 250 people in all) off site for five days and worked through the appreciative inquiry 4-D process.[2] By the end of the week, the group had launched ten cross-functional strategic initiatives to decrease costs, increase quality, improve product cycle time, and enhance working relationships.

As a result of the AI Summit, the plant experienced many successes, including a significant reduction in product cycle time. This provided John Deere with an immediate savings of more than $3 million and projected earnings and millions more in new market share. But perhaps the most significant results were the transformed relationships, particularly between labor and management. Many participants shared that this was the first time that they had the opportunity to sit down as equals with management to plan for the future. They talked about how searching for the best in themselves and others allowed them to feel validated and gave them a whole new perception of the gifts, strengths, and humanity of their colleagues. They said that in the summit they learned more and made more progress in five days then they typically do in five years. One participant said that this was the first time in over twenty years that he had hope for the future.

BENEFITS OF THE AI SUMMIT

The John Deere case is just one example of the Appreciative Inquiry Summit methodology in action, but its results are becoming increasingly familiar. We have used the AI Summit with dozens of organizations in every sector of society, and over and again we see an immediate and sustained boost in levels of cooperation, innovation, and bottom-line results. When we ask ourselves what makes AI Summits so much more effective than traditional approaches to change, six factors keep popping up:

- **They are quicker.** They accelerate change because they produce a "critical mass" of involvement throughout the organizational system. They speed up the change process by directly engaging the entire organizational system in envisioning, designing, and implementing the change.

- **They build organizational confidence.** AI Summits begin by inviting people into a deep exploration of what we call the organization's "positive core"[3]—its greatest strengths, assets, capacities, capabilities, values, traditions, practices, accomplishments, and so on. Access to the positive core bolsters courage and fuels bold innovation throughout the system.

- **They provide immediate and broad access to information.** In any organization, knowledge and information is widely distributed, and people at multiple levels throughout the organization have the information most critical to organizational success. AI Summits, by involving a broad spectrum of people, allow access to a wide range of ideas and information that enrich organizational learning and spur inventiveness throughout the system.

- **They promote a "total organization mindset."** In order to support intelligently the success of the entire enterprise, organizational members need a clear understanding of how their individual contribution fits into the big picture. Rather than relying on the slow and disjointed process of passing this information up and down the chain of command, AI Summits create a forum in which organizational members gain a direct and immediate connection to the "logic of the whole."

- **They result in inspired action.** As Marvin Weisbord writes, people support what they help to create.[4] When everyone is involved in the innovation process, it is implemented with more passion and less resistance. It is not necessary to tell, sell, or force change on organization members.

- **They provide the means to sustain positive change.** For any change to have an enduring impact on an organization, it must be built into the organization's "social architecture"—its systems, structures, strategies, and culture. The AI Summit process supports and energizes enduring change by involving organizational members in designing high-performing systems.

PURPOSE OF THIS BOOK

The purpose of this book is to invite you into the experiment with us, to spark ideas that will help you bring the principles and practices of "whole-system positive change" to your organizations and communities. In this book we provide a framework for understanding and applying the Appreciative Inquiry Summit as a methodology for positive change. We discuss the theories of organization change and large-group processes on which the AI Summit is based; we walk you step by step through the process of planning, conducting, and following up on an AI Summit; we provide a series of case studies of the AI Summit process in action; and we share essential success factors—what we have learned in our work with AI and large-group processes that contributes to success in large-scale efforts.

This book is written primarily for practitioners (internal and external organization change consultants) who want a practical guide to help them plan, design, and facilitate AI Summits. It is also useful for executives, leaders, and managers in organizations who want a primer on the summit methodology and who want to use it to support a process of positive change in their organizations. Finally, it will be of value as a textbook in undergraduate, graduate, and professional programs that offer courses on organization change, appreciative inquiry, or large-group interventions.

To make it easy to use, we have written the book in a conversational style and have included many tables, illustrations, case examples, and practical tools (designs, worksheets, etc.). Our highest hope is that the book becomes a regular companion and good friend to practitioners, a resource to which they turn regularly as they explore the exciting frontier of the AI Summit methodology.

If you are new to appreciative inquiry or new to the field of organization change, you may be wondering, "Is this book for me, or is the AI Summit a more advanced topic?" Our answer is "Yes!" Certainly, to lead an AI Summit requires an understanding of appreciative inquiry and of basic organization change processes. Consequently, we have designed this book to include both an introduction to appreciative inquiry and an explanation of the core organization change principles that give the AI Summit methodology its power. It is an excellent starting point for further exploration.

WHAT YOU WILL FIND IN THIS BOOK

The book is divided into five sections designed to help you understand and implement the AI Summit process.

Part I, "Understanding the AI Summit," provides an introduction to AI and to the AI Summit methodology (Chapter 1), an overview of the AI Summit process from start to finish (Chapter 2), and ten essential conditions for AI Summit success (Chapter 3).

Part II, "Before the Summit," gives an in-depth look at how to prepare for an AI Summit. In our experience, more time is spent in planning for a summit than in actually conducting it. This section covers three important phases involved in getting ready: building sponsorship for the AI Summit (Chapter 4), planning it (Chapter 5), and creating a powerful design for it (Chapter 6).

Part III, "During the Summit," walks you through the process of conducting an AI summit, using the appreciative inquiry 4-D model. It provides descriptions of the discovery (Chapter 7), dream (Chapter 8), design (Chapter 9), and destiny (Chapter 10) phases. This is followed by a discussion of the art and practice of facilitating an AI Summit (Chapter 11).

Part IV, "After the Summit," offers a variety of approaches for implementing and supporting the changes that are initiated in the summit process. It includes specific ways to follow up immediately after the summit (Chapter 12) and our dream of the appreciative organization (Chapter 13).

Part V, the Appendix, contains a sample participant workbook. It includes a number of practical tools and worksheets you can use or adapt for your own applications.

ACKNOWLEDGMENTS

We could hold an enormous AI Summit just to thank the many people whose contributions have made this book possible. The innovative research, practice, and theory building by members the Department of Organizational Behavior at Case Western Reserve University laid the foundation for the AI Summit. We are deeply grateful to our colleagues David Cooperrider, Suresh Srivastva, and Ronald Fry for their willingness to invent new ways of working and their courage to put forth appreciative inquiry as a bold, positive approach to organization change. We wish to thank David especially for his deep and abiding commitment to open, affirmative, inclusive ways of knowing, being, and organizing. He is a true visionary who "lives the change he wants to see in the world."

Thousands of people in organizations around the world have experimented with appreciative inquiry in large groups and have aided in the development of the AI Summit process. Specifically, we would like to thank our clients who generously allowed us to include their stories in this book. They include Andy Gianulis at John Deere Harvester Works; Phil Gray at McDonald's; Tom White at GTE; Judy Fantham, Tony Burman, and Harold Redekopp at the Canadian Broadcasting Corporation; Dave Erich at British Airways; Rick Pellett at Hunter Douglas; Neil Samuels and Kenny Lang at BP's Upstream Technology Group; Bob Stiller at Green Mountain Coffee Roasters; Monique Boudrais and Robert LeGris at the Department of National Defense, Canada; John Cwiklik at the

Santa Ana Star Hotel and Casino; Dan Plauda, Penni Gebke, and Melanie Murphy at the Illinois Credit Union League; Michael Landgarten and Shari Goupil at Bob's Clam Hut; Bishop Bill Swing and Charles Gibb at the United Religions Initiative; Andy Ryskamp at CRWRC; Paul Wilson and Albert Vermeulen at Park Center; John Sundquist and Stan Slade at American Baptist International Ministries; David Jewel, Terri Petersen, Malcolm Fraser, and Frank Szuch at the Organization Development Network of Chicago (ODNC); Joy Salmon at the Nevada Child Welfare Agency; Kathleen Davis at Lovelace Healthcare System; Sr. Marilyn Jean Runkel at Sacred Heart–Griffin High School; Tom Morrill at Fairview Elementary School; and Suzanne Moratta at the West Springfield Public School System.

Colleagues who have shared stories, insights, and wisdom for this book include Frank Barrett, David Cooperrider, Eileen Conlon, Keith Cox, Ron Fry, Jim "Gus" Gustafson, Jen Hetzel, Gina Hinrichs, Claudia Liebler, Rodrigo Loures, Ada Jo Mann, Mike Mantel, Debbie Morris, Ravi Prahdan, Cheryl Richardson, Judy Rodgers, Bob Roberts, Marge Schiller, Tony Silbert, Jackie Stavros, Amanda Trosten-Bloom, Ilene Wasserman, and Susan Wood. Warm thanks to each of you.

We are grateful also to the fantastic team at Berrett-Koehler Publishers who made this book possible. In particular, we want to thank Steve Piersanti, Jeevan Sivasubramaniam, and Rick Wilson. They were tremendously supportive the whole way and repeatedly helped us to elevate our vision for the book to higher and higher levels. We are also grateful to Frank Basler, Jim Evers, Peggy Holman, Lisa McLeod, Perviz Randeria, and Alis Valencia for their insightful reviews and helpful comments on the first draft. Finally, our thanks go to Susan Yates and her colleagues at Publication Services in Champaign, Illinois, for the outstanding job they did on the copyediting and layout of the book.

From Jim

In addition to those listed above, I want to thank my colleagues at Benedictine University for their support and for their commitment to create a dynamic learning environment in which the best of theory and practice can be brought together to advance innovations like the AI Summit. Special thanks go to President Bill Carroll, former Provost Mary Daly Lewis, Dean John Cicero, Fr. David Turner,

Fr. Philip Timko, Peter Sorensen, Ram Tenkasi, Therese Yaeger, and Vera Lukas.

I also want to thank my wife, Beverlee, and our children, Christina, Michael, and Nicole, for their constant encouragement throughout the writing process. Their love, care, sense of humor, and engagement in the world were an enduring source of inspiration for me. I dedicate this book to my parents, Kenneth and Johanna Ludema, who taught me at a young age the importance of finding the best in others and leveraging strengths to build a better world.

From Diana

Much of what is written in this book comes naturally to me. For this I want to thank my family of origin; my children, Brian and Shara Kaplin; and my spiritual family. The first whole system any of us knows is our family. Growing up in a big Italian family was great preparation for working with large groups. Thank you to my extended family and especially to my brothers Louis Cocciolone and Stephan Cocciolone. I dedicate this book to my brother Fredrick Cocciolone, 1953–1985.

In addition, I want to thank my sister Amanda Trosten-Bloom and my partner Maury Calvert for their ever-present love and support. May Peace Prevail on Earth.

From Bernard

For years I wondered about the influence of my parents' careers on my own. I now increasingly suspect that my mother's lifelong passion as a professional artist has helped me search for ways to engage people in the creation of vibrant images of possibility for themselves in their communities and organizations. My father's deep commitment, as an intellectual and teacher extraordinaire, to the search for meaning through the exploration of language was, of course, a supremely nourishing platform for my own intrigue with how we speak our world into being. For this, all their sacrifices and more, I am forever grateful.

I also want to thank my children, Alexandra and Joshua, who each day fill my life with the elixir of discovery and potential of yet-to-be-created futures. And finally, thanks to Karen, without whose support, understanding, and encouragement none of this would have been possible.

From Tom

I would like to express my deepest appreciation to my wife and best friend, Mary. She has provided me with the lasting emotional, moral, and encouraging support needed to complete this project. It is to the memory of my mother Catherine (Kay) that I dedicate this book. She taught me many things growing up, but the most valuable was the importance of *going the extra mile in everything that you do*. Many people went the extra mile in order for us to complete this book, so a special thanks must go to all the AI practitioners who have contributed in large and small ways.

PART I

UNDERSTANDING
THE AI SUMMIT

Tony Burman, the Canadian Broadcasting Corporation's (CBC) chief journalist and executive director of CBC Television News—an 1,100-person global unit responsible for news and current affairs programming—wanted to create a vibrant culture of change. He had already begun a process of renewing his department through working committees. But he wanted a change movement that was more inclusive, more pervasive and ongoing. Tony decided to hold an AI Summit. He believed that bringing together reporters, cameramen, journalists, producers, managers, and hosts to invent new ways of collecting, editing, producing, and evaluating the news was the way to engage and ignite employees.

Some were skeptical about bringing together staff without a clear vision of the end game by senior management. Some journalists were wary of a process that adopted an affirmative approach. But Tony, his team, and the Learning and Development Department were confident about the summit's positive potential. Following the three days of intense dialogue, debate, creative dreaming, invention, and planning, they could not have been more pleased. The group presented their initiatives to the Executive Vice President of Television, Harold Redekopp. Harold responded, "In all my years at CBC I've been trying to explain what deep organization transformation is really about. This is the first time I have really seen it in practice—we have done it and we should all be very proud of ourselves."

As the CBC case illustrates, the AI Summit process creates conditions to enable deep transformation in people, organizations, and communities. It does this by bringing members of the "whole system" together to learn from their strengths, envision new possibilities, and co-create the future. It is based on the simple yet profound assumption that human communities enable extraordinary performance when they combine and develop the capacities of every member in service of the whole.

The first part of this book provides a brief overview of how and why the AI Summit process works. We share stories and learnings from early experiments with the AI Summit. We connect it to other approaches of whole-scale change. We walk through a summit from start to finish. Finally, based on our and others' experience and on leading-edge organization change theory, we offer ten essential conditions for AI Summit success.

CHAPTER 1

WHAT IS THE APPRECIATIVE INQUIRY SUMMIT METHODOLOGY?

Whenever we introduce the Appreciative Inquiry Summit methodology, people have questions. What is appreciative inquiry, and precisely what is an AI Summit? How does the AI Summit process relate to other ways of using appreciative inquiry, and how does it relate to other large-group processes, such as Future Search, Open Space Technology, Whole-Scale Change, Real Time Strategic Change, the Search Conference, and the Conference Model?

In this chapter, we respond to these questions by looking at the emergence and key characteristics of the AI Summit methodology. First, we introduce appreciative inquiry and its various forms of engagement. Second, we provide a brief definition of the AI Summit methodology. Third, we offer a short history of the AI Summit methodology and highlight some of its central characteristics. Finally, we compare the AI Summit with other large-group processes.

A BRIEF INTRODUCTION
TO APPRECIATIVE INQUIRY

Appreciative inquiry got its start in the early 1980s when David Cooperrider, then a doctoral student in organizational behavior at Case Western Reserve University, and his faculty mentor,

Suresh Srivastva, were doing an organization change project with the Cleveland Clinic in Cleveland, Ohio. They found, first of all, that when they used the traditional organization development (OD) approach of problem diagnosis and feedback, it sucked the energy for change right out of the system. The more problems people discovered, the more discouraged they became; and the more discouraged they became, the more they began to blame one another for the problems.

Second, they discovered that their work as an intervention was more powerful when they let go of the very idea of intervening. Instead of *intervention* they framed their task as *inquiry*—simply to be students of organizational life, to learn, to discover, and to appreciate everything that gave "life" to the system when it was most vibrant, effective, successful, and healthy in relation to its whole system of stakeholders. In their analysis of the data, Cooperrider and Srivastva engaged in a radical reversal of the traditional problem-solving approach.

Influenced by the writings of Schweitzer[1] on "reverence for life," they focused on everything they could find that appeared to empower and energize the system, everything contributing to excellence and high performance at the clinic. Even though, in the early stages, they still asked some very traditional diagnostic questions (such as "Tell us about your largest failure as a chairman of your department"), they decided later, in preparing their feedback report, to include analysis of all the generative themes: moments of success; experiences of high points; and stories of innovation, hope, courage, and positive change. Instead of doing a root-cause analysis of failure, they let go of every so-called deficiency and turned full attention to analysis of root causes of success.

The results were immediate and dramatic. Relationships improved, cooperation increased, and measurable business performance hit an all-time high. When Cooperrider and Srivastva presented the outcomes of the inquiry to the clinic board, the report created such a powerful and positive stir that the board asked to use the method with the entire organization of 8,000 people. They called the approach "appreciative inquiry," and the term first appeared in a footnote in this feedback report to the members of the Cleveland Clinic board. A few years later they published their classic article "Appreciative Inquiry into Organizational Life,"[2] articulating the theory and vision of appreciative inquiry as an exciting paradigm shift for the field of organization development and change. It was a call, as they wrote, "for a scholarship of the positive."

Toward a Positive Revolution

Since the early 1980s, AI has grown extensively around the world. It has been used by thousands of people and hundreds of organizations in every sector of society to promote transformative change. For example, it has been used in a variety of applications by:

- Major corporations such as Avon Mexico, Blue Cross Blue Shield, Boeing, Bristol Myers Squibb, British Airways, BP, British Telecom, Canadian Broadcasting Corporation, Cap Gemini Ernst & Young, DTE Energy Services, GE Capital, GlaxoSmithKline, Green Mountain Coffee Roasters, Hunter-Douglas, John Deere, McDonald's, Motorola, Nutrimental Foods (Brazil), Roadway, Square D Corporation, U.S. Cellular, USG Corporation, Verizon, and Wendy's.

- Government organizations such as the Canadian Department of National Defense, City of Berkeley, City of Denver, City of Minneapolis, Hampshire County Council Social Services Department (UK), Inner London Magistrate's Courts Service (UK), NASA, Nevada Child Welfare Services, the Pearson Peacekeeping Centre (Canada), the U.S. Department of Health and Human Services, the U.S. Environmental Protection Agency, the U.S. Agency for International Development, the U.S. Navy, and the U.S. Postal Service.

- Health care institutions such as Children's Hospital of Philadelphia, Cleveland Clinic, Consorta, Eau Claire Family Medicine Clinic, JCAHO, Lovelace Health Systems, Methodist Medical Center, North Berkshire Health Systems, Park Center Inc., Riveredge Hospital, Texas Health Resources, Trinity Health System, and Wheaton Franciscan Services.

- Institutions of higher education such as Benedictine University, Case Western Reserve, Front Range Community College (CO), University of California–Berkeley, University of Minnesota, and University of Wisconsin.

- School systems such as Cleveland Public Schools, National Association of Independent Schools, Northeast Catholic High School (Philadelphia), Sacred Heart Griffin High School (Springfield, IL), and West Springfield (MA) Public Schools. Recently AI consultant Marge Schiller launched an initiative called the Positive Change Corps designed to promote transformation in school systems across the United States.[3]

- Religious and spiritual organizations such as the United Religions Initiative, the Episcopal Church, Spirit in Business, the Brahma Kumaris World Spiritual Organization, and many local congregations.
- Social service and community development organizations such as American Baptist International Ministries, the American Red Cross, CARE, Catholic Relief Services, the Christian Reformed World Relief Committee, the GEM Initiative, InterAction, Lutheran World Relief, the Mountain Institute, MWENGO (East Africa), MYRADA (India), PACT, UNDP, UNICEF, Save the Children, TechnoServe, United Way, World Vision, andWilgespruit Fellowship Centre (South Africa).

Appreciative inquiry has also given birth to a variety of public-dialogue projects to engage a broad range of people in imagining and enacting their desired futures. For example, in the mid-1990s, Bliss Browne launched Imagine Chicago, a citywide inquiry designed to promote civic discourse and innovation.[4] Since then, similar inquiries have emerged in locations around the world: Imagine Dallas, Imagine Gotland (Sweden), Imagine Nagaland (India), Imagine South Carolina, and Imagine Western Australia.

In 1999, under the leadership of Judy Rodgers, the center for Social Innovations in Global Management (SIGMA), the Brahma Kumaris World Spiritual Organization, and the Visions of a Better World Foundation launched Images and Voices of Hope, a worldwide inquiry to strengthen the role of media as agents of world benefit.[5] Since 1999, conversations have opened in over twenty cities on five continents.

In 2001, David Cooperrider began Business as an Agent of World Benefit (BAWB), a world dialogue designed to engage executives, thought leaders, and change agents in reflecting on and convening around the subject of how the business sector might put its extraordinary imagination, capacity, and resources to work on behalf of the world.[6] These public-dialogue projects are intended to last many years and to include millions of people in rethinking and acting to heighten the positive potential of citizens, the media, and business as forces for world benefit.

Appreciative inquiry is also quickly developing a robust theoretical foundation. A variety of master's-level programs in management, organization development, education, and social change have incorporated AI into their coursework. At least two Ph.D. programs in organization development/behavior, at Benedictine University[7] and Case Western Reserve University,[8] have made AI a cornerstone of their curricula. A growing number of master's theses and Ph.D. dissertations are devoted to appreciative methodologies and applications, and scholarly papers on AI have received awards from the Academy of Management, the International Management Association, the Organization Development Network, the Organizational Development Institute, and the American Society of Training and Development. Emerging movements in positive psychology[9] and positive organizational scholarship[10] provide additional theoretical grounding to appreciative inquiry.

Finally, the community of AI practitioners around the world is growing dramatically, and an increasing number of resources are being made available. Benedictine University, Case Western Reserve University, NTL,[11] and the Taos Institute[12] offer a variety of training programs for AI practitioners. Appreciative Inquiry Consulting, LLC (AIC),[13] a global network of AI consultants, was launched in 2001 to advance AI, create transformational business and philanthropic opportunities, and promote rapid learning on AI. The AI Listserv[14] allows anyone interested in AI to engage in online dialogue with others. AI Practitioner is an up-to-the-minute quarterly journal that features new advances in the practice of AI from around the world.[15] Appreciative Inquiry Resources (AIR) is an online "market" that offers a range of products on appreciative inquiry and positive change, including books, manuals, videotapes, and DVDs.[16] The AI Commons website[17] is a free, open-access resource bank at Case Western University that includes all things AI. As University of Michigan professor Robert Quinn writes in his book *Change the World*, AI is "revolutionizing the field of organization development."[18]

The Power of Appreciative Inquiry to Transform

At its core, appreciative inquiry is the study and exploration of what gives life to human systems when they function at their best. It is based on the assumption that every living system has a hidden and underutilized core of strengths—its positive core—which, when revealed and tapped, provides a sustainable source of positive energy for both personal and organizational transformation. David Cooperrider and Leslie Sekerka relate this to the concept of *fusion energy* in the sciences.[19] Fusion is the power source of the sun and the stars. It results when two positively charged elements combine into one. In organizations, when joy touches joy, strength touches strength, health touches health, and inspiration combines with inspiration, people are liberated and empowered to create ascending spirals of cooperative action. According to Cooperrider and Whitney, "Link the positive core to any change agenda, and changes never thought possible are suddenly and democratically mobilized."[20]

The Appreciative Inquiry 4-D Cycle

As an approach to organization change, AI involves the cooperative search for the best in people, their organizations, and the world around them. This is significantly different from conventional managerial problem solving. The key task in problem solving is to identify and remove gaps or deficits. The process usually involves (1) identifying problems, (2) analyzing causes, (3) searching for solutions, and (4) developing an action plan.

In contrast, the key task in AI is to identify and leverage strengths. The steps include (1) discovery, (2) dream, (3) design, and (4) destiny (see Exhibit 1.1).

Exhibit 1.1

The "4-D" Cycle

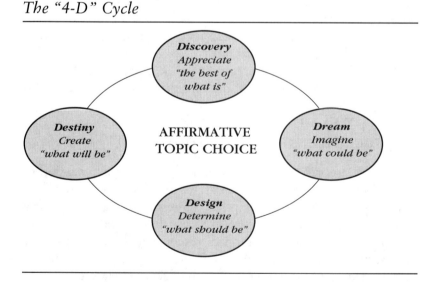

The purpose of the **discovery** phase is to search for, highlight, and illuminate those factors that give life to the organization, the "best of what is" in any given situation. The list of positive topics for discovery is endless: high quality, integrity, empowerment, innovation, customer responsiveness, technological innovation, team spirit, and so on. In each case the task is to promote organizational learning by sharing stories about times when these qualities were at their best and analyzing the forces and factors that made them possible.

The second phase is to **dream** about what could be. When the best of what is has been identified, the mind naturally begins to search beyond this; it begins to envision new possibilities. Because these dreams have been cued by asking positive questions, they paint a compelling picture of what the organization could and should become as it conforms to people's deepest hopes and highest aspirations.

The third phase is to **design** the future through dialogue. Once people's hopes and dreams have been articulated, the task is to design the organization's social architecture—norms, values, structures, strategies, systems, patterns of relationship, ways of doing things—that can bring the dreams to life. It is a process of building commitment to a common future by dialoguing and debating, crafting and creating until you get to the point where everyone can say, "Yes this is the kind of organization or community that I want to invest my energies in. Let's make it happen." The key to this phase is to create a deliberately inclusive and supportive context for conversation and co-creation.

The final phase, **destiny**, is an invitation to construct the future through innovation and action. Appreciative inquiry establishes momentum of its own. People find innovative ways to help move the organization closer to the ideal. Because the ideals are grounded in realities, the confidence is there to try to make things happen. This is important to underscore because it is precisely because of the visionary content, placed in juxtaposition to grounded examples of the extraordinary, that appreciative inquiry opens the status quo to transformations in collective action.

Forms of Engagement of Appreciative Inquiry

The AI Summit is one of many different ways to use appreciative inquiry to promote positive change in organizations and in communities. Each AI process is designed to meet the unique needs and goals of the people, organization, or community involved. Table 1.1, adapted from Diana Whitney and Amanda Trosten-Bloom's book *The Power of Appreciative Inquiry,* contains a brief description of the core forms of engagement of AI.[21]

Table 1.1

Forms of Engagement of Appreciative Inquiry

AI Summit: A large group of people (30–3,000) participate simultaneously in a three- to five-day AI 4-D process.

Whole-System 4-D Dialogue: All members of the organization and some stakeholders participate in an AI 4-D process. It takes place at multiple locations over an extended period of time.

Mass Mobilized Inquiry: Large numbers of interviews (thousands to millions), on a socially responsible topic, are conducted throughout a city, a community, or the world.

Core Group Inquiry: A small group of people select topics, craft questions, and conduct interviews.

Positive Change Network: Members of an organization are trained in AI and provided with resources to initiate projects and share materials, stories, and best practices.

Positive Change Consortium: Multiple organizations collaboratively engage in an AI 4-D process to explore and develop a common area of interest.

AI Learning Team: A small group of people with a specific project—an evaluation team, a process improvement team, a customer focus group, a benchmarking team, or a group of students—conduct an AI 4-D process.

Progressive AI Meetings: An organization, small group, or team goes through the AI 4-D process over the course of ten to twelve meetings that are each two to four hours long.

Although there are many different ways to use appreciative inquiry, for us and for many other AI practitioners the AI Summit is rapidly becoming a methodology of choice because of its power to get everyone involved, strengthen relationships, and quickly produce remarkable results.

WHAT IS AN APPRECIATIVE INQUIRY SUMMIT?

The Appreciative Inquiry Summit is a method for accelerating change by involving a broad range of internal and external stakeholders in the change process. It is typically a single event or series of events that bring people together to (1) discover the organization's or community's core competencies and strengths; (2) envision opportunities for positive change; (3) design the desired changes into the organization's or community's systems, structures, strategies, and culture; and (4) implement and sustain the change and make it work. AI Summits vary in size anywhere between 30 and 1,000 people, and could include more.[22] Most of the summits we have conducted have been in the 100–500-person range. Our experience has been that because of the power of wholeness, the closer we get to including every member of the system, the more dramatic and sustainable the impact.

The AI Summit methodology represents a radical shift away from traditional change management approaches that put the responsibility for change in the hands of just a few individuals and are based on the assumption that the best way to move forward is to solve problems. The Appreciative Inquiry Summit begins with the premise that organizations change fastest and best when their members are excited about where they are going, have a clear plan for moving forward, and feel confident about their ability to reach their destination. In other words, quick and effective organization change is a product of having the "whole system" aligned around its strengths and around ideas that generate energy for action.

A SHORT HISTORY OF THE APPRECIATIVE INQUIRY SUMMIT

The seeds of the AI Summit methodology were planted in the mid-1980s when John Carter, David Cooperrider, and Mary Ann Rainey, all doctoral students at Case Western Reserve University, were asked by Touche-Ross Canada to lead an important strategic planning process. Two key executives were close to retirement, and they wanted to empower a culture of co-leadership throughout the organization before stepping down.

Based on their growing interest in the appreciative approach, John, David, and Mary Ann created a set of positive questions designed to identify and highlight everything that gave "life" to Touche-Ross when it was most successful and most capable in terms of co-leadership. But instead of using the traditional OD approach of doing the interviews themselves, they trained 40 junior partners to go out and interview the other 310 partners in offices around the country. Junior partners interviewed senior partners to promote dynamic cross-generational learning. The logic was that if indeed the 350 partners were the future leadership of the organization, who was there better to understand at a deep level the forces and factors that support organizational excellence at Touche-Ross?

Once the interviews were completed, John, David, and Mary Ann brought together the 40 junior partners to develop a set of "provocative propositions"[23] that represented the collective image of the ideal organization. A month later, all 350 partners met to validate the provocative propositions and to develop a plan to put them into practice. They called this event the Partners Roundtable because it was a fully participatory, open, dialogical process. Every partner was an equal participant in the co-creation of the future. The Partners Roundtable was the first experiment in large-group, "whole-system" appreciative inquiry, and many valuable lessons were learned.[24]

The first lesson was simply the remarkable power of a process that invited full participation and full voice on the part of organizational members. Both junior and senior partners said they accelerated their learning and experienced immediate growth in their effectiveness by being able to interview each other across the "generational divide." Similarly, in a matter of two short days, the partners developed a comprehensive strategic plan that engaged their energies and redirected the focus of the organization.

Second, John, David, and Mary Ann were amazed by the power of storytelling at the Partners Roundtable. When people shared stories of peak performance and extraordinary contribution, not only did it delight the listeners, but it promoted learning by revealing the root causes of success. It also made the seemingly impossible, suddenly possible. If they did it very well once, they could do it even better the next time.

Third, they discovered the power of a positive guiding image of the future. When the partners wrote their provocative propositions, they were in essence writing a set of comprehensive design principles that would shape the future of their organization. Taken together, these design principles constituted a robust, practical image of the future. It described their commitments around systems, structures, strategies, organizational culture, approaches to leadership, and so on. It set the stage for concrete action in the organization.

Today, a large-group appreciative dialogue with 350 people seems almost ordinary. It happens consistently and frequently. In the mid-1980s, however, it was a bold new invention. According to David Cooperrider, "John Carter was, and continues to be, one of the most creative consultants in the field of OD. Much of the early innovation with what eventually became the AI Summit methodology, grew out of John's courage and belief in people in large-group dialogues."[25]

The Organizational Excellence Program (OEP)

Another important moment in our learning process around large-group AI took place in the early 1990s when the Global Excellence in Management (GEM) initiative was launched with a large six-year grant from the U.S. Agency for International Development (USAID) by David Cooperrider, Ada Jo Mann, Claudia Liebler, and others at Case Western Reserve University.[26] One of GEM's most successful initiatives was the Organizational Excellence Program (OEP), a five-day residential institute for executive teams of international development organizations. The OEP was offered twice a year, included anywhere from 30 to 100 people each time, and was designed according to the appreciative inquiry 4-D model. Its purpose was to allow senior executive teams to come together to discover their strengths, build a compelling vision for the future, share best practices, and launch action initiatives to enhance the effectiveness of their organizations. Those of us working with the OEP were amazed by its success. The amount of learning that took place during the events as people shared their experiences and wisdom was astounding.

When we asked participants what made it a great learning experience, they zeroed in on three things:

- **The appreciative approach.** The participants said that by focusing on examples of success, they had more fun, learned more, and strengthened their organizational capacity more effectively than they had in previous experiences. Many of them talked about it as the most important "paradigm shift" of their career.

- **The combination of in-group and cross-group learning.** Participants said that the work they did in their own executive teams was essential because it allowed them to focus on specific opportunities and actions for their organizations. At the same time, the "knowledge exchanges" in mixed groups were enriching because they allowed them to learn from the best experiences of others, see things in new ways, and understand their organizations in a broader context.

• **The amount of progress made in just five short days.** The combination of having the key people in the same room face to face, taking the time to work through complex issues, and following through on the entire 4-D cycle, allowed participants to walk out of the OEP with fully developed plans for implementation.

The Christian Reformed World Relief Committee (CRWRC)

The remarkable results of the OEP aroused our curiosity about what it would be like to use a similar approach with a single organizational system focused on a single change agenda. Would the learning and successful change be multiplied if not only the executive team but the whole organization were focused on a common purpose or task? With this question in mind, in 1994 we took the AI large-group approach "on the road." A group of us were working with the Christian Reformed World Relief Committee (CRWRC), an international development organization based in the United States and Canada, to develop an appreciative approach to building and measuring organizational capacity. At the time, CRWRC worked in partnership with over 120 local nongovernmental organizations (NGOs) worldwide, and we, along with many CRWRC field staff, felt that because the new capacity-building system would be used by them, it was essential to engage all of the NGOs—the whole system—in developing the final product.

To accomplish this, we designed a three-year global learning process that consisted of four large-group AI meetings per year, one in each of four regions of the world: East Africa, West Africa, Asia, and Latin America. Heavily influenced by Marvin Weisbord and Sandra Janoff's work on Future Search,[27] we created a design for the meetings that blended Future Search with AI and called the meetings Appreciative Future Search Conferences.[28] The results from the conferences were powerful. Over the three-year period, CRWRC and its partners improved their working relationships, created an appreciative capacity-building process that was "owned" by the entire system, and launched hundreds of new initiatives to strengthen performance through training, consultation, advocacy, new sources of funding, coalitions, and access to global markets.[29]

We learned many valuable lessons from CRWRC about what it takes to make appreciative large-group processes successful, but three in particular stand out.

- **The importance of wholeness.** As stated in the Preface, AI Summits provide a direct and immediate link to the "logic of the whole." For example, many community development organizations promote small business formation in the communities they serve, but because these businesses have few links to sources of capital or to markets beyond their local area, they flounder. CRWRC included business leaders in the AI Summit process, and as a result, a new organization called Partners for Christian Development was created that links established entrepreneurs with small businesses to provide loans, management consulting, and development of new markets. Having businesspeople, an essential part of the "whole system," present at the summits opened up a whole new world of possibilities for participants.

- **The value of a relevant, clear, and compelling task.** The topic for this series of summits was "partnering to build and measure organizational capacity." It was selected by the project's planning team, which was composed of people from around the world to represent the "whole system." They selected this topic because it was relevant to them at a deep strategic level. It would allow them to grow and to better accomplish their missions as organizations. This singular focus allowed all 120 organizations to learn more about building capacity than they ever imagined possible. And because of its attractiveness as a topic, it enabled them to align their actions and sustain their energies for many years.

- **The power of high-quality connections.** Recent research by Jane Dutton and Emily Heaphy at the University of Michigan suggests that high-quality relationships boost performance for both individuals and organizations.[30] They provide an exchange of resources; contribute to the growth, learning, and development of those involved; and lead to cooperative action. We saw this distinctly in the CRWRC summits. The appreciative focus created the possibility for participants to discover and affirm the best in each other. This set the stage for new levels of trust and a willingness to risk and to collaborate around previously unexplored initiatives.

The United Religions Initiative (URI)

The name Appreciative Inquiry Summit was coined by David Cooperrider and Diana Whitney in 1995 in the process of working with Bishop William Swing of San Francisco on a five-year project to create the United Religions Initiative (URI), a global organization dedicated to promoting interfaith cooperation, peace, and healing.[31] It was selected to communicate the idea that large-group AI meetings are intended to help human systems reach the highest level attainable on change agendas of essential importance to them. They enable organizations to achieve peak performance in pursuit of elevated purposes.

From 1995 to 2000, we along with many others collaborated on the design and facilitation of five global summits and approximately ten regional summits of 100 to 250 people each to draft a preamble, purpose statement, set of organizing principles, charter, and plan for the global evolution of this newly emerging organization. In June 2000, the global summit served as the center of a worldwide charter signing, through which the URI came into being as a legally chartered organization.

The URI added enormously to our understanding of what makes the AI Summit methodology work. We mention here three lessons of particular importance.

- **Appreciative dislodgment of certainty.** Change requires a willingness to let go of certainty and head into the unknown. The AI Summit, because it invites and rewards curiosity, builds confidence in people to step courageously forward. This was certainly true in the case of the URI. To create a brand new global organization that crossed boundaries of all kinds, especially those of faith tradition, required enormous amounts of openness and trust, and a willingness to explore. Muslims, Jews, Christians, Buddhists, and a host of others came to know and appreciate each other in new ways that opened up the potential for new forms of cooperation. Together they also left behind the certainty of traditional organizational forms and created a global alliance like the world had never seen.
- **Holographic beginning.** A good AI interview guide touches on all four D's: discovery, dream, design, and destiny. We call this a holographic beginning because it allows people to anticipate the entire summit within the first hour or so of the four-day meeting. We learned in the URI process that this is important. First, it allows all participants to express their ideas and share their hopes for the organization early in the meeting. Second, it appeals to all learning styles; people who like to reflect on the past can reflect, those who like to dream can dream, and those who are hungry for action can jump quickly into design and destiny. Third, a holographic beginning allows everyone to see the flow of the meeting. The link between dis-

covery, dream, design, and destiny is established as the path forward for the meeting and for the organization's future.

- **Leadership levels the playing field.** By design, AI Summits are intended to be a dialogue of equals. This is based on the idea that people will give their best effort and most energy when they are full co-creators of their common future. In an AI Summit, there are few if any presentations by "experts." People sit at round tables of six to eight with a mix of functions, levels, and areas of expertise. Leaders are expected to join in as peers. We learned the power of this from Bishop Swing. In all of the URI summits, he would kick things off by standing up at his table, welcoming everyone in the room, and then saying, "Let's get to work." For the rest of the time, he participated as a fellow inquirer. This allowed the will of the group to emerge and gave the URI a "collective power" that would not have developed had Bishop Swing or others imposed a personal agenda.

THE RAPID GROWTH OF THE AI SUMMIT METHODOLOGY

Since the early 1990s, hundreds of organizations worldwide in the corporate, nonprofit, government, and community sectors have used the AI Summit methodology. Examples include McDonald's, John Deere, U.S. Cellular, GTE (Verizon), British Airways, British Telecom, Hunter-Douglas, Roadway Express, Vermont Coffee Roasters, Nutrimental, Avon Mexico, U.S. Navy, Canadian Broadcasting Corporation, Canadian Department of National Defense, World Vision, American Red Cross, United Way, United Religions Initiative, and dozens of NGOs and communities around the world.

These organizations have employed the AI Summit methodology to address a variety of agendas, including leadership development, strategic planning, organization design, culture transformation, business process redesign, brand building, vision and values clarification, customer service, knowledge management, labor-management relations, quality, safety, the formation of partnerships and alliances, and the integration of mergers and acquisitions. Some organizations—such as Hunter-Douglas, Nutrimental, and Syntegra, a division of British Telecom in the Netherlands—have begun to use the AI Summit as an ongoing way of managing. They hold regular AI Summits to address specific topics, pursue new business opportunities, or realign the organization along a common strategic direction.

We have learned much from these organizations and the courageous experiments they have done with the AI Summit methodology. Throughout the rest of the book, we will share many of these stories in detail, highlight what we learned, and take you through a step-by-step process of how to plan, conduct, and follow up on an AI Summit. But before we do this, we want briefly to draw a link between the AI Summit and other large-group processes.

THE RELATIONSHIP OF THE AI SUMMIT TO OTHER LARGE-GROUP PROCESSES

In his book *Productive Workplaces,* Marvin Weisbord shows how managing has evolved from experts solving problems *for* other people toward everybody improving the whole system.[32] In the early 1900s, Fredrick Taylor had "expert" consultants solving organizational problems using principles of scientific management. In the 1950s, Kurt Lewin's followers involved organizational members in solving their own problems—participative management. In the mid-1960s, experts discovered systems thinking and began improving whole systems *for* other people. Finally, in the late twentieth century, managers and OD practitioners began to experiment with getting everybody involved in improving whole systems.

This participatory whole-system approach gave rise to a variety of large-group intervention methodologies, including the Search Conference,[33] Future Search,[34] Open Space Technology,[35] Whole-Scale Change,[36] Real Time Strategic Change,[37] the Conference Model,[38] and others. For excellent reviews of large-group interventions, see Bunker and Alban's *Large Group Interventions*[39] and Holman and Devane's *The Change Handbook.*[40]

The AI Summit builds on these methodologies but breaks new ground by stressing the relational nature of innovation and by highlighting the power of the positive to unleash extraordinary organizational performance. The AI Summit is based on the understanding that the future is truly unknown and un-knowable, and that people in organizations are continuously in the process of building something new. When they are most alive and most vital, they are not simply improving systems, they are jointly inventing surprising new ways of organizing. This perspective is particularly important in today's world, in which vigorous global competition, instantaneous electronic communication, and the elimination of previously polarizing political, cultural, and geographic boundaries are rapidly re-configuring the social and economic landscape. As Gary Hamel recently put it in his book *Leading the Revolution,* "The world is increasingly divided into two kinds of organizations—those that can get no further than continuous improvement, and those who have made the jump to radical innovation."[41]

To extend Weisbord's model, we are now in an era that calls for methods of organization change that allow everybody to in-novate for extraordinary performance. The AI Summit is de-signed to meet this challenge. Exhibit 1.2 illustrates the evolution of thought on managing change that has prepared the way for the AI Summit methodology.

Exhibit 1.2

Evolution of Thought on Managing Change[42]

1900:	1950:	1965:	1980s:	2000+:
Experts solve specific problems	Everyone solves specfic problems	Experts improve whole systems	Everyone improves whole systems	Everyone innovates for extraordinary performance

Common Features

Although it is important to distinguish the AI Summit from other large-group processes, we have drawn on these processes in many ways for ideas and inspiration. We have been particularly influenced by the work of Marvin Weisbord and Sandra Janoff on Future Search, Harrison Owen on Open Space Technology, Kathleen Dannemiller on Whole-Scale Change, and Robert Jacobs on Real Time Strategic Change.

The AI Summit shares the following common features with these pioneering approaches.

- **The importance of getting the whole system in the room.** When people see interconnections among departments, processes, people, and ideas, they know better how to participate and therefore are able to make commitments that were previously impossible or unlikely. If anyone is missing, there is much less potential for new discoveries and innovative action.

- **A focus on the future.** Ronald Lippitt and Eva Schindler-Rainman,[43] in their work with community futures conferences, concluded that problem solving depresses people, whereas imagining ideal futures creates hope and energy. In all large-group interventions, the focus is on helping people generate energy for action by imagining the future rather than focusing directly on problems.

- **Dialogue, voice, and the search for common ground.** When people are free to listen to each other and to share their unique experiences, they get a much clearer picture of one another's perspectives and are more likely to build shared understandings. They are also more likely to discover common dilemmas and shared aspirations that are larger than their own agendas, which leads to common ground.

- **A commitment to self-management.** People will invest huge amounts of energy into real business issues that are of passionate concern to them. Shared self-management contributes significantly to the amount of work people do, the quality they produce, and the high degree of implementation that follows large-group interventions.

How the AI Summit Adds to the Field of Large-Group Processes

Although the AI Summit has much in common with its peers, it is distinctive in five important ways: its social constructionist assumptions, appreciative approach, commitment to continuous inquiry, search for higher ground, and attention to values-based organization design.

Social Constructionist Assumptions

The concept of *social constructionism* sounds complex in theory, but in practice it is really quite simple. The idea is that the future of our organizations and our communities has not yet been invented. Within reason, we can make of them anything we want. When we engage in meaningful conversation with others, we can "socially construct" them in the direction of our ideals. For example, in the John Deere case introduced in the preface, on the first day of the AI Summit nobody believed that they could create new ways of relating or invent new approaches to improving business results. As one participant told us, "You're nice people and everything, but this isn't going to work. We've been through it all before, and nothing ever changes."

But once people began to talk to one another as equals and to co-construct new systems, structures, strategies, and processes to support innovation and healthy relationships, they made enormous progress toward their ideals. In essence, they socially constructed their destiny by engaging each other in meaningful conversation around topics that were important to them. The constructionist emphasis of the AI Summit is different from the "systems improvement" focus of other large-group processes because it takes seriously the idea that anything, including systems that seem fixed and immutable, are open to reinvention through purposeful conversation about our highest ideals.[44]

Appreciative Approach

Our observation has been that the fastest, most direct route to positive change is to learn from examples of the best. Illustrations of failure tell you what not to do, but they do not teach you how to succeed. For example, in the John Deere case, at a deep level everybody wanted to learn how to work together positively to produce significant results. We could have spent our time studying the root causes of low morale and poor performance and then trying to intervene to fix the system. But as Gina, the internal OD consultant, says, "If we had done that, I will guarantee you, we would never have gotten past day one!"

Not only would such an approach have further fragmented relationships, but it would have stifled creativity and created few new ideas for innovation. Instead, we mobilized a systemwide inquiry into moments of exceptional pride and performance and then invited organization members to co-create a future for their system that nurtures and supports even more pride and performance. The AI Summit is premised on the belief that it is much faster and more straightforward to go through the front door of extraordinary performance than to go around the block and through the back door of pitfalls and problems.

Commitment to Continuous Inquiry

One of the most important insights we have learned with AI to date is that the seeds of change are implicit in the very first questions we ask. According to Ludema, Cooperrider, and Barrett, "human systems grow in the direction of what they most persistently, actively, and collectively ask questions about."[45] In the case of John Deere, we worked with a planning team to develop a set of positive questions to guide the AI Summit process. One of the questions was this:

> Describe an incident when you or someone you know went the extra mile to be responsive to a customer need, improve quality, cost competitiveness, or introduce a new product. What made it possible? What did you do? What did others do? What did the organization do to make it possible?

This question (along with many others) was asked of all 250 people to bring forward best practices from across the plant. It unleashed systemwide learning about effective models of organizing and the forces and factors that made them possible. The AI Summit is based on the assumption that perhaps *the* most important thing a manager or change agent does is articulate questions. The questions we ask set the stage for what we "find," and what we find becomes the knowledge out of which the future is constructed.

Search for Higher Ground

The AI Summit is about action inspired by human hope and aspiration. Hope theory claims that people are energized to take action when they have (1) an elevating purpose, (2) a sense of collective confidence in their capacity to accomplish the purpose, and (3) a set of practical strategies for moving forward.[46] High hope, in turn, is related to a range of performance indicators, including more active visioning capacity; the ability to set, pursue, and achieve a greater number of goals; increased levels of creativity, persistence, and resilience in the search for alternative strategies; more adaptability to environmental change; a higher propensity to interact and collaborate with other people; better physical and emotional health; a greater sense of meaning; and even profitability and employee satisfaction and retention.[47] An essential resource for generating constructive change is our collective imagination and discourse about our highest ideals for the future.

At the end of the second day of the John Deere summit, people shared their dreams of the ideal future. Of course, those dreams were filled with all kinds of ideas about product innovations that would thrill their customers and boost their profits, but more important, they were rich with imagery about their ideal workplace. They painted a picture of a community based on principles of pride, honor, respect, cooperation, and excellence. They held spirited discussions about how to shape pay systems, supervisory roles, and the assembly line floor to enact and support these principles. And they talked about how to create a dramatic shift in the "internal dialogue" of the organization from one of complaint, blame, and hopelessness to one of support, encouragement, and the search for positive alternatives.

This conversation was a watershed moment in the summit. Prior to it, people had little hope for change. After it, they shared a compelling image of what they wanted and where they wanted to go. This image, grounded in their principles of the ideal workplace, served ever so slightly to transcend animosities and to energize a willingness to act. One of the most important actions a group can take to liberate the human spirit and construct a better future is to embark on a continuing search for higher ground.

Attention to Values-Based Organization Design

One of the reasons it is important for AI Summits to be three to five days long is to provide time for values-based organization design.[48] Organization designs are expressions of values embodied in structures, systems, strategies, relationships, roles, policies, procedures, products, and services. If done well, they liberate cooperation, support the best in people, and sustain the principles and aspirations that are generated in the discovery and dream phases of the summit. In the John Deere case, the third and fourth days of the summit were dedicated exclusively to design.

One group worked on redefining the supervisor's role to allow greater self-management throughout the plant. Another group worked on revising the profit-sharing plan to support more cooperation and higher individual performance. A third group worked on redesigning the new product development process to make it faster without compromising quality. During this time, each group also coordinated with other groups and individuals in the room, so that by the end of the fourth day, all of the groups had the support of the whole system to take action on their new designs. This unleashed unbelievable energy. Not only had the group discovered its positive core, not only had it strengthened relationships and invented new possibilities for the future, but it made those possibilities real and meaningful by designing them into the very fabric of the organization.

AN INVITATION TO EXPERIMENT WITH THE AI SUMMIT

In this chapter we have provided a brief introduction to AI, a short history of the AI Summit, and a quick comparison of the AI Summit with other large-group processes. But the AI Summit methodology is still in its infancy. There is much to learn and many experiments to be done. We hope that you will join with us and with other practitioners around the world in taking the AI Summit to new heights and co-constructing it in ways that give it ever more potential to transform organizations and human communities.

CHAPTER 2

THE APPRECIATIVE INQUIRY SUMMIT PROCESS: START TO FINISH

When we refer to the AI Summit process, we include all the activities that occur before, during, and after the actual meeting. As a transformational process involving hundreds or even thousands of people, an Appreciative Inquiry Summit requires extensive, thoughtful planning as well as committed follow-up. The work done to sponsor, plan, and craft an agenda for an AI Summit sets the bar for the meeting's success. Follow-up activities ensure systemic innovation and impact over time. In this chapter we provide an overview of the activities that occur before, during, and after a summit. By understanding the whole process from start to finish, you can more easily determine whom to involve, how much time to allow, and what resources to plan for each step along the way. Table 2.1 provides an overview.

Table 2.1

Activities Before, During, and After an AI Summit

Before	During	After
• Sponsoring the summit	• Day 1: Discovery	• Communicating outcomes
• Forming a planning team	• Day 2: Dream	• Supporting innovation teams
• Defining the summit task	• Day 3: Design	• AI training
• Selecting participants	• Day 4: Destiny	• Positive change network
• Creating a summit design		• Second-wave inquiry

BEFORE AN APPRECIATIVE INQUIRY SUMMIT

Activities before a summit generally take place over a three- to four-month period of time. For a typical four-day AI Summit process we estimate at least eight days of work before the summit, four days during the summit, and four or more days after the summit. This means that it takes twice as much time to organize support, engage participants, design the meeting, create handout materials, and attend to logistics than it does to actually conduct the meeting. It is our experience that time spent up front pays off during the summit. When we take time to get all the stakeholders present and committed before the summit, dialogues, decisions, ideas, and inspiration flow easily during the summit.

Sponsoring an AI Summit

An AI Summit begins when an organization's leadership learns about appreciative inquiry and decides to apply it to an organizational issue, challenge, or opportunity. The first task is to enlist the support of a key group of sponsors for the summit.

Sponsors are people who ensure the success of the AI Summit process in their organization or community. In corporations they typically include key leaders such as CEOs, division VPs, plant GMs, union stewards, and so forth, and in communities they include the leaders of constituencies that have a stake in the topic to be addressed. These people provide financial and other resources, garner support for the summit in their organization or community, and work closely with the facilitators to make sure that the AI Summit process is on track.

Although the support of senior leaders is essential, no one person, function, or level within an organization can be the sole sponsor of an AI Summit. A broader group is needed to enable the necessary participation, information, and leadership. Once sponsorship is established, we create an advisory team made up of sponsors who will provide resources, ensure participation, and offer general guidance for the success of the process. For example, we recently conducted an AI Summit with Park Center, Inc., a comprehensive mental health system in Fort Wayne, Indiana. The CEO, Paul Wilson, was 100 percent behind it and willing to fund it, but to gain broader support, he formed a small advisory team (four VPs and three managers) to shape the AI Summit process and promote it with others in the system. The advisory team is less hands-on than the planning team, which is formed later to design and orchestrate the entire summit process. See Chapter 4 for more on sponsoring an AI Summit.

Forming a Planning Team

The planning team for an AI Summit is the working team whose job it is to design, orchestrate, and carry out the entire process from start to finish. They are the ones who link appreciative inquiry to the organization's core issue or opportunity, and who ensure that the AI Summit is tailored to meet the needs and culture of the organization. We have worked with planning teams as large as forty and as small as three. The ideal size depends on the size of the organization conducting the summit. In general, however, a planning team of twelve to twenty people can represent the interests and functions within an organization.

An effective planning team includes a broad and diverse group of people. Its membership is representative of all those who will attend the summit, internal and external stakeholders alike. For example, in the case of Park Center, the CEO, two VPs, and the three managers all joined the planning team. Then they invited two board members (representing the community), three clients (representing different services), and four employees (representing different levels, programs, and functions in the organization) to join, for a total of fifteen people representing multiple core constituencies.

We find that it usually takes at least two to three full days with the whole planning team plus many phone calls, e-mails, and smaller meetings to adequately plan a summit. We make the initial two-day meeting as similar to an AI Summit as possible so that the planning team members can gain a deep experiential understanding of what a summit is like. During the two-day meeting we introduce AI, do one-on-one interviews concerning the summit topic, create a stakeholder invitation list, create a customized design for the summit, discuss summit pre-work and post-summit follow-up expectations, agree on how to document and communicate outcomes, develop a plan for promoting the summit, and work out logistics. See Chapter 5 for more on forming a planning team.

Defining the Summit Task

One of the most important, if not *the* most important, activities to take place before an AI Summit is the identification of a clear, relevant, and compelling task. Appreciative inquiry leads us to define the summit task as an affirmative call to action. Effective AI Summit tasks are actionable and engaging and command the attention of the whole organization.

Park Center, like all mental health care systems, was facing dramatic cutbacks from federal and state funding sources. They wanted to use the AI Summit to explore ways to "do more with less." One of their strengths was the outstanding reputation and strong set of relationships they had at the local, state, and federal levels. Consider the differences in intention and motivation implicit in the following two summit tasks they could have chosen:

1) Finding ways to minimize the effect of budget cuts on our programs
2) Extraordinary collaboration: Investing in relationships to multiply our impact

Clearly, "extraordinary collaboration" carries more energy, focus, and potential than "finding ways to minimize the effect of budget cuts." It is a dynamic summit task that draws people to it and brings out their best. It is a task that motivates people to get involved and to contribute. See Chapter 5 for more on defining the summit task.

Selecting Participants

Participation at an AI Summit is holistic. Ideally, the entire organization and members of its entire value chain participate. This means that everyone in the organization and representatives from all stakeholder groups attend the summit meeting.

However, there are instances when not all members of the entire organization can attend simultaneously. This happens when the organization is too large to bring everyone together, such as a 67,000-person company, or when the business cannot be shut down for four days, such as an airline or hospital. In these cases, at a minimum, all stakeholder groups are represented. This means that people from all levels, all functions, all business units, and all staff groups, as well as customers, suppliers and community members, participate.

In the case of Park Center, the summit included representatives from every program, level, and function in the organization. Also included were clients; parents of clients; board members; representatives from local hospitals, social service organizations, and the judicial system; liaisons from state and federal agencies; and representatives from local businesses and other potential funding sources—a total of about 150 people. See Chapter 5 for more on selecting participants.

Creating an AI Summit Design

Once the planning team has defined the task and selected the participants, it is time to create a customized design for the summit. We never do this alone. We do it with the planning team as part of the two-day meeting prior to the summit. By creating their own customized design, the planning team is able to make it fit their unique situation and context. They also gain ownership of it, understand it more deeply, and can explain it more fully to other members of the organization.

We usually begin this conversation by walking through a generic AI Summit design with the planning team. Then we go back through and let them mold it in a way that makes sense to them. By the time the planning team gets to this point, they already have some idea of what a summit design looks like because they are in the middle of a two-day "summitlike" meeting, and because we have shown them videos and shared experiences of other summits. Specific tasks include determining the format for the summit, crafting the agenda, and revising the interview guide.

Creating a customized design always involves a very rich and engaging conversation. It invariably results in innovations from which we learn. For example, in a summit we did with McDonald's on global staffing and retention, Cheryl Richardson[1] and her colleagues created a friendly competition. They invited all of the participants (about 300 HR and operations managers, restaurant owner-operators, and vendors from around the world) to submit their best practices of staffing and retention. Of those submitted, the top thirty were invited to present their best practices at the summit. Each was given a presentation table and asked to present his or her best practice three times for thirty minutes each time so that every participant could visit at least three presentations. This process was not part of our "generic" AI Summit design, but it was one of the most powerful inquiries into an organization's positive core that we have ever seen. See Chapter 6 for more on creating an AI Summit design.

DURING A TYPICAL FOUR-DAY APPRECIATIVE INQUIRY SUMMIT

Although each AI Summit is unique, there are some common aspects. A summit generally takes place over three to five days and is designed to flow through the appreciative inquiry 4-D cycle of discovery, dream, design, and destiny. A brief outline follows as a sample of a typical four-day AI Summit design. It is offered only as a starting point. In practice, each summit is tailored to address the unique culture, purpose, and circumstances of the sponsoring organization or community.

Day 1: Discovery

The focus of the first day is on the discovery of many facets of the organization's "positive core." The focus on discovery includes the following questions: Who are we, individually and collectively? What resources do we bring? What are our core competencies? What hopes and dreams do we have for the future? What are the most hopeful macro trends impacting us at this time? In what ways can we imagine going forward together? Specific activities include:

- *Setting the task focus:* A brief introduction to the context and purpose of the meeting
- *Appreciative interviews:* All participants engage in one-on-one interviews organized around the topics of the meeting
- *Who are we at our best:* Small-group recollection of highlight stories and best practices discovered during the interview process
- *Positive core map:* A large-group process to illustrate all of the strengths, resources, capabilities, competencies, positive hopes and feelings, relationships, alliances, and other assets of the organization
- *Continuity search:* A large-group process to create organization, industry, and global timelines to identify factors that have sustained the organization over time and are desirable in the future

See Chapter 7 for more on discovery.

Day 2: Dream

The second day is a day of envisioning the organization's greatest potential for positive influence and impact in the world. Dialogues are stimulated by questions such as:

- *You are in the year 2010 and have just awakened from a long sleep. As you wake and look around, you see that the organization is just as you have always wished and dreamed it might be. What is happening? How is the organization different?*
- *Imagine it is 2010 and your organization has just won an award for outstanding socially responsible business of the year. What is the award for? What is said about your organization as the award is presented? What are customers saying? What are employees saying? What did it take to win the award?*

Specific approaches include:

- *Creative dreaming:* A series of activities to create a common guiding images of the future for the whole organization
- *Opportunity mapping:* A series of activities to mobilize action around a set of specific strategic opportunities
- *Consensus visioning:* A series of activities to achieve consensus on a purpose, mission, or vision statement for the whole organization

See Chapter 8 for more on the dream phase.

Day 3: Design

During day 3 participants focus on creating an organization in which the positive change core is boldly alive in all of the strategies, processes, systems, decisions, and collaborations of the organization. Provocative propositions (or "design statements," as some clients have called them) are crafted. These are affirmative statements that create a bridge between the organization's positive core and its dreams. For example, one of the provocative propositions created as a part of the McDonald's global staffing and retention summit was the following one on building a dynamic learning environment for all employees. It reflects both the best of who they are and their aspirations for who they want to become.

> McDonald's is a borderless, learning-rich organization where opportunities for growth abound all over the world. It provides the training, tools, and development opportunities necessary to enable all people to excel in their careers and in life. McDonald's state-of-the-art learning architecture allows learning and sharing of "best bets" to occur instantaneously and continuously throughout the world and provides McDonald's a reputation as the world's most respected global corporation. The dynamic learning environment stimulates creativity, innovation, and achievement and makes work at McDonald's challenging and intellectually fulfilling. McDonald's attracts the best and trains the best to be the best.

Such a statement is a visionary proclamation but also a call to action. It will require action to fulfill. It represents the organization's commitment to move in that direction.

Specific activities include:

- *Creation of the organization design architecture:* The large group identifies the organization design architecture (strategies, systems, structures, processes, best practices, etc.) best suited to their business and industry.
- *Selection of high-impact organization design elements:* The large group draws on interviews and dreams to select high-impact design elements.
- *Crafting provocative propositions for each organization design element:* Small groups draft provocative propositions (design statements) incorporating the positive change core into the design elements.

See Chapter 9 for more on design.

Day 4: Destiny

The final day is an invitation to action inspired by the prior days of discovery, dream, and design. For some this is the day they have been waiting for, a time to finally get to work on the specifics of what will be done. At this point we seek to invite personal and group initiative and self-organization. We seek to demonstrate the large group's commitment to action, and support for those who choose to go forward working on behalf of the whole.

Specific activities include:

- *Generation of possible actions:* Small groups brainstorm possible actions and share with the large group.
- *Selection of inspired actions:* Individuals publicly declare their intention for action and specify the cooperation and support needed.
- *Formation of innovation teams:* Groups meet to plan the next steps for cooperative innovation.
- *Large-group closing*

See Chapter 10 for more on destiny.

AFTER AN APPRECIATIVE INQUIRY SUMMIT

After the four-day summit meeting there is still much to be done. At a minimum, follow-up activities such as communication of outcomes and support for innovation teams must occur. Most organizations, however, decide to expand their use of appreciative inquiry following an AI Summit. This leads them to initiate AI training, a positive change network, or new applications of AI, thereby embarking on a second wave of AI.

For example, during their summit, Park Center identified eight broad strategic areas on which they wanted to focus, including attracting top talent, vigorously pursuing new partnerships, and encouraging fresh entrepreneurial programming. These became the basis of their strategic and operational activities in subsequent years. They also established a goal of incorporating appreciative and strength-based ways of doing business into their organization. This led to extensive AI training, using AI as the basis for staff meetings, and building AI into some of their measurement systems. (See Chapter 12 for more on AI Summit follow-up.)

Another client began by using AI for culture change, and went on to use AI for strategic planning and then for process improvement. After six years of applying AI to a series of business agendas, this organization can truly be said to have become an appreciative organization! See Chapter 13 for more on the appreciative organization.

CONCLUSION

The AI Summit process, from start to finish, engages the whole organization in inquiry and dialogue to create a more desirable future. A successful summit takes time and attention. Before, during, and after a summit care must be taken to create conditions for equal, open, and committed participation. When people come together in large groups, with the enthusiasm and safety that AI creates, hope flourishes and high levels of inspired action are unleashed.

CHAPTER 3

TEN ESSENTIAL CONDITIONS FOR AI SUMMIT SUCCESS

People are often surprised when we tell them that we prefer working with large groups of 200–500 people for most of the organizational change work we do. They wonder how we do it— how we keep order among so many people, how we arrive at consensus, and how we ensure commitment to consistent follow-up. These are good questions but not the questions we ask ourselves when planning, facilitating, or assessing the success of an AI Summit. Instead, we ask: How can we create a safe and inviting context for open, authentic conversation? How can we help the large group honor diverse ideas and opinions, bond emotionally, and move together to higher ground? How can we build excitement and trust in a co-created future? In other words, how can we help build an organization's capacity for ongoing positive change?

With these questions as our guide, we find that there are ten essential conditions for the success of an AI Summit (see Exhibit 3.1). Certainly, there is much more to a summit than these ten conditions, but we consider them to be an essential starting point.

If this is your first read through this book, these ten essential conditions may seem a bit abstract, not yet clearly connected to the practice of conducting an AI Summit. We acknowledge this and encourage you read them anyway. Throughout the rest of the book we refer back to them again and again, and we use many examples and illustrations to bring them to life. We offer them here in consolidated form so that in the future, as you are planning, conducting, and facilitating AI Summits, you can find them quickly without having to wade through the entire book.

Exhibit 3.1

Ten Essential Conditions for AI Summit Success

---

1) A relevant, clear, and compelling task

2) An unconditional focus on the positive

3) Robust planning

4) The whole system in the room, the whole time

5) Commitment to support success of decisions and outcomes

6) A healthy physical and relational space

7) Minimal and mindful facilitation

8) Begin with appreciative interviews

9) Flow through the AI 4-D cycle

10) Create a narrative-rich environment

CONDITION 1: A RELEVANT, CLEAR, AND COMPELLING TASK

As we mentioned in Chapter 1, human systems move in the direction of what they study. During an AI Summit, the task focus serves to organize inquiry and dialogue, and hence to establish direction for the organization's transformation. A clearly stated task and a process designed to keep the group on track are essential to a successful AI Summit.

Embedding the Task in the AI Summit Title

In general, we like the task to be clearly stated in the title of the meeting. This makes the purpose of the summit clear, and it builds energy for people to contribute their stories, ideas, and opinions. Some examples of AI Summit tasks and titles include:

- A Time for Action: Discovering the Steps for a United Religions Charter
- Focus 2000: A Working Session to Create Our Future

- Partnership: Creating the Principles and Practices That Align Our Strengths
- From Vision to Strategy: Planning for 2005

Multiple Summits, Multiple Tasks

In organizations that have used AI Summits repeatedly, the task for each successive summit changes to meet the evolving needs of the organization. At Nutrimental, five annual summits have focused on visioning, strategic planning, organization design, revolutionizing customer responsiveness, and creating a culture of innovation. As for the United Religions Initiative, annual summits have taken the organization from Discovering the Steps, to Visioning, to Drafting the Purpose and Principles, to Living into the Organization Design, to Charter Signing. Each successive summit serves as a forum for inquiry and dialogue into the organization's most emergent high-priority task. See Chapter 5 for more on defining the summit task.

CONDITION 2:
AN UNCONDITIONAL
FOCUS ON THE POSITIVE

When an organization decides to embark on an AI Summit process, it is committing to an unconditionally positive approach to organization change. Based on the principles of appreciative inquiry, everything involved in an AI Summit—before, during, and after—is focused on the positive.

Deep Exploration into the Positive Core

At the heart of a successful AI Summit is deep exploration into the organization's positive core. Questions are crafted and activities designed to guide participants in discovering and learning about their organization at its best. One of the reasons this is so important, according to Ronald Fry, Professor of Organizational Behavior at Case Western Reserve University, is that organizations find their point of highest vitality at the intersection of continuity, novelty, and transition.[1] Vital organizations know how to innovate and create unexpected newness (novelty). They know how to launch and manage planned change (transition). But perhaps even more important, vibrant organizations are expert at connecting the threads of identity, purpose, values, wisdom, and tradition that already support extraordinary performance (continuity). This attention to continuity is enhanced via the deep exploration of the positive core in the AI Summit, resulting in the knowledge and confidence necessary to inform intelligent collective action.

The Appreciative Dislodgment of Certainty

When we mention "appreciative dislodgment," we are talking about change that is inspired by images of possibility rather than driven by fear of failure. Clients often ask, "Don't we have to make the case for change by creating a burning platform? Don't we have to put the fear of God in people before they'll take any action?" Our answer is clearly "no." The case for change comes through the discovery, dream, and design of positive possibilities that are so inspiring that they activate, provoke, and invite action in their direction. It is based on a logic of attraction[2] rather than a rationale of reaction.

The Continuous Search for Higher Ground

The AI Summit is about action fueled by human hope and aspiration. Barbara Fredrickson, Professor of Psychology at the University of Michigan, has done groundbreaking research on the power of positive emotions—such as hope, joy, inspiration, elevation, and pride—to heighten human performance.[3] According to her "broaden and build" model, negative emotions such as fear, hostility, anxiety, and apathy lead directly to "fight or flight" behaviors, in essence narrowing a person's response options. Positive emotions, on the other hand, broaden a person's capacities. They spark interest, curiosity, creativity, resilience, cooperation, and energy for action. Over time, the repetitive broadening of options associated with positive emotions builds an enduring set of personal resources that sustain health and high performance long term.

But perhaps the most compelling part of Fredrickson's theory is her claim that the most direct route to positive emotions is the intentional creation of positive meaning. When people connect with something bigger than themselves, something they care about deeply, it invariably leads to a flourishing of positive emotions. In an AI Summit, people are continuously encouraged to pursue ideas and opportunities that excite, inspire, and compel them. When considering action, they are asked not only "Does it have market value?" (Will it help achieve bottom-line business results?) and "Does it have organizational value?" (Will it help create a people-focused, high-performance organization?), but also "Does it have affinity value?" (Does it hold meaning for you? Does it excite you, compel you, and call you to action? Will it inspire pride in you, in the organization, and among stakeholders?). As a result, decisions made at the summit multiply the organization's performance potential by connecting with people's highest aspirations.

CONDITION 3: ROBUST PLANNING

As mentioned in Chapter 2, it usually takes twice as much time to plan an AI Summit than it does to conduct one. This is true because the power of a summit is directly related to whether it is focused on the right task, has the right stakeholders in the room, and creates the right conditions for safe, open, and inclusive participation. It is also true because, during the planning phase, many people are being introduced to AI for the first time. It is important to take the time necessary to help people understand and get into the spirit of this new, and sometimes radically different, approach.

Inclusive Co-Creation: All Stakeholders from the Beginning

If the summit is going to be meaningful to the whole system, the system needs to be reflected by the planning team from the start. This is true both for representational reasons and because it produces a better product. In the case of Park Center, only clients knew what was really important to clients, and only community members knew what was really important to community members. They guaranteed the success of the summit by making sure it met their needs and addressed their aspirations.

As It Begins So It Goes

It has been our experience that the planning team has tremendous power to influence what happens with the rest of the organization during the summit. If the planning team begins with a spirit of curiosity, curiosity will flourish at the summit. If the planning team continuously affirms the best in its members, affirmation and productive relationships will grow at the summit. If the planning team embodies inclusion and openness, inclusion and openness will be in full bloom at the summit. The spirit of the planning team reverberates throughout the whole organization and sets the tone for the activities that follow.

CONDITION 4:
THE WHOLE SYSTEM
IN THE ROOM, THE WHOLE TIME

What is it about the experience of "wholeness" that brings out the best in people, teams, and organizations? This question has been with us since the inception of our work with the AI Summit as we watched, over and over again, tension turn to enthusiasm, cynicism to hope, and apathy to cooperative action. When we ask it of our clients and colleagues, their answers typically include:

- It eliminates false assumptions and evokes trust. When everyone is there, you gain a new level of understanding for their perspective, and you can more fully share your own perspective. It becomes easier to develop compassion for different perspectives instead of forming judgments.
- It allows people to gain a sense of interdependence with others. Relationships are strengthened, what's common becomes apparent, and people realize they really need one another to accomplish their goals.
- It lets people see, experience, and connect with a purpose greater than their own or that of their group or department.
- It satisfies the fundamental human need to be part of a larger community. It provides a sense of belonging.
- It brings an ecological perspective. All the pieces of the puzzle come together in one place, and everyone can gain an appreciation for the whole. This creates new possibilities for action, possibilities that previously lay dormant or undiscovered.
- It establishes credibility in the outcomes. When everyone is part of the decision, it has a stronger chance of being put into practice. Public commitments engender personal responsibility.

Whitney and Cooperrider write:

For people in large organizations, the experience of "wholeness" is akin to John Glenn's spiritual experience as he looked upon the whole planet earth from outer space. When the "consciousness of the whole" is evoked in us, we human beings want to organize our life and our work to serve the highest good of humanity. In large scale meetings like the Appreciative Inquiry Summit, getting the whole system in the room brings out the best in people, it facilitates the "whole story" coming together and it inspires highly committed actions on behalf of the whole.[4]

The ROI of Having the Whole System in the Room

When we tell people that an AI Summit requires three to five days of intense, energizing off-site work to be successful, they generally gasp, look at each other in astonishment, and say, "There's no way we can afford to pull our people away from their work for that period of time!" This response, of course, is understandable in many ways. Most organizations keep their operations running 365 days a year, in some cases 24/7. To shut down the whole organization for five days is never easy and sometimes impossible. Similarly, no one wants to spend more time in meetings than is absolutely necessary, especially when it means being pulled away from the "real work" of the organization.

There are four important things to point out in this regard. First, AI Summits are always focused on the "real work" of the organization. This makes them different from other types of meetings, such as training sessions, retreats, pep rallies, and conferences, that pull people away from the core task of the organization. AI Summits are designed to help the organization make a strategic and tactical leap forward in its "real work." For example, a series of summits David Cooperrider and Ron Fry did recently with Roadway Express focused on the topics of terminal throughput, quality of freight handling, load factors, and optimal margins. Groups came together for three to four days at a time in multiple sites to discuss, plan, coordinate, innovate, and design their organization and work to increase performance in the highly competitive long-haul trucking industry. There is nothing more real for Roadway

Express than their margins and time-to-delivery vis-à-vis the competition.

Second, our experience with more than 100 summits to date suggests that three or more days makes a dramatic difference in the quality of the relationships that get established, the focus and depth of conversations that take place, and the impact of the change that occurs. It takes time for people to get to know each other, build trust, hear each other's point of view, see new connections, imagine new possibilities, develop new strategies, create new designs, and launch new initiatives to radically transform the organization. Inevitably, when organizations try to cut corners and "get it done" in a day or two, they are disappointed with the results. The change is superficial, and after a couple of months, people begin to feel like the whole event was just another "flavor of the month."

Third, much of the important work in a summit is done during breaks, lunches, and overnights as people connect with each other informally and hatch new ideas. We strongly support Marv Weisbord and Sandra Janoff's notion of at least two overnights.[5] This allows much needed time for personal reflection, informal dialogue, community building, and whole-group synthesis.

Finally, AI Summits cost less and take less time than traditional change processes precisely because they get the whole system in the same place at the same time. They circumvent the usually slow and time-consuming process of passing attempts at change up and down the chain of command. Roadway earning millions of dollars in new revenue, John Deere saving millions in reduced cycle time, and many other examples in this book show that the return on an AI Summit is directly related to how much time and energy you invest in it.

Making Sure You Get the Right People— People Who Really Care about the Topic

By now it is probably clear that an AI Summit is a roll-up-your-sleeves, hands-on working session focused on a task of strategic importance to the organization. For this reason it is essential to have the right people in the room—people who have a significant stake in the topic. Either they have a vested interest in the summit outcomes, or they have information, influence, or resources that are crucial to the success of the summit task. There is nothing more limiting to the impact of an AI Summit than to have a group of people there who are not seriously committed to the outcome. See Chapter 5 for more on selecting summit participants.

Full Attendance over the Entire Session

Participation in an AI Summit is a full-time affair. Everyone who attends a summit attends the entire meeting. This holds true for everyone from all levels and functions in the organization. The meeting is designed for active involvement, open dialogue, and co-creation of the future. It is essential that everyone who attends be present for the entire process. An organization's leadership must commit to being present for the entire meeting, or the meeting might as well not be held. Full participation is essential to AI Summit success.

CONDITION 5:
COMMITMENT TO SUPPORT
SUCCESS OF DECISIONS AND OUTCOMES

The AI Summit is a broadly catalytic process. It taps into people's passions and unleashes high levels of energy for action. By the end of a summit, many new ideas have been hatched and initiatives launched. People have made commitments to themselves and to the whole to take responsibility for action. Hopes for the future are high. To honor the investment people are making and to maximize the impact of the summit process for the good of the organization, it is essential to provide institutional support to decisions and outcomes.

Primary responsibility for this support lies with the summit sponsors, those who championed the summit in the first place. They can provide strategic legitimacy, resources, rewards, integration across initiatives, and perhaps most important, encouragement. But it cannot stop with senior leaders. Formal and informal leaders at all levels must support the commitments made at the summit *and* be on the lookout for what we call "improvisational initiatives"—surprises, innovations, and new opportunities that open up as a result of new connections, new ideas, and fresh understandings. See Chapter 12 for more on supporting summit success.

CONDITION 6: A HEALTHY PHYSICAL AND RELATIONAL SPACE

A healthy physical and relational space allows people the comfort and facilities they need to be able to focus on what's really important—other people and the summit task. For example, the summit room should have windows to let in natural light and plenty of space to accommodate seating and lots of moving around. Food should be healthy to support people's energy and attention, and it should be served quickly and on time. There are a host of other details that require attention, such as sight and sound, lighting, air quality and temperature, wall space, parking, and bathrooms. If handled well, all of these amenities combine to make the summit experience a lively one. See Chapter 6 for a full description of summit logistics.

CONDITION 7: MINIMAL AND MINDFUL FACILITATION

Facilitation of an AI Summit is akin to being an MC (master or mistress of ceremonies) rather than a traditional small-group facilitator. The summit facilitator's primary job is to guide the large group through a predesigned series of activities. The group itself generates the ideas, establishes the relationships, decides on what's important, and manages its own process. The facilitators provide focus, enthusiasm, and clarity to engage the large group and to create a clearly understood path forward. Their attention is on the flow of activities, the energy levels, and the commitment to action within the large group.

To accomplish this requires a willingness not just to do AI, but to "be" AI. This implies being curious, looking for what is life giving for oneself and for others, working relationally, trusting in cooperation, focusing on meaning rather than methodology, reframing deficit dialogue into affirmative possibilities, and organizing around values and generative, life-giving factors. It all boils down to an unconditional commitment to finding and encouraging the very best in yourself, in others, and in the system as a whole. See Chapter 11 for more on appreciative facilitation.

CONDITION 8: BEGIN WITH APPRECIATIVE INTERVIEWS

There have been many times when people have asked us, "Is it really all that important to start every summit with one-on-one appreciative interviews? Couldn't we just go to small-group discussion of themes or jump directly to dreaming?" Our response is always "Do the interviews! They are essential to a productive start!"

Holographic Beginning

A holographic interview that goes through the full 4-D cycle sets the stage for a full-voice meeting. All participants have the opportunity to tell their stories about the organization. They feel that they are listened to and that they and their ideas are valued. Information, ideas, and stories that are generated during the interviews are referred to throughout the meeting. According to Gurudev Khalsa:

> The holographic appreciative interview process serves several purposes: (1) it gives everyone equal voice from the beginning; (2) it establishes a model of both sharing and listening in a deeply focused way; (3) it offers every participant a chance to explore their own thinking in the relative safety of a one-on-one dialogue; (4) it quickly generates a deep sense of connection among participants; and (5) it draws out the appreciative foundations of the work to be done.[6]

Deep Analysis of the Root Causes of Success

Appreciative interviews are not icebreakers. They do much more than simply set the tone of the meeting. They go to the core of the summit task and initiate a deep study and analysis of the root causes of success for that task. For example, when the Organization Development Network of Chicago (ODNC) wanted to revitalize its purpose, programs, and ways of organizing, they identified four factors that contributed to their success when they were at their best: (1) a strong sense of community; (2) high-quality opportunities for learning and growth; (3) pride, enthusiasm, and voluntary energy on the part of their members; and (4) bold, visionary leadership. Then, in their summit interview guide, they created questions around each of these topics. For example, they created these questions on learning and growth:

> ODNC is an organization dedicated, above all else, to the learning and development of its members. High-quality programs, rich interactions, and hands-on opportunities to "practice the practice" of OD give ODNC its substance and allow it to be an organization that transforms lives.
>
> (a) Think of the most powerful moment of learning and growth you have experienced in your life. Tell the story. What made it possible?
>
> (b) What are the three best programs, activities, or learning opportunities you've been involved in with ODNC, opportunities that delighted you or that enabled you to grow personally and professionally in a transformative way? What was it about you, others, and ODNC as an organization that made them great?
>
> (c) What are ODNC's greatest strengths and best practices when it comes to creating extraordinary opportunities for learning and growth?
>
> (d) Imagine your ideal ODNC five years from now. Imagine that it has a national and international reputation as being the place to go for enriching, life-changing opportunities for learning and growth. What does it look like? Who's there? What's going on that's new and different? What new things are you doing? What are others doing? What is the organization doing to create and sustain these opportunities (new systems, structures, relationships, ways of working, etc.)?

Questions like these allow people to develop an ever more nuanced and textured understanding of what gives life to the organization when it is at its best.

Creating High-Quality Connections

Appreciative interviews allow participants to get to know one another and to quickly feel themselves to be part of the larger group. In our experience, when 200 or more people have the experience of being listened to by another for an hour or more each, the sense of inclusion is palpable in the room. The feeling of being attended to, heard, and respected carries over from the interview to the large group. In addition, meeting another person and hearing his or her story via an appreciative interview creates a sense of mutuality and intimacy. An appreciative interviewer feels responsible for ensuring that the ideas, values, and deepest concerns of his or her partner are considered in the larger group. The appreciative interviews create a deep and abiding sense of cooperation, based on knowing and respecting the interests and differences of another.

CONDITION 9: FLOW THROUGH THE AI 4-D CYCLE

The 4-D cycle walks a group of people through the phases necessary to accomplish strategic change quickly in a way that is consistent with their values and aspirations. Each phase—discovery, dream, design, and destiny—adds essential ingredients to the total process. Taken together, they create an ascending spiral of learning, energy, and action. Neglect any one of them and the process suffers.

We strongly recommend the 4 × 4 summit design (4 D's in 4 days). In this format, a full day is spent on each D of the 4-D cycle. This allows time for work at the individual, small-group, and large-group levels and provides space for new connections, surprises, and innovations to emerge. It also permits the kind of rich, meaningful dialogue that leads to deep, sustainable change. Chapters 7–10 provide a comprehensive look at each of the 4 D's.

CONDITION 10: CREATE A NARRATIVE-RICH ENVIRONMENT

As mentioned in the Touche-Ross example, we are consistently amazed by the power of storytelling in AI Summits. Stories are compelling because (1) they are easy to relate to; (2) they spark spontaneity, humor, and joy; (3) they connect people with each other because they grow out of personal experience; (4) they promote advanced learning because they provide much more vivid detail than formalized forms of communication;

and (5) they are remembered over time. Because of this, a successful summit is always designed to be "narrative rich," that is, rich with storytelling.

Great Stories Make
Impossible Actions Seem Possible

In addition to being fun and full of information, great stories make impossible actions seem possible. We learned this with Touche-Ross, and we've seen it over and over again. A particularly clear example was the United Religions Initiative. For centuries people have been saying that cooperation among the religions is impossible. But when hundreds of people from around the world came to the summits with story after story of deep respect and courageous collaboration, often in highly polarized situations (blacks and whites in South Africa, Israelis and Palestinians, Christians and Muslims in Sudan), all of a sudden cooperation did not seem so unreasonable. In fact, as people shared what made their collaboration possible, and as they worked together in real time in the summits, the prospect of cooperation among the religions became not only possible but indisputable.

Communication Informs Capacity

Storytelling is important also because forms of communication predominant in an organization inform its capacities and potentials. When negotiation is the dominant form of communication within a human system, an environment of separateness and fragmentation is created. People talk and act as if they must each look out for their own interests. Information is withheld, and people seldom know what is happening in other parts of the organization. Few if any people have a sense of the whole. Cooperation and teamwork suffer as people experience a need to protect their place, their ideas, and their identities.

In contrast, narrative forms of communication create environments that are inclusive and invitational. They allow values to be expressed, explored, and adapted. They ignite the human spirit of curiosity and creativity. They contain seeds of wisdom grounded in experience. And they promote social bonding and cooperation.

Organizations as Stories-in-the-Telling

Finally, stories define organizational potential. As Jim Ludema points out in his article "Appreciative Storytelling," organizations follow certain "storylines" that shape their identities, priorities, values, and directions.[7] For example, when we were working with Tom White, President of Telephone Operations at GTE, he characterized GTE's storyline as "the best problem solvers on the planet." They had over 2,000 measurable indicators to pinpoint deficiencies in their processes and systems. They prided themselves on finding problems and fixing them. But, said Tom, the consequence of this storyline was that people began to follow it in their relationships with one another. Before long, GTE Telephone Operations had created "a negative culture, a descent into a paralyzing sense of hopelessness." Tom's conclusion was that organizational culture is in essence "the stories we tell ourselves about ourselves and then forget they are stories."

This is important because in an AI Summit, organizations and communities "re-story" themselves from the perspective of their strengths. They learn from stories of when they were at their best, they share stories about hopes for the future, they design their organization to support the priorities embedded in their "new" stories, and they launch action to make them happen. They begin to live a new strength-based story about who they are and what they aim to accomplish.

CONCLUSION

Together these ten essential conditions provide a general framework for AI Summit success. They serve to create a safe, open, inviting context for dialogue in which people can form healthy relationships, bring out the best in one another, and move together toward their common aspirations. The remainder of this book provides additional detail for you to consider. Chapters 4–6 look at sponsoring, planning, and creating a design for a summit; Chapters 7–10 at conducting a summit; Chapter 11 at facilitating a summit; Chapter 12 at following up after a summit; and Chapter 13 at creating the appreciative organization.

PART II

BEFORE
THE SUMMIT

You are in a meeting with your management team. The topic of discussion is the need for strategic planning. The director of marketing comments on how important it will be to include his whole organization. He notes, "They all work with different customers and different industries, and they care about where we are going. Furthermore, they will all have to carry out whatever we put in the plan." "At the same time that we want to be inclusive," adds the CEO, "we must move quickly. The markets have shifted dramatically in the past six months. We can't afford to fall behind." The director of engineering nods his approval and comments, "There is so much we need to learn from each other and be able to talk over together right now, I don't want to get into finger pointing and blaming one another, like we have in the past."

This scenario may not be exact, but it is real. It raises questions that we hear often. How can the needs expressed—speed, inclusion, and positive knowledge sharing—be addressed in strategic planning? How might an AI Summit be used to meet these needs?

The materials presented in this section will help you transform conversations like this one into a clear commitment to go forward with an AI Summit. They will guide you in helping potential sponsors understand the possibilities of an AI Summit and align it with their goals and aspirations. Chapter 4 covers the basics of establishing commitment and sponsorship for a summit. Chapter 5 provides an understanding of how to plan a summit. Chapter 6 explains what is needed to create a viable summit design. Taken together, these chapters tell you what must be done before an AI Summit to ensure its success.

CHAPTER 4

SPONSORING AN
APPRECIATIVE INQUIRY SUMMIT

Over the past ten years we have worked with leaders who have chosen to sponsor AI Summits for a wide variety of purposes. Organizational culture change, strategic planning, merger integration, superior customer service, and improved time to market are but a few. In our experience leaders choosing to sponsor a summit seek three key benefits: accelerated change within their organization; broad employee involvement in setting a course for the future; and integration across functions, departments, business units, and external stakeholder groups. Consider the case of the West Springfield Public Schools.

In West Springfield, Massachusetts, the Superintendent of Schools, Dr. Suzanne Moratta, and AI consultant Marge Schiller launched a multi-year appreciative inquiry (AI) effort to support the school district's strategic planning process. The purpose of the initiative was to involve the whole system (students, parents, teachers, administrators, and members of the community) in studying the successes of the system, reinforcing relationships, and fostering a strength-based environment of excellence.

Suzanne and Marge began the process with an AI Summit. Their first step was to form an advisory team that included leaders with diverse perspectives from throughout the school district. It included the head of the teacher's union, the head of curriculum, a middle school English teacher, an elementary school principal, and an elementary school teacher. Once this team was introduced to AI and had established the focus for the summit, they created a broadly representative planning team, which included parents, teachers, administrators, community members, and volunteers.

Marge, along with fellow AI consultants Debbie Morris, Gina Hinrichs, and Jackie Stavros, organized a group of volunteer AI consultants called the Positive Change Corps to support the work. Then, to build internal capacity, a fifteen-hour pre-summit training event was held with 150 teachers, students, parents, administrators, and community members who would attend the summit. Finally, hundreds of interviews were conducted during the summer with all stakeholder groups.

The summit itself was held in early September, just prior to the beginning of the school year. Some 650 people (about 400 teachers and administrators, 100 students in grades 6–12, and a cross-section of parents and members of the community) gathered in the high school gym to *discover* moments of greatness, *dream* about what could be, *design* new proposals to guide the district toward its dreams, and *plan* the first steps that each school could take to start moving in that direction.

As a result of the summit, the district established a nine-point strategic framework, and each school launched a series of action initiatives to translate the framework into practice. But more important than the tangible programmatic outcomes were the new relational bonds that were formed among stakeholders. Said one participant, "Each time a child spoke the entire audience in the gym would get quiet, the student was heard and he/she would get a heart-felt round of applause. These moments continuously reconnected the whole community to the voices of students and teachers who can indeed change their world."

Once Suzanne and Marge decided to sponsor the summit, a great deal had to occur in order to make it happen. This chapter provides you with an overview of the key activities, listed in Table 4.1, that are required for ensuring effective sponsorship of the AI Summit and maximizing its potential for success.

Table 4.1

Key Activities for Ensuring Effective Sponsorship

- Gaining the support of sponsors
- Introducing the Appreciative Inquiry Summit process
- Forming an active advisory team
- Focusing the summit on a significant change agenda
- Clarifying advisory team roles
- Ensuring commitment to resources
- Communicating the importance of the summit
- Selecting a summit planning team

GAINING THE SUPPORT OF SPONSORS

As we mentioned in Chapter 2, sponsors are usually a small group of leaders who have a change agenda in mind and want to use the AI Summit process to accomplish that agenda. They provide financial and other resources, give visible and enthusiastic support to the process, and use their influence to ensure its success.

It is essential that sponsors have a passionate interest in the summit topic. If the topic is not of strategic importance to them, they will not give it the time and focus it needs. For example, in the case of the West Springfield schools, if Marge had recommended a summit focused exclusively on curriculum redesign, Suzanne and her colleagues might have been intrigued, but it would not have commanded their full attention. They wanted to engage in a comprehensive process of strategic planning that involved all the major constituencies. At that time, nothing else would do.

A second important factor in gaining and maintaining the support of sponsors is to have a direct and open line of communication with them. Often, the person who invites us into a system is an HR or OD professional or some other person responsible for organization change. Although these folks are essential to the process, we have found that it is a mistake to rely on them as mediators between us and the key sponsor(s). We need to discuss our ideas and questions with sponsors and allow them to discuss their ideas and questions with us regularly and directly to shape the process and keep it on track.

INTRODUCING THE APPRECIATIVE INQUIRY SUMMIT PROCESS

When potential AI Summit sponsors contact us, they generally begin by telling us what they hope to accomplish and why they think appreciative inquiry and a summit might help them. In addition, they often have questions about appreciative inquiry and the summit process. As a result, our starting point is almost always an introduction of the AI Summit process to members of the organization.

Right from the start, in all that we do, we model the philosophy and practices of appreciative inquiry. It is our deep belief, based on many years of experience, that the process we use for gaining sponsorship of, planning, and facilitating an AI Summit must be congruent with the desired outcomes. So the way we introduce the AI Summit to an organization is highly participatory, experiential, and organized around the AI 4-D cycle.

Who Attends the Introduction?

It is our goal to engage as many people as possible in the introduction of the AI Summit. In most cases it is an iterative process. It may begin on a conference call with one or two executives, grow to a conference call with six to eight people—perhaps a team who is planning a change initiative or the annual strategic planning—and then become an actual presentation. We ask that a broad cross-section of the organization be invited to the initial introduction of the AI Summit. At British Airways, for example, after a handful of executives learned about and discussed appreciative inquiry with us via conference calls, they invited forty people to attend a two-day introduction to appreciative inquiry. Participants included vice presidents, frontline employees, customer service representatives, union leadership, and supervisors. Having a microcosm of the organization at the initial introduction gave everyone an opportunity to experience the potential of appreciative inquiryand to express concerns as well. It also gave participants an experience of wholeness and the opportunity to sense the positive benefits of whole-system involvement.

What Makes a Meaningful Introduction?

Whether it is a two-hour introduction, as outlined in Exhibit 4.1, or a two-day introduction (see Chapter 5) to the AI Summit process, there are some common characteristics. First, it should provide a balance of concepts and experience. We share the principles of appreciative inquiry and the summit, and we give participants an opportunity to experience appreciative interviews. The best way to learn about AI is to do it, so the experience of appreciative interviews, at a minimum, is essential. In a longer introduction we may give participants the experience of writing appreciative questions, sharing stories from their interviews, or even selecting potential topics for a summit.

Exhibit 4.1

Sample Agenda for a Two-Hour
Introduction to the AI Summit Process

1. Introduction to Appreciative Inquiry	20 minutes
a. What Is AI? Definitions and Success Stories	
b. Deficit-Based Change vs. Positive Change	
c. Overview of the 4-D Cycle	
2. Mini Appreciative Interviews	45 minutes
a. One-on-One Interviews (15 minutes each way)	
b. Debrief of the Interviews	
c. The Power of Positive Questions	
3. The AI Summit Process	20 minutes
a. Small-Group vs. Whole-System Approaches	
b. Conditions for Success	
c. A Typical Four-Day Summit Agenda	
4. Open Discussion: How Might a Summit Benefit You?	20 minutes
5. Next Steps	15 minutes

Second, the introduction should be narrative rich—full of stories about how the summit process worked in other organizations. Appreciative inquiry is a story-based process, so an effective introduction involves a generous amount of storytelling. We share stories and we ask participants to share stories. As they hear each other tell stories of their own organization at its best, they gain an understanding of the power of sharing best practices.

Third, an effective introduction gives participants an opportunity to discuss how the summit might be used in their organization—what purpose it might serve, the results it might achieve, who might be involved, and when it might occur. During this time some groups actually make a decision to proceed with an AI Summit. In more than one instance we have been asked to leave the room only to be invited back within ten to fifteen minutes to hear that a decision had been made to move forward with the summit process.[1]

Experiencing the Introductory Interview

The prime reason we facilitate appreciative interviews during introduction of the AI Summit is because it gives people insight into appreciative inquiry and provides the greatest testament to its power. Participants repeatedly tell us that they learned the most about the benefits of AI when they engaged in appreciative interviews. Exhibit 4.2 shows three sets of appreciative interview questions that can be used in introducing the AI Summit.

Exhibit 4.2

Sample Introductory Appreciative Interview Questions

Example 1	Example 2	Example 3
Opening	**Opening**	**Opening**
I'd like to learn about your beginnings with the organization. Please tell me a little bit about yourself and how you got started with your organization. What were your first impressions?	To start, I would like to learn about your beginnings with the organization. What attracted you to the organization? What keeps you here?	Tell me about yourself. What brought you here? How long have you been here? What keeps you going? Please elaborate.

(continues)

Exhibit 4.2 *(continued)*

Sample Introductory Appreciative Interview Questions

Example 1	Example 2	Example 3
High Point	**Work Experience**	**Valuing**
Looking back at your entire work experience, reflect back on a high point, a time when you felt most alive, most inspired, and most proud. What was it about that experience that made it a high point? Who was involved? Please tell me the story.	Think of a time in your entire work experience when you felt best about coming to work, when your work group was performing extraordinarily well. What were the circumstances that led to that high level of performance? Please tell me the story.	What do you value most about yourself as a person? What are your special talents, gifts, or attributes? What do you like most about the people you work with? And finally, what do you value most about this organization? What are its best practices?
Trends, Valuing	**Core Factors**	**Positive Changes, and Opportunities**
What is it that you most value about yourself, this organization, and the work that you do?	As you think about what it takes to be successful in this industry, what are the core factors (life-giving forces) that help make this organization unique? What gives life to your organization?	As you reflect on your experiences in this industry, what are some of the most significant changes you've seen? What are the most important trends, and opportunities that you see coming?
Sense of the Future	**Image of the Future**	**Hopes for the Future**
If you were given three wishes to improve the health and vitality of this organization, what would they be?	Imagine that three years from now this organization has achieved everything it had set out to do during that time. What has changed? What is different? How do you know?	Imagine that tomorrow you wake up and on the front page of your local newspaper is a story about the immense success of your organization. What is the headline and what story has been told?

Introductory interviews not only give an experience of appreciative inquiry but also allow participants to begin to identify what gives them life when they are at their best. As a result, it is important to debrief the interview experience. We ask people to share what the experience was like and what they learned about their partner and their organization in the process. In most cases participants are amazed at how easily and quickly their conversations became meaningful, how much they discovered they had in common, and how much they learned about their partner's contribution to the business. On one occasion even we were surprised by the enthusiasm generated as a vice president of sales known to be a bit of a loner described his introductory interview as powerful and productively intimate, and he called for all 1,200 employees to be given the opportunity to experience an appreciative interview. At that point our agenda was thrown out and the group began discussing their summit.

FORMING AN ACTIVE ADVISORY TEAM

Once the decision is made to sponsor an AI Summit we suggest the formation of an advisory team[2]—a small group of no more than eight people who will provide oversight, direction, and resources for the summit. In some cases the existing management team may take on the role of the advisory team. Such was the case at Hunter Douglas Window Fashions Division when the business unit managers, also known as the BUMS, took on the responsibility of sponsoring their AI initiative, Focus 2000.[3]

In most cases, however, a cross-functional advisory team is formed. The advisory team for the Nevada Child Welfare Services Integration summits was made up of leaders from the state, the county, and various child welfare agencies. At Santa Ana Star Hotel and Casino, the advisory team consisted of the general manager, the assistant GM, the director of human resources, the manager of training and development, and the chairman of the board.

Once the advisory team is formed, we usually meet with them for one full day to focus the summit process on a significant change agenda, clarify advisory team roles, ensure commitment to resources, plan for communicating the importance of the summit, and select a planning team.[4] We find it useful to start this meeting with an appreciative inquiry into "leadership for positive change." In the interview guide, we ask questions that invite participants to share stories of the most successful change initiatives they have been a part of and to identify the forces and factors that made them possible. We ask them to envision the future of *this* change initiative—to focus it on a specific change agenda; to imagine how people are working together before, during, and after the process; to imagine the impact and outcomes; and so on. And finally, we invite them to get practical about key tasks and activities that need to be accomplished to ensure success. We then spend the rest of the day putting all of the pieces into place.

FOCUSING THE SUMMIT ON A SIGNIFICANT CHANGE AGENDA

One of the first things that needs to be done in the advisory team meeting is to come to agreement on the strategic focus of the summit. It is not necessary or even desirable at this point to finalize the title or name of the summit; that is the job of the planning team. But it is essential to get clear about the change agenda. As discussed earlier, to be successful a summit must be focused on a clear task of strategic significance to the organization or community sponsoring it. Whatever the change agenda is, the higher a priority it is for all the stakeholder groups involved, the better suited it will be as the focus for a summit.

Examples of tasks initially established by advisory teams or sponsors include leadership at all levels in the U.S. Navy; optimal margin and employee-driven throughput at Roadway Express; strategic competitive advantage at McDonald's; the future of the Human Resources function at the Department of National Defense, Canada; merger of state and county child welfare services in Nevada; nursing retention at Lovelace Health System; diversity at the National Association of Independent Schools; superior customer service at Santa Ana Star Casino; and strategic planning at Nutrimental. These tasks are specific enough to define the change agenda but broad enough to allow extensive dialogue on the part of the planning team and other stakeholders to determine the specific topic for the summit. For example, in the case of the Navy, our colleagues Frank Barrett and David Cooperrider worked with the planning team to transform the broad strategic focus of leadership at every level into a specific topic that everyone could support passionately: "Bold and Enlightened Naval Leaders at Every Level: Forging an Empowered Culture of Excellence."

CLARIFYING ADVISORY TEAM ROLES

It is always important to help the advisory team understand its unique role and to clarify it vis-à-vis the planning team, facilitators, and others. This is especially true if the advisory team has not been through this kind of large-scale change process before. The appreciative inquiry into "leadership for positive change" is of great value in this regard. Given the opportunity to interview one another and to share stories about times of leading change, advisory team members can generate a list of what they must do to sponsor the summit successfully.

Typical roles of the advisory team—before, during, and after a summit—are shown in Table 4.2. Before a summit the advisory team has four key roles: to ensure that the summit is focused on a significant organizational change agenda, to communicate the importance of the summit, to provide resources needed for success, and to select and empower a planning team.

Table 4.2

Key Roles of the Advisory Team
Before, During, and After an AI Summit

Before	During	After
• Focus the summit task on a significant organizational change agenda.	• Be a full participant—take turns performing the various self-management roles.	• Continuously demonstrate an appreciative focus in every follow-up activity.
• Communicate the importance of the AI Summit.	• Meet with and provide feedback to the summit facilitators.	• Communicate the importance of vigorous follow-through—adopt an action focus.
• Provide the resources (time, money, and people) to ensure success.	• Be vulnerable—share thoughts and feelings with others.	• Require documentation of AI Summit activities and establish follow-up meetings to ensure progress.
• Empower a diverse, cross-organization planning team.	• Listen intently and deeply to the many voices of the organization—be curious and inquisitive.	

(continues)

Table 4.2 *(continued)*

Key Roles of the Advisory Team
Before, During, and After an AI Summit

Before	During	After
	• Exude energy and enthusiasm for the process—model what you want others to do. • Encourage others to share thoughts and perspectives. • Contribute passionately to co-creating the future.	• Lead the transition by creating an environment that facilitates open sharing and supporting. • Continuously reinforce and communicate, and track progress—use measures, targets, and results to keep the momentum going. • Provide resources and support to teams moving the process forward.

ENSURING COMMITMENT TO RESOURCES

It takes a lot of resources and support to run an AI Summit effectively. The advisory team needs to clearly understand and be willing to commit the resources required to ensure its overall success. The resources required to run the AI Summit should be discussed right from the outset.

Beyond money, the resources required to effectively sponsor an AI Summit include people, supplies and equipment, dedicated time, venue, and food. Table 4.3 provides a resource matrix that can be used to help clarify the resource requirements for a summit.

Each summit is unique, and so are the resources invested. The change agenda, the length of the summit, the number of people invited, and the organization's culture and financial state will all influence the level of resources committed. We have worked with organizations that hosted their summits at hotels, on university campuses, and in convention centers. Some have catered elaborate meals; others have had simple box lunches donated.

Table 4.3

Resource Matrix for an AI Summit

	Before the Summit	During the Summit	After the Summit
People	• Advisory team (6–8 people) • Planning team (12–20 people) • Facilitators (2 per 100 summit participants) • Interview team (if conducting pre-summit interviews) • Organization members (if conducting pre-summit interviews) • Stakeholders (if being interviewed pre-summit)	• Advisory team • Planning team • Facilitators • Organization members • Stakeholders	• Innovation teams (if initiatives are developed) • Advisory team: ongoing guidance and support for continuing positive change • Planning team: communication of summit successes and next steps
Time	• Advisory team: one day per month • Planning team: five days per month • Interview team: twenty hours—two hours per interview for ten interviews conducted • Organization members: one hour each for an interview • Stakeholders: one hour each for an interview	• Whole-system involvement: three to five days • Planning team: full participation, plus brief morning huddle, end-of-day review with facilitators • Advisory team: full participation, plus end-of-day feedback to facilitators	• Innovation teams: TBD per initiative • Advisory team: one day per month • Planning team: four to five days to communicate about the summit and wrap up; more if they form a positive change network or launch second-wave AI

| Venue: Rooms, Equipment, and Food | • Conference dates and time
• Lodging requirements (how many rooms)
• Transportation (to and from location)
• Room arrangements for the event:
  • Size and shape (windows preferred)
  • Additional breakout rooms
  • Lighting requirements
  • Tables and chairs (round preferred)
  • Food arrangements and quality
  • Wall space and/or foam boards
  • Audiovisual equipment
  • Adequate rest room facilities | • Daily room setups, including breakout rooms
• Audiovisual equipment setup:
  • Easels, flipcharts, and markers
  • Projectors (computer and overhead)
  • Video cameras (if videotaping)
  • Microphones
  • Computer voting equipment (if using)
• Access to copiers, computers, and printers
• Food and refreshments
• Lodging and transportation as needed | • Break down rooms and equipment, etc.
• Meet with facilities manager and provide feedback
• Arrange for transportation from venue to airport if required
• Arrange for transportation to return equipment to home facility if needed |
| Supplies and Materials | • Participant invitation letter
• Registration process
• Seating designations
• Workbooks and handouts
• Needed supplies | • Participant rosters and name badges
• Participant workbooks and handouts
• Participant table supplies
• Foam boards for wall maps (if needed)
• Evaluation sheets
• Participant gifts (if desired) | • TBD during summit |

Audiovisual equipment has ranged from easels with flipchart pads and markers to professional video documentation.

Taking the time to clarify and provide resources up front builds trust, eliminates potential surprises, and increases the chances of a successful AI Summit. At Nutrimental, a part of the food processing plant was emptied out, and picnic tables and 750 rented chairs were brought in. A stage was built at one end of the large space and a sound system was set up temporarily. For three days the entire company met with community leaders, suppliers, and customers. Together, in one room and all wearing identical t-shirts created for the summit, they charted a new direction for the company. Six months later the company's revenues were up 300 percent and morale was up 200 percent. Their resource investment paid off both in employee morale and in business results.

COMMUNICATING THE IMPORTANCE OF THE AI SUMMIT

Once the change agenda has been selected, roles clarified, and resources committed, the advisory team must clearly communicate the importance of the summit throughout the organization. A combination of formal vehicles, such as newsletter articles, memos, and staff meetings, and informal vehicles, such as testimonials and statements of personal hopes for the process, has been found to be most effective. In keeping with an appreciative spirit, be creative about how you promote the summit. In one organization where people did not have access to e-mail on a regular basis and the company newsletter was not well read or appreciated as a source of news, posters were made and hung in the cafeteria, at the time clock, and in the break rooms.

Sometimes we recommend that a series of "kickoff" meetings be held to inform every employee about the appreciative inquiry process and the AI Summit that will occur. During that time we solicit volunteers who will make up the planning team, serve as interviewers, and be AI coordinators in the various business units and functional departments. Kickoff meetings are especially useful when the organization has never conducted a whole-system initiative and when full commitment among employees is crucial for success. They ensure that everyone knows about the summit, why it is important, and why their involvement is essential.

SELECTING A SUMMIT PLANNING TEAM

The summit was over and the planning team was debriefing. Shoes had been kicked off as business casual turned to casual. As each team member spoke, it became clearer and clearer: The summit had been a great success, and serving on the planning team had been even better. This group of people were a typical planning team. They were from different functions in the organization—some staff, some line. They represented all levels in the organization, including a vice president, a human resources manager, a communications representative, two frontline supervisors, a director, a union steward, and two additional frontline employees. They had worked hard for the past four months, sharing hopes, resources, frustrations, and a clear intention. And they had just pulled off a first for their company—a 250-person AI Summit. It all began when they were invited to serve as the planning team by the advisory team.

It is the advisory team's responsibility to select and to empower a planning team for the AI Summit. The advisory team should take great care in creating a planning team, as its role is to do everything that is needed to make the summit happen. Without an effective planning team there can be no summit. Table 4.4 identifies team and individual characteristics of a planning team. We use this tool to help an advisory team select the best possible members for the planning team. It is not meant to be exhaustive, but to serve as a general guide.

Table 4.4

Characteristics of an Effective AI Summit Planning Team

Team Membership Characteristics	Individual Member Characteristics
• Diverse membership representing multiple levels, functions, and units • Includes corporate staff such as HR and internal/external communications and line employees • Includes both formal and informal leaders (management, frontline, and union)	• High credibility within the organization • Strong interpersonal communication and listening skills • Strong action and follow-through orientation • Understanding of and support for the vision and strategic direction of the organization

(continues)

Table 4.4 *(continued)*

Characteristics of an Effective AI Summit Planning Team

Team Membership Characteristics	Individual Member Characteristics
• Includes all groups whose buy-in is critical to the success of the AI Summit	• Enthusiasm toward AI Summit participation • Valuing of teamwork, participation, and cooperation

As consultants we include ourselves as active members of both the advisory team and the planning team. We meet at least monthly with the advisory team and more often with the planning team. We work hand in hand with the planning team and guide their efforts throughout the AI Summit planning process to ensure success.

With the selection of a planning team the infrastructure is in place to successfully sponsor an AI Summit. In Chapters 5 and 6 we discuss all that a planning team must do before the summit actually occurs.

CHAPTER 5

PLANNING THE AI SUMMIT

The first United Religions Initiative summit occurred when the idea of the URI was just a burning hope in the hearts and minds of Bishop William Swing and a handful of his interfaith colleagues. They had reserved a conference room and invited sixty-five religious leaders to a four-day meeting to discuss the feasibility of a global interfaith organization dedicated to peace among religions. Just six weeks before, David Cooperrider and Gurudev Khalsa had introduced them to appreciative inquiry. Quickly a decision was made to use appreciative inquiry as the foundation for the scheduled meeting.

As planning conversations proceeded, two critical success factors became increasingly evident: The task must be clear and compelling, and all the stakeholders must be in the room. If Bishop Swing, as quoted in the newspapers, had committed to the formation of a United Religions Initiative, then the question of feasibility was moot. The task for the summit had to be redefined to evoke commitment and action, not ponder feasibility. And if the URI was to become a truly global organization, the list of relevant stakeholders had to include world leaders, global organizers, and the media, along with religious leaders. As a result, the meeting, which was initially set to consist of religious leaders discussing the feasibility of a URI, became a meeting of world leaders considering "The URI: A Time for Action."

Planning for an AI Summit is important because it plants the seeds for what will happen at the summit and thereafter. As the case of the URI illustrates, planning can itself be transformative for an organization and its members. It shifts their focus and mobilizes people, energy, and resources to aim higher and accomplish more than previously imagined.

Summit planning activities fall into seven broad categories:

- Forming the summit planning team
- Defining the summit task
- Identifying the summit participants
- Determining the summit format
- Creating the summit design
- Preparing the summit communication strategy
- Arranging the summit logistics

Exhibit 5.1 shows the categories and the considerations that are necessary within each. In this chapter we cover the first four: forming the planning team, defining the task, identifying the participants, and determining the format. In Chapter 6 we discuss the final three: creating the design, preparing the communication strategy, and arranging the logistics. Taken together, these two chapters provide a broad overview of summit planning and design, not a formula. They are intended to help you adapt the summit process to your organization and change agenda.

Exhibit 5.1

Essential Summit Planning Activities

Summit Planning Team

- Introducing the planning team to appreciative inquiry
- Clarifying the roles of the planning team

Summit Task

- Cooperating to define the summit task
- Creating a powerful summit task

Summit Participation

- Framework for identifying stakeholders
- Creating a stakeholder map
- Selecting internal stakeholders
- Selecting external stakeholders
- The power of improbable pairs
- Sending out invitations
- Ensuring attendance
- Planning for on-site registration

Exhibit 5.1 *(continued)*
Essential Summit Planning Activities

Summit Format

- Multiple mini-summits
- Multiple mini-summits connected virtually in real time
- Pre-work, post-work sequence
- A rolling process of shorter AI meetings

Summit Design

- Creating a summit agenda
- Crafting an appreciative interview guide
- Planning pre-summit interviews
- Creating the summit participant workbook
- Determining how to document summit proceedings

Summit Communication

- Branding the summit task and process
- Determining how to market the summit

Summit Logistics

- Who does logistical planning?
- Selecting the site for your summit
- Room shape
- Tables, chairs, and seating arrangements
- Wall space
- Equipment and technical support
- Breakout rooms
- Meals and refreshments
- Travel, transportation, and parking

SUMMIT PLANNING TEAM

Once the planning team members have been selected by the advisory team, the planning team begins to meet to learn about appreciative inquiry, scope out its roles and responsibilities, and plan the AI Summit process. This work usually takes place over a two- to three-month period of time. Usually, some planning team members are familiar with appreciative inquiry whereas others are new to it. So the first thing we do is level the playing field by introducing appreciative inquiry and the AI Summit.

Introducing the Planning Team to Appreciative Inquiry

We introduce AI in any number of ways. On some occasions we conduct an "in-house training" specifically designed for the planning team. An in-house training is an opportunity for both learning and planning. At British Airways during the initial two-day workshop for the planning team, interview topics were selected and a draft interview guide was created. In addition, people volunteered to help with communication, invitations, logistics, and the summit agenda. During this workshop, planning team members learned about AI and organized themselves for planning. Our experiences is that a minimum of two days with the planning team is necessary to launch the AI Summit process. In many cases, especially when the organization is new to AI or when the change initiative is large and complex, three days for the initial planning meeting is better. Exhibit 5.2 contains a sample agenda for a two-day planning team meeting.

A second option for introducing the planning team to AI is to invite the team to one of our public workshops on appreciative inquiry. The benefits are learning, planning, and team development. When seven people from different levels and functions of Hunter Douglas Window Fashions Division attended the appreciative inquiry workshop we teach annually in Taos, New Mexico, they learned about AI, bonded as a team, and drafted their plan. They left the workshop prepared to introduce AI to their organization, launch an organization-wide inquiry, and host an AI Summit.

In still other situations we are able to have some or all members of a planning team attend a summit being held by another organization. For example, when the U.S. Navy hosted its first summit on "Leadership at all Levels," people from Cisco Systems, Veterans Affairs, Cap Gemini Ernst & Young, and the URI attended to experience the summit firsthand. Whatever the method used, it is essential that the entire team gain an understanding of appreciative inquiry and the AI Summit in order to plan for its use in their organization.

Clarifying the Roles of the Planning Team

As mentioned earlier, the role of the planning team is to do whatever is needed to hold a successful AI Summit. Typically,

Exhibit 5.2

Sample Agenda for a Two-Day Planning Team Meeting

Day 1

8:30–9:00	Opening, welcome, introductions
9:00–9:30	Brief introduction to appreciative inquiry, with stories (facilitators)
9:30–11:00	On-on-one appreciative interviews (break included)
11:00–11:15	Debrief interview process (facilitators)
11:15–12:00	Introduce AI 4-D cycle and AI Summit approach, with stories (facilitators)
12:00–1:00	Lunch
1:00–2:15	Share stories from interviews (small groups) and map positive core (large group)
2:15–3:15	Define summit task/topics (first small groups, then large group)
3:15–3:30	Break
3:30–4:45	Identify summit participants (first small groups, then large group)
4:45–5:00	Wrap-up

Day 2

8:30–8:45	Opening, reflections
8:45–9:30	Confirm summit task and stakeholders (first small groups, then large group)
9:30–10:15	Visioning activity: our ideal summit (first small groups, then large group)
10:15–10:30	Break
10:30–11:00	Present sample summit agenda (facilitators)
11:00–12:00	Customize summit agenda (first small groups, then large group)
12:00–1:00	Lunch
1:00–2:30	Create interview guide (back and forth between small and large group)
2:30–2:45	Break
2:45–4:30	Form subgroups to work on summit workbook, documentation, communication, and logistics
4:30–5:00	Closing reflections and wrap-up

---

this includes attending to the seven categories outlined earlier. Each of these activities requires both thoughtfulness and the input from many people throughout the organization. In addition, at each step of the way, it is advisable for the planning team to coordinate with the advisory team. In some instances we establish regular meetings between the planning and advisory teams. In other situations we serve on both teams along with one or two key leaders and are able to keep the two teams coordinated. In all cases the planning team should call on the advisory team for resource checks and balances, input on whom to invite, and help with communication.

The larger the intended summit, the larger the planning team. For a small summit of up to 200 people, the planning team may work as one united team with various members taking on specific tasks. For larger summits, we suggest the formation of subteams responsible for different aspects of the planning.

SUMMIT TASK

An AI Summit's potential for success is maximized when its purpose is clear, compelling, and directly related to the business of the organization. Defining the summit task is one of the most important steps in the planning process. It defines the scope of the inquiry and provides the framework for subsequent interviews, data collection, action taking, and follow-up. An effective summit task is one that excites, energizes, and invigorates participants to contribute at the highest level.

Cooperating to Define the Summit Task

Defining the summit task is a collaborative effort between the advisory team and the planning team. The advisory team usually provides broad input such as the overarching issue, challenge, or opportunity at hand as well as their expectations for the summit. Their input is usually framed around questions like: What do we really want from this summit? What are our ultimate hopes and aspirations? What will success look like? The planning team uses the advisory team's input and ultimately defines the unique summit task. Exhibit 5.3 provides a list of sample AI Summit tasks.

Exhibit 5.3

Sample AI Summit Tasks

- Enhancing Customer Service through an Appreciative Eye
- Excellence in City Leadership
- Becoming the World's Best HR Business Partner
- Just-in-Time Learning
- Ultimate Teamwork
- Excellence in Action: Celebrating Our Past and Creating Our Future
- Called to the Future Together: Planning for Mission in the New Millennium

Creating a Powerful Summit Task

Based on the idea that organizations move in the direction of what they study, the summit task should be a bold proposition of the desired future. Questions to ask when selecting a summit task include:

1) *Is it stated in the affirmative?* All too often organizations put a lot of time, money, and attention into studying problems—from loss of market share to employee turnover to poor performance to financial downturns to low productivity. Studying deficits such as these tends to lead to finger pointing and blame, dissension and demoralization. It is essential that the summit task be focused on the positive.

   Getting to an affirmative summit task may require reframing a problem. For example, we worked with one group that reframed their main concern of overcoming obstacles to sales to define their summit task as "Increasing Sales through Creativity and Collaboration." In another case, the problem of declining market share led to a summit task of "Industry Leadership through Product Innovation." The reframing of a problem into an affirmative statement shifts the focus of the summit and of the organization away from deficits and toward positive potentials.

2) *Do you really want it?* Few things are more fatiguing than having to sit through a four-day meeting talking about a topic that you really don't care about. For example, when the 300 global participants from McDonald's came together to talk about how to enhance global staffing and retention, they really wanted it. The quick-service restaurant industry is highly competitive, and attracting and keeping the best employees is a distinct competitive advantage. If they had had to sit through a summit on, say, teamwork or collaboration, they may have been interested, but it would not have engaged them in the

passionate way that staffing and retention did. Summit tasks should always be focused on something the organization really wants at a deep strategic level.

3) *Is it driven by true curiosity?* Good summit tasks stretch the status quo and require learning from one another. They invite people to inquire, explore, hear, and learn what others value and what others know about the business, customers, and processes.

   Consider the summit task "Creating a Culture of Superior Customer Service." This task implies the need to learn about, discuss, and ultimately define what is meant by superior customer service, as well as what a culture of superior customer service would look like. We used this task recently for a series of summits that involved close to 1,000 people in the creation of a set of service principles for their organization. The principles in turn became the foundation for the organization's performance and measurement systems.

4) *Does it require collaborative action?* Very little work gets done these days without high levels of interaction and interdependence. We suggest that summit tasks be defined using relational language such as "collaboration," "cooperation," "partnership," "mutual," "we," "our," "together," or "united," as illustrated by the following examples: "Building a Partnership for the Future," "Creating Our Future," and "United We Strive for Excellence."

Keep in mind that your summit task will serve to guide discussion and actions at the summit and beyond. Like a seed planted in the spring, it will grow and spread over time. In order to reap a bountiful harvest, take time in the beginning and choose your summit task wisely.

SUMMIT PARTICIPATION

Determining whom to invite to an AI Summit can be a powerful learning activity for the planning team and an early test of the organization's commitment to full participation. To decide whom to invite, the planning team must first list all of the stakeholders— those people or groups, internal and external to the organization, that have a stake in the decisions and actions that will take place at the summit.

When a cross-level and cross-functional planning team takes the time to do this, they learn a lot about their business and who must be involved to create the future. A medical center, for example, realized that patients and community health advocates, as well as doctors, nurses, policymakers, and administrators, needed to be involved in creating the future of health care. They invited representatives from all these groups to their summit. Similarly, a university invited faculty, administration, board members, full- and part-time students, parents of students, and high school guidance counselors to their strategic planning summit.

Framework for Identifying Stakeholders

The framework we like to use for identifying stakeholders is called the "Five I's of Involvement."[1] It's simple, comprehensive, and easy to use. In this framework, planing team members list the people and groups along the organization's value chain who have:

1) **Interest** in the summit task and potential outcomes. For example, community members may be very interested in having a say about where a new manufacturing site will be located.

2) **Influence,** formal and informal, to provide resources to achieve the summit task. For example, in a union work environment, both union leadership and management must participate for the summit to be effective.

3) **Information** or access to information needed for summit success. For example, customers have essential information about their preferences for any organization that provides products or services.

4) **Impact** or a high probability of being impacted by what happens during the summit. For example, county planners and citizens would both be on a community planning summit invitation list.

5) **Investment,** financial or emotional, related to the summit task and outcomes. Shareholders, distributors, and product designers would all be invited to a strategic planning summit focused on market leadership for re-inventing an industry.

Creating a Stakeholder Map

Once a list of all potential stakeholders is generated, the next step is to create a stakeholder map. It is a way to illustrate all the people and groups who might be invited to attend, the value they would bring, and how they would benefit from participation. At this point we begin to identify specific people, by name, as well as groups or departments.

When creating a stakeholder map, it is not necessary to identify internal stakeholders if the organization has already decided to invite all employees to attend the summit. If, however, the organization, for reasons of size or cost, has decided to invite only a representative number of employees, then the stakeholder map must also include internal stakeholders. Exhibit 5.4 shows a variation of a stakeholder map that includes both internal and external stakeholders, what they have to offer to the summit, and the benefits they might receive by participating.

Exhibit 5.4

Stakeholder Map

Stakeholder Group—Internal	Recommended People	What They Bring to the Summit	How They Might Benefit
Stakeholder Group—External	Recommended People	What They Bring to the Summit	How They Might Benefit

Selecting Internal Stakeholders

Having completed a stakeholder map, the planning team must now create an invitation list stating which internal and external stakeholders will actually be invited to the summit. When it comes to selecting internal stakeholders (employees), there are three broad alternatives:

1) *Invite everyone:* All employees in the organization are invited.

2) *Invite representatives:* People from all groups, departments, functions, and levels in the organization are invited.

3) *Invite a selected population:* People are chosen and invited from certain groups, departments, functions, or levels in the organization that are deemed relevant and important to the summit task.

Table 5.1 shows the relative advantages and disadvantages of different ways of selecting employee participants.

Table 5.1

Methods of Selecting Internal Stakeholder Participants

Method	Advantages	Disadvantages
Everyone	• All viewpoints valued • People can speak for themselves • Generates ownership • People gain a holistic perspective • Dramatically speeds up change—no convincing others "back home"	• Costs for shutdown or temporary staff
Drawing or lottery for representatives	• Viewed as most open and fair • Generates excitement	• May not get the critical or required knowledge • People must represent their group or department
Nomination or referral for representatives	• Viewed as more open and fair • Generates self-pride in participants • Builds informal leadership	• May not get the critical or required knowledge • People must represent their group or department
Direct selection	• Gets the critical or required knowledge	• Viewed as least open and fair

One method we have found to be especially powerful for generating participants is self-referral. At British Airways, Hunter Douglas, and the Canadian Broadcasting Corporation we solicited volunteers to attend the summits. In each case people wrote thoughtful letters volunteering and explaining what they had to offer and why they wanted to attend. After reading through stacks of self-referral letters, planning team members commented on how much they learned about the creative capacities and dreams of the people who volunteered. Previously untapped creativity and commitment were discovered, informal leaders were identified, and self-responsibility and risk taking were reinforced in the organization. At the Canadian Broadcasting Corporation, the enthusiasm of the letters caused a rethinking of the summit size—from 125 to over 300 participants.

Selecting External Stakeholders

Selecting external stakeholders is a quite different process. It usually requires extensive input from people throughout the organization. In most organizations, different stakeholder groups work with different parts of the organization. For example, the vendors who provide meals for airlines work much more closely with airline purchasing departments and the ramp crew than they do with pilots, customer service reps, or executives. Each stakeholder has specific and unique relationships with the organization and will need to be sought out by the planning team.

If the planning team has been formed to be broadly representative of the various stakeholder groups, one way to collect stakeholder names is to simply have planning team members meet with their colleagues in the organization to collect names. Another way is to ask department heads to spend fifteen minutes at a staff meeting asking for recommendations.

The Power of Improbable Pairs

David Cooperrider defines improbable pairs as people or groups that represent opposite extremes of a perceived dilemma. It is often precisely these people who need to come together in an AI Summit to make significant new progress on a particular agenda. For example, in the cases of John Deere and GTE, labor and management needed to come together. In the case of the URI it was Muslims and Jews, Christians and Buddhists, spiritual expressions and indigenous traditions. But in all these cases, had the "opposing" points of view not joined in dialogue, meaningful, lasting, sustainable progress would not have been made. They would have had to settle for "business as usual."

In the same way, in any summit it is of essential value to include people who bring dramatically different points of view to the process. In this way all the voices get heard, new connections and relationships get made, and innovative solutions that were previously unimaginable get created. Summits are no place to be timid. They are forums for meaningful dialogue and vital action on significant business issues.

Sending Out Invitations

Once the planning team has decided who will be invited to the summit, they create an invitation list and send out invitation letters. The invitation list describes the people, functions, and organizations they represent. It will also serve as the database to track:

- Who has been invited
- If they are planning to attend
- Special needs, if any
- Names and contact information for a participant roster

Exhibit 5.5 shows a sample invitation list that can be adapted to fit any summit situation.

Exhibit 5.5

Sample Invitation List

Stakeholder Group	Invitee's Name & Title	Contact Information	Attending: Yes or No	Special Needs, if Any
Executives				
Customers				
Vendors				
HR staff				
Manufacturing				
Summit staff				

Once the invitation list is built, an invitation letter is created and sent out to all invitees. The invitation letter should contain the following information:

- Summit purpose and potential outcomes
- Reason for attendance—value and benefits
- Dates, time, length, and location of summit (be specific; don't leave out anything)
- RSVP information
- Pre-summit preparation activities
- Expression of thanks

Ensuring Attendance

Beyond the invitation letter, there are many things that can be done to ensure attendance at the summit. To foster internal participation, flyers can be sent to employees at home. Supervisors can discuss the importance of the summit at regular staff meetings. Articles can be put in the company newsletter. Planning and advisory team members can attend department meetings to explain the summit's importance and what to expect at the summit. At the Canadian Broadcasting Corporation, advertisements for the summit showed pictures of the planning team in action and carried the message "Space is limited—our future will be defined." The response was like a run on tickets for a hit Broadway show!

Another excellent way to foster external participation is by sending invitation letters from the organization's leadership and then following up with a phone call. It is most effective when members of the organization who have a personal relationship with the external invitees call them to express gratitude for their attendance and to answer any questions they may have. In most cases external invitees will know little or nothing about appreciative inquiry or the AI Summit. We suggest that the booklet *Appreciative Inquiry* by David Cooperrider and Diana Whitney[2] or the booklet *The Essentials of Appreciative Inquiry* by Bernard Mohr and Jane Watkins[3] be sent to all external invitees along with their invitation letter.

Planning for On-Site Registration

The final activity related to summit participation is on-site registration. Before the summit, planning team members who will be responsible for on-site registration need to devise a process for registration. This process will include:

- A way for participants to check in and be accounted for on a daily basis (if needed).
- A way for participants to obtain predetermined seating assignments. This is important because seats are often assigned to optimize diversity in each of the working table groups. One easy way to do this is to have predetermined table numbers written on name tags in advance. Another way is to have predetermined table numbers listed on the roster and be written on name tags as participants check in. The second way provides a bit more flexibility to reassign people if needed as a result of last-minute cancellations or no-shows.
- A vehicle for validating and correcting information on the participant roster, if one is to be created.

SUMMIT FORMAT

Our experience shows that if you really want the kind of deep, long-lasting innovation and change that a summit can produce, a minimum of three days is required. If you want to go even deeper, to involve the whole system in significant organization design work or in tactical planning around action initiatives, four or five days are better. We recommend the 4×4 summit format (4 D's in 4 days), which is described and illustrated in Chapters 7–10. If, however, you are in a situation in which it is truly impossible to pull the whole system aside for four days, the following are alternative formats to consider:

1) Multiple mini-summits, each of which includes a subset of the whole system
2) Multiple mini-summits connected virtually in real time
3) A pre-work, post-work sequence
4) A rolling process of shorter AI meetings, each focusing on one of the 4 D's

These are four of many formats that have been developed by innovative practitioners around the world. In the following sections we provide a case illustration of each of the four.

Multiple Mini-Summits

We recently did some work on customer service with the Santa Ana Star Hotel and Casino, a Native American–owned operation in Bernalillo, New Mexico (just outside Albuquerque). Recognizing that Albuquerque, unlike Las Vegas or Atlantic City, is a local market depending primarily on repeat customers from the surrounding area, Santa Ana Star general manager, John Cwiklik, wanted to use the AI Summit process to develop a level of customer service that would distinguish the Santa Ana Star from its competitors. But, of course, the casino business is a 24-hour-a-day industry. Greeters, servers, dealers, cashiers, security officers, valet attendants, housekeepers, and a host of others work around the clock to attend to guests and make the operations run smoothly. To pull the whole system off the floor for a four-day summit was impossible.

So we scheduled a series of six two-day mini-summits over the course of three months to include every member of the organization (about 850 people). The topic was "Delivering Superior Customer Service." The first mini-summit included the board of directors and the senior leadership group, 40 people in total. At that meeting, we walked through the normal 4-D cycle, but when we got to "destiny," instead of launching action initiatives around customer service, we formed groups to plan, schedule, and market the subsequent mini-summits.

Next, we held a series of four mini-summits, each to include 200–225 people, strategically selected to represent a range of functions and shifts. Each member of the senior leadership team was expected to attend at least two of the four "all-employee" mini-summits. At each of these meetings, employees worked through the 4-D cycle and emerged with three products: (1) a series of personal and team customer service action initiatives to be implemented immediately in their own jobs and departments, (2) a set of recommended customer service initiatives to be implemented at an organization-wide level, and (3) a set of recommended service principles for the organization.

The recommended organization-wide initiatives and the recommended service principles from the four all-employee mini-summits were then brought to a two-day integration mini-summit. Present at this meeting were the board, the senior leadership group, and 15 representatives from each of the employee mini-summits. The group moved through the 4-D cycle and emerged with a finalized set of twelve service principles and a series of eight organization-wide action initiatives designed to deliver superior customer service. Teams based on interest were formed to sponsor and implement each initiative.

The results from this process were spectacular. Within three months after the integration mini-summit, the Santa Ana Star experienced a dramatic increase in employee satisfaction, customer satisfaction, customer return rate, new customer attraction, coin-in, and profitability.

Multiple Mini-Summits Connected Virtually in Real Time

Tom White, then president of Teleops at GTE, selected appreciative inquiry as the process for engaging the entire workforce—67,000 people—in transforming the culture of the organization from a highly successful telephone company to a highly successful, innovative, fast-paced telecommunications company. At the heart of the change was an effort to train employees at all levels in appreciative inquiry so they could use it to positively impact the business and create a "positive revolution" in the organization.

The challenge, however, was one of scale. Sixty to 100 people attended each of the first three sessions. As appreciative inquiry caught on, more and more people began asking when they could attend. To reach more people more quickly and manage costs, we decided to experiment with simultaneous meetings connected via video and audio. This enabled 600 employees at five locations in three time zones to participate in a single session simultaneously.

We led the program from Dallas. There were over 100 people in the room with us, including a satellite broadcast video crew and audio technicians. At the other locations were both a technical facilitator and an AI facilitator. The use of one-way video allowed participants at all five locations to see us and the rest of the group in Dallas. Two-way audio facilitated an open dialogue and sharing across all five locations.

The question in our mind as we embarked on this experiment related to energy and affect. We wondered if the tremendous positive energy, hope, and enthusiasm that is created at an AI Summit would also emerge at a technology-mediated multi-site session. We were delighted with the results. Each local group did bond and develop a spirit of its own, and at the same time, the

experience of being part of a larger whole was significant and inspiring to many who participated. Among the many notable results stemming from this effort was that GTE won the American
Society for Training and Development's Best Culture Change of
the Year Award.

As the GTE case shows, the use of information technology has
made it considerably easier and more cost-effective to bring large
groups of people together to contribute their knowledge, skills,
and experiences in support of an organization's change agenda.
There are potential disadvantages, such as the occasional technical failures, the lack of face-to-face interaction on the part of all
participants, and the additional time it takes to prepare, but we
believe that the benefits far outweigh the costs. We encourage
you to continue experimenting with the use of technology for AI
Summit applications.

Pre-Work, Post-Work Sequence

A nice example of the pre-work, post-work sequence came from
Keith Cox,[4] president of Tirawa Consulting, Inc. He recently did
some work on employee attraction and retention with FM
Systems. Inc., an electronic security and burglar alarm company
that services Fortune 500 companies throughout northeastern Ohio.
When Keith got involved with the company, it was a functional/
hierarchical organization with an authoritarian culture that left
little room for employee involvement and participation. Growth
had stagnated, morale was low, turnover was high, and the
working relationship between departments was strained. When a
new president took over, he asked Keith to help him create a
"magnetic" work environment characterized by teamwork,
empowerment, employee fulfillment, innovation, and high performance.

Keith created a design that included a two-day mini-summit
with significant pre- and post-work on the part of participants.
First, he conducted a company-wide culture assessment to map the
positive values that the organization was striving to embody (i.e.,
accountability, teamwork, customer satisfaction, commitment,
and integrity). These five positive values then became the focus of
the AI mini-summit process. He formed a cross-functional planning team to create an interview protocol that would explore when
the five positive values had been alive and well in the company.

The planning team also determined all of the stakeholders that needed to be interviewed, including employees, customers, vendors, subcontractors, and community leaders. The interviews were completed by every employee and were used to kick off the first day of the AI mini-summit.

The company closed its doors for a Friday and required that all employees attend a paid Saturday session. The first day of the summit included the discovery and dream phases, with design and destiny covered on day 2. Participants began day 1 by sharing their most positive stories and quotes from their interviews. They then mapped the organization's "positive core" and concluded the day with a guided imaging exercise and a creative presentation of their dreams and dream statements. In day 2, participants were introduced to an organizational architecture model and charged with choosing and redesigning one or more components of their organization "to bring their dreams to life." Each group then formed a one-year action plan for implementing their respective design change.

After the mini-summit, there was still work to be done. The mini-summit process generated twenty-five short-term and long-term initiatives to build and reinforce the new culture. Those initiatives were prioritized, and tactical plans to implement them were created (e.g., the establishment of a customer service department).

Over a year after the AI process, FM Systems had made some considerable strides. Functional silos were eradicated and teamwork increased dramatically. The organization moved to a team-based environment characterized by empowerment and shared leadership. Appreciative inquiry gained significant traction as an organizational mindset. Inquiries were used to address everything from performance feedback to organization design. Financially, the company had one of its best years. And most important, the company strengthened its talent pool by adding some top-rated individuals and continued to drive people, process, and technology changes to support the new culture.

A Rolling Process of Shorter AI Meetings

Ravi Pradhan,[5] president of Karuna Management, Inc., used a rolling process of half-day meetings with twenty-five government-owned and -operated hospitals in South Asia (India, Bangladesh,

Sri Lanka, Nepal, Pakistan, and Bhutan) to help them provide twenty-four-hour quality obstetrics care, particularly to those 15–20 percent of pregnant women who are at risk. The final objective of the project was to reduce the high rate of maternal mortality and morbidity in South Asia, which accounts for one-fifth of the world's population and close to half of all maternal deaths. The project was supported by UNICEF, the Bill & Melinda Gates Foundation, the ministries of health in the respective countries, and the hospitals themselves.

Ravi's first step was to train a group of facilitators in appreciative inquiry in each country. They in turn held four half-day sessions in each hospital. Each session included anywhere from 50 to 100 staff from all levels and focused on a different "D" of the AI 4-D cycle. For example, the first day focused on discovery—appreciative interviews and mapping the positive core. A week later, the second day focused on dream—imagining the ideal future for twenty-four-hour quality care and crafting dream statements. The third day focused on design, and so on. At the end of the fourth day, each hospital formed teams to focus on specific challenges called "breakthrough tasks." A month or so later, the local facilitators met with the leadership team and each of the breakthrough teams to coach them in achieving their results. Five months later, a final workshop was held. Also as a part of the initiative, the maternity/obstetrics departments received specific supplies, equipment, and technical training.

The impact of this approach was seen in the volume and quality of obstetrics care services, the improvement in other medical services, greater cooperation and collaboration between various departments, higher levels of motivation and accountability, more participatory leadership styles, greater involvement of the community stakeholders, reduction in costs, better inventory management, increased pride and ownership, and appreciation of one's own value and capacity to bring about positive changes. Two specific examples include a 300-bed hospital in Karachi, which doubled the volume of its patients in the maternity and obstetrics wing without any increase in staff or budgets. As a result, the hospital was appointed a national "training center." In Bangladesh, one hospital's obstetrics care initiative was featured on national TV as an example of what is possible despite difficult circumstances. Given the history, context, and management culture and performance of government institutions in South Asia, these changes and results represent unprecedented success.

THE SECRET TO SUCCESSFUL PLANNING: MODELING POSITIVE CHANGE

When Hunter Douglas Window Fashions Division wanted to change its organization culture to be one of high employee involvement and learning, it held kickoff meetings and invited all employees to volunteer to help plan their AI initiative. A month later 100 people attended the planning meeting—itself a mini-summit—and formed teams to define the task, select the participants, design the format, conduct pre-summit interviews, establish and maintain communication about the overall endeavor, develop the summit agenda and workbook, and integrate the entire process. This high-participation planning process was the first major enactment of what has now become the Hunter Douglas way of doing things.

To be successful, AI Summit planning must walk the talk. It must model not business as usual, but the most hoped and dreamed for ways of doing business. It must be out in front of the organization, leading it to new ways of working by working in new and different ways. Planning for an AI Summit is a highly creative effort. It takes time and inventiveness to generate innovative approaches while at the same time inviting others in to help discover, dream, and design them. Through the AI Summit process, the words and deeds of the planning team lead the way toward the organization's new destiny.

CHAPTER 6

CREATING THE
AI SUMMIT DESIGN

A n integral part of planning for an AI Summit is the creation of the summit design, that is, the agenda that outlines summit activities day by day and minute by minute. A great design takes into consideration the organization's context, its change agenda, and its resources and combines them with the principles of appreciative inquiry to create a flow of activities that:

- Invites participation while maintaining focus on a specific task
- Includes both serious work and fun so as to be energizing
- Gives people a voice and lets them feel a part of a larger whole
- Creates safety for learning and delight with diversity
- Fosters comfort with uncertainty and spontaneous innovation

Also crucial to the success of an AI Summit is a communication strategy that keeps people informed and interested in the summit process. The most powerful strategies apply the well-known communication adage "same message, multiple channels, over time" and make extensive use of personal relationships. Finally, logistics are key. The flow and timing of an AI Summit should appear seamless to participants. Devoting significant time and attention to logistics helps make that happen. In this chapter we take you through the essential considerations for designing an AI Summit, preparing the communication strategy, and arranging the logistics. These are the final three steps for planning a successful summit.

SUMMIT DESIGN

By now we know what our summit will be about, who will be there, and what format it will follow. It is now time to plan the flow of activities that will take participants through the 4-D cycle during the summit. It is time to:

- Create an agenda
- Craft an appreciative interview guide
- Plan pre-summit interviews (if desired)
- Create the participant workbook
- Determine how to document the proceedings

Although ultimately the responsibility of the planning team, the question of who should actually craft the summit agenda and supporting documents often surfaces. Planning team members may not have much experience or expertise with AI, the summit may need to be planned quickly, or resources may be limited. Depending on the situation, the agenda, interview guide, and workbook may be created by a team of AI consultants alone, a small group made up of AI consultants and other planning team members, or a large group of planning team members and other members of the organization. Table 6.1 outlines the pros and cons of the three different alternatives.

Ultimately, regardless of who creates the agenda, interview guide, and workbook, the key is to create a summit environment that maximizes joy, learning, healthy relationships, self-management, and profound organizational transformation.

CREATING A SUMMIT AGENDA

The best summit agendas are simple and easy for participants to follow. Simplicity, however, requires a great deal of thoughtfulness and conscious decision making about what to do when, how long to take for what, and how to create an environment that inspires. As noted previously, no two summits are alike. They each have a unique context, purpose, and set of circumstances. Creating an effective summit agenda is as much an art as it is a science.

The agenda of an AI Summit flows through the AI 4-D cycle: discovery, dream, design, and destiny. Sample agendas are included in Chapters 7–10 and in the Appendix. Exhibit 6.1 provides a list of questions to consider as you create an agenda for a summit.

Table 6.1

Options for Who Might Create the
Agenda, Interview Guide, and Workbook

Who	Pros	Cons
Appreciative inquiry consultants	• Strong AI expertise • Depth of skill for creating activities • Easier to reach agreement on options • Can be done faster and more efficiently	• Lack of organizational history and context • More time and trust needed to create buy-in for the agenda • Less learning for organizational members
Small team of AI consultants and planning team members	• Blends AI expertise and organization understanding • Models teamwork • Agenda appropriate to organization culture	• Takes time for learning • Takes time to reach mutual agreement on agenda options
Large team including AI consultants, planning team members, and other members of the organization	• Greatest level of organization understanding • Blends AI expertise and organization understanding • Gives voice to multiple stakeholder groups who can provide valuable input • Easier to get buy-in once agenda is done • Builds strong support for the AI Summit • Surfaces potential barriers to the summit • Strong sense of community is built • Potential to create a better agenda	• Requires facilitation to ensure all voices are included and heard • More difficult to get consensus about agenda options • Takes more time to deal with differences • Requires greater resources, costs more

Exhibit 6.1

Questions to Consider When Creating a Summit Agenda

Day 1: Discovery

- How will discovery be introduced? What information about AI will be presented?
- How will the AI interviews be conducted? Where will they be conducted?
- How will the individual interviews be processed? What type of group reflection will be used to share stories and lessons from the interviews?
- What process will be used to produce the positive core map? What type of reflection process will be used? How will the data be captured? Who will capture it? How will the positive core be summarized?
- Is there a need to do a continuity scan? A series of timelines?
- Will previous interview data be used in this Summit? How will it be used and when? What will participants need to know? How can we best prepare them?
- How will we link what is done in the discovery phase to what will be done in the dream phase?

Day 2: Dream

- How will the dream phase be presented and what will be covered?
- How will the data generated in the discovery phase be used in the dream phase?
- What type of group activity will be used to discuss and describe the organization's vision of the future? What type of narrowing process will be used if needed?
- How will participants demonstrate their ideal future (creative presentation, skit, magazine cover story, TV show, etc.)? How many presentations should be performed (all groups or selected groups)?
- How will the collective vision be summarized? How will it be used?
- Will other data sources, such as benchmarking data, be used in support of the dream phase? How will it be used and when? Who will collect it?
- How will we link what is done in the dream phase with what will be done in the design phase?

Day 3: Design

- How will the design phase be presented?
- How will the data captured in the dream phase be used in the design phase?
- What activity will be used to identify the social architecture? The design elements?

Exhibit 6.1 *(continued)*

Questions to Consider When Creating a Summit Agenda

- What process will be used to develop provocative propositions? What type of narrowing process will be used if needed? How do we ensure that the provocative propositions are bold enough?

- Will we begin to identify initiatives or implementation proposals that move the organization toward the images of the ideal organization? How will this be done?

- How will we link what is done in the design phase to what will be done in the destiny phase?

Day 4: Destiny

- How will the destiny phase be presented?

- How will the data captured in the design phase be used in the destiny phase?

- What type of group process will be used to generate potential actions to realize the dream and design? How will actions be narrowed and/or organized?

- How will action/innovation teams be formed? How will action initiatives be launched? How will the teams hold themselves accountable?

- What type of summit report will be generated? Who will do this?

- How will the efforts of the summit be communicated to the rest of the organization?

Timing: An Important Consideration in Outlining an AI Summit Agenda

In addition to the questions in Exhibit 6.1, it is important to consider the amount of time to allocate to each activity. When working with large groups, we like to err on the side of too little time rather than too much. Of course, we aim to plan just the right amount of time. But in large groups there are generally some people who work faster than others. We prefer to set a pace just a bit faster than the average. This way, fast participants are kept interested and involved, and slower participants can use break times to finish up if need be.

In addition, we generally include one or two optional activities in our agendas—things that may be done but are not essential to the overall flow or success of the summit. This way, if one activity takes longer than we planned, we can make up time by eliminating an optional activity without negatively impacting the summit process or goals.

Balancing Individual, Small-Group, and Plenary Activities

One of the most important aspects of creating a summit agenda is balancing individual, small-group, and plenary activities. Good balance among the three allows time for people to reflect individually, engage in dialogue with others, and contribute to a sense of the whole. Individual reflection is accomplished through one-on-one appreciative interviews; activities in which people write their perspective individually on a flipchart, timeline, or opportunity map; and large-group activities in which people get to cast a vote or speak during an open-microphone session. It is important to provide time for "individual voice" at least once a day during a summit.

Most summit activities—discussions, presentations, and creative enactments—are done in small groups. Generally, participants are assigned to "max-mix" groups. These are groups that constitute a maximally diverse mixture of people. For example, at a health system summit, each table would have eight people selected from the stakeholder groups: one doctor, one nurse, one administrator, one manager, one line employee, one patient advocate, one lab technician, and one patient. But, there are also times when we have people work in stakeholder groups (e.g., all the doctors together, all the patients together), design groups (e.g., all the people who want to design a new patient flow process or a revised performance appraisal system), or action teams (e.g., all those who want to launch an initiative to increase nursing retention or improve collaboration among doctors, nurses, and technicians). We provide more detail on these groups in Chapters 7–10.

It is important to plan the small-group process for the entire four days of the summit as an integrated flow of activities. For example, small-group activities on the first day generally allow group members to meet each other and to discover who they are and what they bring to the summit. On day 2, they facilitate group members sharing dreams with each other and creating a collective group dream. On day 3 it's about design, and on day 4 about destiny. This progression of activities creates a safe environment for people to connect and then to co-create.

In addition to individual voice and the small-group process, an effective summit creates a sense of wholeness among participants. This is done through activities in which everyone present participates, either personally or through their small group. Plenary activities—those that involve all participants—can be especially powerful when they are visually documented. When everyone writes on timelines, draws on an opportunity map, adds pieces to a positive core map, or votes using computer-assisted polling, a strong sense of wholeness emerges.

Plenary activities that involve speeches by a single person do not have this effect. Indeed, they work to the contrary. They tend to alienate people who have come to the summit expecting equal participation and co-creation. As a result, we steer away from "talking heads" presentations where executive, experts, or others speak to the participants as an audience.

Bringing in the Voices of Interest Groups

In most cases all the relevant and interested parties participate in the summit. Customers, vendors, community members, governmental groups, and other external stakeholders are all in the room. There are times, however, when this is just not possible. Key customers cannot attend, or children cannot miss school, or nurses cannot leave the hospital unattended. When this occurs, it is important to include their voice at the summit in some way.

There have been summits where customers participated on the first day only or where a customer panel was interviewed about their dreams on the second day. In other cases pre-summit appreciative interviews were done with all the stakeholder groups who could not attend. In still other cases the dream activity asked one-third of the participants to portray the dreams of their children, one-third to portray the dreams of their parents, and one-third to portray their own dreams. Each of these activities is a creative way to include the voice of interest groups unable to attend. None, however, is as good as actually hearing from the interest groups themselves.

Keeping Focused on Positive Change

Creating an agenda for an AI Summit means creating momentum for positive change. The starting point for inquiry, analysis, dialogue, and debate is the positive core (strengths, resources, capacities, assets, hopes, dreams, positive potentials, or competencies) rather than problems. As you create the agenda for your AI Summit, focus all of your activities on the positive core—discovering it, envisioning it, and designing it into the fabric of your organization's future.

Planning for Leadership Involvement at the Summit

When we are outlining a summit agenda, we create two spaces for senior leadership comments: at the beginning of the meeting and at the very end. We find it useful for senior managers to open the session with brief comments (thirty minutes maximum) about the importance of the summit to the business, what they hope to accomplish, and how excited they are to participate and learn along with everyone else. At the end of the summit, senior managers' comments are best when they are authentic descriptions of what they experienced at the summit, the hope it generated for them about the future, and of course, appreciation for everyone's participation and ideas.

A primary principle of an AI Summit is equality of voice. This means that everyone's ideas are valued and given equal attention and space for expression. At an AI Summit there are no speeches by executives who charge the group and then leave. Senior managers participate fully from start to finish. After their opening comments they join their assigned table group and participate on the same terms as anyone else.

CRAFTING AN APPRECIATIVE INQUIRY INTERVIEW GUIDE

All Appreciative Inquiry Summits, no matter what format, begin with an appreciative interview process. We plan to have summit participants engaged in appreciative interviews within the first two hours of the summit. It usually takes one to two hours, maximum, to introduce the summit purpose and the AI process and then get into the interviews. More than two hours is too long.

The purpose of the appreciative interviewing process is to create a "holographic beginning" to the summit. Like a hologram, in which the whole image is contained in any piece of it, the appreciative interview contains questions about topics that will be discussed throughout the whole summit. Table 6.2 shows this relationship between the summit agenda and the interview guide using an example of a summit on customer service. A complete interview guide is included in the Appendix.

Table 6.2

Connecting the Interview Guide to the Summit Agenda

Broad Summit Agenda	Interview Questions	Purpose of the Questions
• Discovering the positive core of customer service	• High-point experiences of great customer service	• To collect stories and data for the positive core map
• Dreaming about an organization that delivers great customer service	• Images of an organization winning an award for great customer service	• To generate ideals for the dream activity
• Designing an organization culture to delight and retain customers	• Leadership, structures, processes, values, and practices used by exemplary organizations recognized for customer service	• To garner information and ideas to apply when writing provocative propositions describing the ideal organization design
• Initiating innovations to ensure outstanding customer service	• Ideas for action, ways to bring exceptional customer service alive	• To generate ideas for actions to be taken after the summit

Creating the interview guide is the planning team's responsibility. They should, however, seek input from the advisory team as well as others in the organization. A good interview guide typically goes through several iterations in its development cycle. Piloting the interview guide with a small group prior to the summit is a good idea. This ensures that it is both relevant and able to be completed within the time allotted on the agenda.

There are three steps in crafting an appreciative interview guide:

1) Selecting affirmative topics
2) Writing appreciative questions
3) Creating the interview guide

Step 1: Selecting Affirmative Topics

An effective interview guide is focused on three to five affirmative topics that are related to the summit task. For example, if the summit task is labor-management partnership, then the interview guide would include questions on topics such as productive partnership, labor-management cooperation, collaborative leadership, leveling the playing field, consensus-based decision making, and democracy at work. As you can see, all of the topics selected have a direct relationship to the summit task.

We begin the process of selecting affirmative topics with what we call "generic" appreciative interviews. We create a generic interview guide consisting of four to five questions about the summit task in general and ask members of the planning team to use it to interview one another. In the case of labor-management partnership, a generic interview guide might include questions on:

- High-point experiences at work
- What you value about yourself, your work, your organization
- Positive trends in labor-management relations
- Dreams for the future of labor-management partnership

Conducting generic interviews and sharing stories from them stimulates the planning team's understanding about the summit task and enables them to select three to five meaningful and strategically powerful affirmative topics. They use the stories heard during the generic interviews as data to determine what topics would lead to learning and action related to the summit task. For more information on affirmative topic selection, we suggest you review *The Appreciative Inquiry Handbook*.[1]

Step 2: Writing Appreciative Interview Questions

Each affirmative topic is turned into an appreciative interview question. Appreciative interview questions have two parts: a positive lead-in and a series of actual questions. A sample question, taken from an interview guide created and used at British Airways, can be found in Exhibit 6.2. It shows the affirmative topic, the lead-in, and the set of questions, all of which constitute the appreciative interview question.

Exhibit 6.2

Sample Appreciative Interview Question

Topic: Timeless Heritage

Lead-in: British Airways has an illustrious heritage as a leader and innovator. From flying boats to flying beds, from three days to three hours, from the community to the world, we are the world's favorite airline. Keeping this in mind, let's explore how we can harness our heritage and take us into the future.

Questions:

1) Think back to when you first joined British Airways.

   • What was the allure and excitement?

   • What was it about our history that appealed to you?

2) What is it about British Airways that makes you proud to work here now? Tell me a story about when you felt the most pride as a member of the British Airways family.

3) As we move into the new millennium, what is your dream, your vision, your greatest hope for British Airways?

4) From our unique heritage, what two or three things must we take with us into the future?

Well-written appreciative interview questions elicit stories, stimulate reflection and learning from experience, and bring out the best of people and the organization. For detailed guidance in writing Appreciative Inquiry questions we suggest you refer to *Encyclopedia of Positive Questions: Bringing Out the Best in Your Organization.*[2]

Step 3: Creating the Interview Guide

The final interview guide has three parts to it: opening questions, affirmative topic questions, and closing questions. Exhibit 6.3 shows the general structure of a typical appreciative interview guide. It includes sample questions for the opening and closing sections.

Once created, the appreciative interview guide is printed up. It may be printed as a separate document, or it may be included in the summit workbook. Either way, be sure to leave sufficient

Exhibit 6.3

Structure of an Appreciative Inquiry Interview Guide

I. An *opening* section that sets the stage for individual and organizational valuing.

- What attracted you to the organization? What were your initial impressions?

- What do you value most about yourself, your work, and your organization?

- Tell me about a high point/peak experience in the organization. What made it a high point/peak experience for you?

- What factors give life to this organization?

II. A *middle* section that inquires into the topics of choice.

- This section usually contains two to three questions for each of three to five affirmative topics.

- Affirmative topics can cover any aspect of the "positive core" that the organization wants to study and enhance—leadership, teamwork, collaboration, respect, excellent quality, outstanding service, blinding speed, magnetic culture, social contribution, market growth, etc.

III. A *closing* section that articulates a new future.

- What is our most inspiring image of the future? What are we called to become?

- Imagine that tonight you fall into a deep sleep and don't wake up for three years. While you are asleep a miracle has happened and the organization has become everything you always wanted it to be. This has resulted in many positive and highly effective changes in the organization and its culture. You feel elated. As you awaken and open your eyes, what do you see happening that is new, positive, and different? How do you know—what are people doing or saying that lets you know?

- Looking toward the future, if you could transform the organization in any way, what three wishes would you make?

---

space between questions for note taking by the interviewer. In addition, we often include an opening statement about the purpose of the interview on the first page of the interview guide. This statement answers the questions: Why are we doing this? What will happen to what I say? It also provides a few simple guidelines for appreciative interviewing.

Once your appreciative interview guide is complete, you are ready for interviews either at the summit or as pre-summit work. If you are going to conduct interviews at the summit only, we suggest you include the interview guide in the summit workbook. If you are going to conduct pre-summit interviews, then it is best to print your interview guide as a separate document.

PLANNING PRE-SUMMIT INTERVIEWS

If your AI Summit format calls for pre-summit interviews, you will need to carefully think through the process for data collection, meaning making, and reporting. The following questions must be thoughtfully answered:

- How many people will be interviewed as part of pre-summit data collection?
- Should everyone in the organization be interviewed or a representative sample?
- Will stakeholders be interviewed? If so, how many and who will be interviewed?
- Who will do the interviews?
- Will interviewers be trained? How and when will they be trained?
- Will interviewers bring data to the summit to be processed as part of the summit activities, or will the data be summarized ahead of time and put into a report that will then be utilized in the summit?
- Will the interviewers bring the entire AI interviews with them, or will they bring an annotated summary of the best thoughts, quotes, and stories they heard?
- If a report is being produced prior to the summit, to whom do the interviewers send the information and exactly what should they send? How will the data be consolidated and reported?

For a detailed example of one company's pre-summit interview process, we suggest you read about Hunter Douglas Window Fashions Division in *The Power of Appreciative Inquiry.*[3] Prior to their first summit, on cultural transformation, they conducted in-terviews with 600 employees and 100 customers, vendors, and community members. They held four data synthesis and meaning-making meetings. The results of the interviewing process were summarized in a report that was distributed to all employees and all stakeholders who were invited to the summit.

CREATING THE
SUMMIT PARTICIPANT WORKBOOK

The final document to be created by the planning team in ad-vance of the summit is the participant workbook. It includes all materials and worksheets that will be used by participants dur-ing the summit. A table of contents for a summit participant's workbook might include:

1) Summit Purpose, Objectives, and Agenda
2) What Is Appreciative Inquiry?
3) The AI 4-D Cycle
4) The Appreciative Interview Guide
5) Worksheet 1: Introducing Your Interview Partner
6) Worksheet 2: Mapping the Positive Core
7) Worksheet 3: Creating a Shared Dream
8) Worksheet 4: Writing Provocative Propositions
9) Worksheet 5: From Inquiry to Action: Forming Innovation Teams

This is a simple overview of a possible table of contents. It is not all-inclusive by any means. A well-developed summit workbook includes all of the information the facilitators will share or teach and worksheets for all summit activities. See the Appendix for a sample participant workbook.

DETERMINING HOW TO
DOCUMENT SUMMIT PROCEEDINGS

Another aspect of summit design has to do with what and how to record the proceedings and important output of the summit. The possibilities range from video recordings to digital photos to real-time computer transcriptions to flipcharts and wall drawings. There are two questions that guide what we plan to document and save from an AI Summit: (1) What will aid the summit process? That is, what kinds of documentation will help participants follow the process and understand what is being shared and discussed? What will help energize the discussions? (2) What needs to be documented for future use? In other words, what will be developed during the summit that will be followed up on or finalized at another time?

What to Save and Why

What gets documented and saved varies from summit to summit. Because appreciative inquiry focuses on what works, interview data and stories carry organizational wisdom and should be collected and disseminated throughout the organization. At different times we have found it useful to save and disseminate the following:

- *Stories.* We capture stories of best practices and exemplary organizations on video as well as in writing. They are great to show in the cafeteria or break room following the summit. They can also be used in the company newsletter. Some organizations have made books of best-practice stories and given them to customers and vendors as a thank-you gift.
- *Quotable quotes.* We often draw great quotes from interview data and summit discussions. They are used after the summit in a variety of ways. They can be made into posters and distributed across the organization. They can be used on public relations documents ranging from recruitment brochures to marketing materials to annual reports.
- *Positive core map.* Most organizations find their positive core map to be both informative and energizing. Consequently, they want to save it and display it after the summit. Positive core maps have been laminated and hung in the company cafeteria and reproduced in poster size and distributed to all departments. At British Airways, "Best Practice Banners," made by each of the twenty-two stations in North America, circulated from station to station for a year until all banners had visited all stations.
- *Dream images.* Dream skits can be videotaped and played after the summit. By watching the video, people who did not attend the summit can be included and be brought up to date with the process. In addition, people who did attend are revitalized when they see things like the dream skits on tape.
- *Provocative propositions or principles.* It is essential that provocative propositions or design principles be saved. They can be put into a computer during the summit or taken from flipcharts after the summit. Either way they are important to preserve, to refine, and to use throughout the organization following the summit. The URI principles

are posted in all meeting spaces and are read at the beginning of
many meetings.

- *Commitments to action.* In most cases we ask people who commit to
  action to submit a worksheet describing their intentions. This serves
  as a record of commitments and an action plan for the initiatives that
  will take place. This set of documents is passed on to the advisory
  team, which tracks and supports progress.

Graphic Facilitation

Whenever possible, we plan to partner with a graphic facilitator,[4]
who documents the entire summit proceedings in big, colorful
mind maps, illustrations, and symbols. Graphic facilitation
serves the summit process by focusing and drawing meaning
from the whole-group discussions. When participants see their
ideas illustrated on the walls, they gain a sense of pride and accomplishment. Graphic facilitation is a way of demonstrating
that people's ideas are valued and that something tangible is oc-
curring through the dialogue process.

Videotaping

Whenever possible, we suggest that the AI Summit be profes-
sionally videotaped. A video makes a great communication tool
for anyone who is not able to participate in the actual summit.
For those who cannot be there, a video is the next best thing.
More significant, however, is that a video can be replayed in cafeterias, break rooms, and meeting rooms after the summit as a reminder of the summit experience. It can also be used as a teaching tool for new employees who join the organization after the
summit occurs. At the Canadian Department of National
Defense, all new internal OD consultants learn about AI and
about the organization's dreams and plans for the future by
watching its ever-expanding library of summit videotapes.

SUMMIT COMMUNICATION

Once the planning team has determined the summit task, participants, format, and design, it is time to plan a strategy for
communication and promotion of the summit throughout the

organization and stakeholder groups. The purpose of communication before the summit is simple: to inform people about the summit and to generate enthusiasm for it. This means that people need to know what it is, why it is happening, and why their participation is essential. They also need to have an early indication that:

- It will be practical—that they will have an opportunity to speak about what matters to them.
- It will be safe—that they can speak out without negative consequences.
- It will be fun—that four days in a meeting will be energizing and inspiring.
- It will be powerful—that what gets discussed and decided will be of strategic significance to the organization.

As Marshall McCluhan said, "the medium is the message." This is very much the case when it comes to summit communication. The vehicles used must illustrate the significance of the summit as well as its fun, participatory, and inclusive spirit. Summit communication can most effectively be thought of as an internal marketing campaign.

Branding the Summit Task and Process

As an organization adapts the AI Summit process to its own situation, the desire often arises to create a tag line, rallying cry, or brand that is uniquely its own. It is a way of making the summit task "sing," as one planning team member suggested to us. Some examples are:

- "United We Strive for Excellence," the project name for a merger that involved every employee in one of three summits
- "Focus 2000: All Voices, All Opinions, All Ideas," the title of a highly successful two-year effort to transform a corporate culture
- "The Power of Two," the name used for a customer service initiative that involved 1,200 employees in appreciative interviews prior to a 100-person summit

These examples are all the creations of employees of organizations sponsoring AI Summits. "United We Strive for Excellence" was a contest winner. The organization put out a call for titles for its series of summits. A vote was held and employees selected their favorite from all the submissions. The winning title was put on banners, t-shirts, and posters and became a rallying cry for the summits and other AI activities.

"Focus 2000: All Voices, All Opinions, All Ideas" was invented by a communication subteam to emphasize the importance of everyone's participation in the process. They also named their newsletter the "Focus 2000 Inquirer" and used it to keep everyone up to date with appreciative inquiry activities in their organization.

Determining How to Market the Summit

Communication materials used to market the AI Summit should be clear, concise, and consistent in message content and quality. The summit message should be framed appreciatively and invite questions that promote additional conversation. An effective summit communications plan will include what you want to communicate, who is responsible to communicate it, by when, the specific method used to communicate it, and the intended communication outcomes.

Some of the various methods that can be used to market an AI Summit are shown in Exhibit 6.4. Whatever you decide to do, remember: "same message, multiple channels, over time."

Exhibit 6.4

Methods of Marketing an AI Summit: Getting the Message Out

Word of Mouth

Spreading the word to others through informal networks is a great way of getting the message out. Planning/advisory team members can do a lot to informally market the summit and promote the benefits of the summit approach. Making presentations at meetings and other organizational functions can also help stimulate enthusiasm and interest for the summit. Conducting one-on-one meetings with critical stakeholders is also an effective and highly recommended method for promoting interest and participation in the summit.

E-mail/Voicemail

Broadcast e-mails and voicemails are a great means of getting the word out quickly and efficiently about the summit. These methods can also include information on where to go to get additional information.

Direct or Mass Mail

Direct mail to all organizational members is another way to get the summit message out quickly and effectively. Mail sent directly to organizational members can be highly customized and based on preferred methods and styles.

Brochures or Flyers

Brochures and flyers can be produced in highly attractive trifold formats and placed in many strategic locations. Brochures and flyers can contain a great deal of information if designed well, and are a proven method for promotional efforts.

Exhibit 6.4 *(continued)*

Methods of Marketing an AI Summit: Getting the Message Out

Newsletters

Company newsletters can be a powerful means of increasing awareness and conveying the purpose and intent of the summit. Newsletters can contain stories or short articles that pique interest and stimulate inquiry.

Posters and Bulletin Boards

Posters should be placed where people will notice them. Bulletin boards are usually places that people frequent and offer ideal locations for posters and other communication vehicles. Posters placed on bulletin boards should be refreshed often and arranged so that passersby will notice them.

Videos

Short video spots that promote the summit can be effective. One organization created a six- minute video of the planning team meeting, in which they did many of the same activities that would be done in the summit, and ran it on a continuous loop for a time in the employee dining room.

Internal Websites

Internal websites are commonplace today and are an effective way to get the summit message out. They can be accessed anytime right from a person's desktop. Establishing hyperlinks that go directly to the information location facilitates the accessing of information about the summit.

Novelties

Novelties (pens, pencils, coffee cups, t-shirts, etc.) can be a powerful means of stimulating enthusiasm and interest for the summit. They can also serve as a remembrance of the event and foster conversation for a long time to come.

SUMMIT LOGISTICS

Devoting significant time and attention to logistics helps the summit flow smoothly for everyone. Space, seating arrangements, workbooks, name tags, pens and pencils, microphones, computers, parking, and food service—all the details—must be finely organized and coordinated. Logistics are essential. They can make or break your summit. Table 6.3 is a checklist showing the most important logistical considerations for planning a summit.

Table 6.3

Logistics Checklist

Item	Item Details
Room configuration	• Round tables—no more than eight participants per table, max-mix seating arrangement. • No visible obstructions for good eye contact and participant comfort. • The positive core map is on the wall (or foam core boards if necessary). For a 250-person summit the positive core map is a large sheet of paper on the wall that covers an 8-foot by 20-foot rectangular area. • For an opportunity map session, if the whole group is 150 people or less, one large map 6' × 12' will do. For more than 150, a 4' × 4' sheet of paper hung on the wall for each stakeholder group is better. If there is not enough wall space, three foam core boards for the large map or one foam core board for each small map will work. Each stakeholder group will also need at least six different colors of magic markers. Each individual in the room will also need seven Avery dots (a different color for each stakeholder group). • Large enough space for all activities and ease of movement. • Refreshment tables out of the way. • Breakout space or breakout rooms
Equipment	*Technical* • Audio sound system: at least four cordless microphones—two for facilitators and two for roving. • TV/VCR if needed. • Computers/printers/copiers if needed. • Projector(s)—overhead and/or proxima for PowerPoint presentations. • Projection screen(s)—the larger the group, the larger the screens. • Music equipment if not provided by the facility. *Nontechnical* • One easel with paper for each table, stored out of the way against the wall until needed; two easels for facilitator use. • Spare flipchart paper (a lot gets used). • Registration table with several chairs—typically set up right outside the meeting room. Distribute registration

Table 6.3 *(continued)*

Logistics Checklist

Item	Item Details
	packets including name tags, participant workbooks, table assignments, and any individual materials.
	• Supply table stocked with additional supplies to be used for specific summit activities (positive core and opportunity map) when needed: scissors, glue sticks, multiple-colored Avery dots, colored paper, rubber bands, staplers and staples, etc.
	• Foam core boards if wall space is lacking—about fifteen foam core boards, 4 feet × 8 feet × 1/2 inch thick, if needed (five for the positive core map, one for each of the opportunity maps).
	• If you plan to have participants do creative presentations (skits, etc.) during the dream phase, a table full of props is nice (hats, costumes, etc.).
	• Coat racks.
	• Facilitator platform/riser (12") for summits of 150–300 people, a stage for over 300.
	• Summit banners if appropriate.
	• Message boards.
Table materials	One basket or bin per table with supplies:
	• One box of multi-colored markers.
	• One roll of masking tape.
	• Pens/pencils for each participant.
	• Several packages of different colored Post-it notes.
	• Table numbers.
	• Pipe cleaners and soft toys to play with are nice.
Participant materials	• Registration packets.
	• Preprinted name tag for each participant.
	• Summit workbook for each participant.
Facilitator materials	• Table up front for equipment and materials.
	• Separate facilitator table.
	• Two boxes of multi-colored markers.
	• One roll of masking tape.
	• Prepared flipcharts:
	• Welcome
	• The summit task
Food	• Daily menus and refreshments planned; consider special requests (times and locations predetermined).

Who Does Logistical Planning?

In most cases members of the planning team attend to logistics. In some cases a subteam is formed to devote itself exclusively to logistics. This team may include some planning team members along with people from the organization's meeting planning function, training department, or education center. We have found that most organizations have people who are knowledgeable and helpful for identifying sites, hiring caterers, producing workbooks, and arranging for audiovisual equipment. It is always good to get them on board right from the start. In addition, most venues large enough to host a summit have dedicated staff willing to adapt their resources to meet summit logistical needs.

Selecting the Site for Your Summit

The number one consideration in selecting a summit site is space—the size of the primary meeting room. AI Summits require a lot of space. The primary meeting room needs to be able to hold the number of people attending your summit when seated at round tables of eight, plus extra space for screens, a platform (if needed), walking around, writing on wall charts, preparing and enacting skits, and so on. A formula that has worked for us is to calculate an area of 12 feet × 12 feet (144 sq. ft.) for every eight participants. This covers the seating. Then add 50 percent more space for everything else.

Most often summits are held in hotel ballrooms, large conference rooms, or auditoriums, but there are times when you need to be more creative. As mentioned in the previous chapter, Nutrimental has held four annual all-employee summits in their own food processing facility. Colleagues at a California financial services company could not find a hotel ballroom to meet their budget, so they held their first 100-person summit on one level of the company's parking garage. They reported their only challenges were too much fresh air and getting the sound system just right! The United Religions Initiative, unable to rent a large enough room during the week of their third annual global summit, rented a tent and had it put up on the Stanford University campus. Residence halls, university cafeterias, and lounges were used for participant housing and meals.

Room Shape

We have found that large, square rooms work best for a summit meeting. They allow participants to see the facilitators and each other. The room should have windows, good lighting, temperature control, a good sound system, and no visual barriers. The facilitators and the front of the room need to be visible to everyone. All participants should be able to clearly see all working areas of the room and to hear all speakers, no matter where they are standing.

In general, we create a front part of the room with a large projection screen or screens and a table for computers, microphones, and materials. We often have a seating area up front for the facilitators when they are not presenting. We do not use podiums or tables or anything that would hide the facilitators from view.

Stages, Platforms, and Screens

With groups of 150 or less, we use no stages or platforms. This puts us on the same level as the participants and allows us to move about freely. With groups of 150–300 we request a 12" platform or riser that allows people at the back of the room to easily see the presenters. This also permits us and other presenters to step down and wander around among the tables. With a group of 300 or more a stage is best. It is the only way for the whole group to see those who are presenting throughout the course of the summit. But even with a stage, it is important to have easily accessible stairs and ramps that allow people to move quickly back and forth between the table level and the stage. In all cases, it is essential to have the appropriate number of projection screens showing what is going on up front.

Tables, Chairs, and Seating Arrangements

We suggest using round tables with cushy chairs to enhance participant comfort and satisfaction. Round tables are ideal because they create a face-to-face space for good dialogue and interaction between participants. Five-foot rounds with space for eight people at each table are ideal for this purpose. An alternative that we have used successfully is to eliminate the tables altogether and put the chairs in circles of eight. Make sure the chairs are comfortable. Participants spend much of their time sitting, and to have nice chairs makes a big difference. Chairs with wheels are a great but often expensive addition to summit flexibility.

Wall Space

The room needs plenty of wall space to hang butcher paper that will become positive core maps, opportunity maps, and continuity scan timelines. In addition, it needs wall space for participant groups to hang their work. If a room does not have enough wall space, a less desirable alternative is to make fake walls out of foam core boards. Boards that are 4 feet by 8 feet by a half-inch thick are very light and can easily be taped together. They are rigid enough to stand against existing walls or pillars.

Equipment and Technical Support

Typical audiovisual equipment used in most AI Summits includes laptop computer(s), projectors, projection screens, TV/VCR, video recorders, and a sound system. For ease of mobility, we recommend cordless microphones whenever possible. Other, non-audiovisual equipment includes printers, easels with flipchart paper, and enough additional tables for supplies and registration activities.

Make sure that you have the right technical support people on site and always close at hand, including audiovisual technicians, camera operators, and computer experts, especially if you are linking together summits from various sites. Do not assume that the meeting venue will provide this. We cannot stress this too much. There have been many times in our experience when the audio or video systems worked one minute and not the next, or when there was a computer crash or incompatibility. The only thing more frustrating than interrupting a summit because of a technology snafu is not having anyone available who can fix it.

Breakout Rooms

If the meeting room is not large enough to accommodate breakout configurations effectively, you will need to ensure that enough breakout rooms are available. Breakout rooms will need to be fairly close to the main meeting room for ease of travel and time purposes.

Signs of Inspiration, Fun, and Vitality

Making a hotel ballroom or other large meeting venue your own space takes thoughtful consideration. We like to create a room that is distinctively set for work and that evokes creativity and fun. We do this with a wide range of things, such as inspirational posters, photos of participants, boxes of building materials, tables of art supplies, costumes, and plants. People get curious and energy rises in anticipation when they walk into a room and are surprised by what they see.

At British Airways, for example, we collected quotes from employees and made posters with the quotes and photos of British Airways employees. We hung them on the walls of the meeting room so that as people entered they were greeted by the words and images of their colleagues. In many cases we prepare a running slide show with images of members of the organization at work on the job or at prior summits if there have been some.

Whatever we use to decorate the room generally serves as props for activities that will take place during the summit. Corners of the room or tables may be covered with a library of inspirational children's books; magazines for making collages; markers, tape, and art supplies to illustrate the positive core; musical instruments and costumes to use for dream skits; or building blocks and Tinkertoys, which are useful for organization design activities.

Meals and Refreshments

Always provide a healthy menu. Healthy food keeps the energy up and gives people a feeling of well-being, which in turns stokes the fires of creativity and active participation. Too much sugar and caffeine can trigger cycles of energy followed by late afternoon lethargy. As energy drops, so does enthusiasm for the process and hope in the future.

Meals and breaks are best served in a room other than the main summit room. This allows setup and cleanup without interrupting the summit activities. The goal is to get people served as quickly as possible. Whether the meals served are plated, buffet, or box lunches, ensure that there is a very streamlined method for making this happen. Make sure the meeting venue contact understands the importance of process efficiency during meals and breaks.

Travel, Transportation, and Parking

When selecting a summit site, also take into consideration travel time, access to public transportation, and parking. At one of our summits about thirty people got parking tickets because we had not known to supply them with complimentary parking stickers!

CHANCE FAVORS A PREPARED MIND—AND A WELL-PLANNED SUMMIT

When you bring 200 or 300 or 1,000 people together for four days, you cannot predict or plan for all that will happen. Thoughtful and thorough planning creates flexibility and enables the facilitators to easily adapt to the needs of the group as they arise during the summit. Just as discipline grants freedom, so robust planning fosters safety, spontaneity, and creativity during the summit.

The work of the planning team may seem to go unnoticed, and that is good. As we said earlier, a well-planned summit will appear seamless to the participants. Successful planning will be evident in the compliments received about the high level of energy, the excitement of new relationships, the easy flow of the process, and the quick progress made on important issues, not to mention the food, the practical workbooks, and the absence of annoyances. Don't forget to thank your planning team!

PART III

DURING
THE SUMMIT

This is the moment you've been waiting for! You, the advisory team, and the planning team have organized things well, and now the entire organization is ready to get to work. As you stand in the reception area, you are excited to see people starting to arrive. Along with the facilitators and members of the advisory and planning teams, you say hello to familiar colleagues, greet other members of the organization, and welcome external stakeholders.

As you stand back, you see people approaching the registration table, collecting their name badges, venturing into the conference room to check out their seating assignments, and wandering back out into the reception area for coffee and lively conversation. You know that some people are uncertain and a few are skeptical, but your communication campaign has been effective and, for the most part, the energy is good and people are enthusiastic.

As you stroll into the conference room for a last-minute check, you see forty round tables each surrounded by eight comfortable chairs. On each table you see a table number, participant workbooks, pens, a box of markers, a roll of masking tape, several pieces of multicolored construction paper, and a little basket full of pipe cleaners and soft toys for fun.

At the front of the room you see a platform. On the platform is a small table and two chairs for the facilitators, two flipchart stands, and an equipment table containing two digital projectors, a laptop computer, a VCR, and two lavalier microphones. On either side of the platform are two large projection screens that can be seen clearly from every vantage point. One says "Welcome!" and the other displays the summit task. Positioned against the wall off to the side of each screen is a 16 ft.-long table covered with playful props such as hats, masks, boas, costumes, plastic flowers, and musical instruments to be used for the dream presentations.

On one wall you see an 8 ft. × 20 ft. piece of white butcher block paper. On the top is written in big, bold letters "Our Positive Core of Strengths." On the opposite wall you see a huge collage of baby pictures and present-day pictures of your colleagues and dozens of posters filled with quotable quotes and compelling stories gleaned from the pre-summit interviews. Along the back wall is an 8 ft. supply table, a tower of sound equipment, and a table for the four additional facilitators containing two laptops, two digital cameras, and four cordless microphones. In the far back corner the video crew is methodically setting up their lights, cameras, and boom microphones. Forty flipchart stands are positioned out of the way against the walls. Everything is precisely organized and ready to go.

This is it . . . the big moment . . . the start of your AI Summit!

In this section, we get to the heart of the matter: how to conduct a successful AI Summit. We follow the 4 × 4 summit model: 4 D's in 4 days. In Chapter 7 we provide an in-depth look at discovery, in Chapter 8 dream, in Chapter 9 design, and in Chapter 10 destiny. Finally, in Chapter 11 we explore the spirit and practice of appreciative facilitation. Taken together, these five chapters provide a comprehensive look at what to do during an AI Summit.

CHAPTER 7

DISCOVERY

A few years ago, the executive director of American Baptist International Ministries (ABIM), John Sundquist, felt it was time to establish a fresh vision and direction for his organization. He had been through a similar process ten years earlier when he joined the organization, but new times called for new measures, and John wanted to engage a wide range of stakeholders in discovering what those measures should be. He turned to ABIM Director of Planning, Stan Slade, and to us to get the job done.

Because ABIM works in dozens of countries and has a long and distinguished history of strong collaboration with its international partners, our first step was to form a twenty-five-person "global planning task force" to reflect the diversity of ABIM's programs and relationships. The task force members fanned out around the globe and trained interviewers, who in turn interviewed some 1,200 partners. The purpose of the interviews was to discover ABIM's positive core—the purpose, principles, programs, practices, and qualities of relationship that gave life to their ministries when they were at their best—and to hear from partners about their aspirations for ABIM and its future. The results of the interviews were brought to a January AI Summit in Green Lake, Wisconsin.

The summit was characterized by one staff member as "a full body experience . . . a great big bodacious planning party!" It included all ABIM staff and their children from around the world (about 300 people) and consisted of four full days of playing in the snow, singing, worshiping, networking, discovering strengths, discerning trends, and envisioning the future.

As a result of the summit, ABIM established a new ten-year strategic plan complete with mission priorities, strategies, and measurable goals, many of which represented significant new directions for the organization. John Sundquist said, "The AI Summit was truly a mountaintop experience for all of us. We came away from the time together energized, inspired, and with a profoundly renewed sense of calling and direction." Stan added, "For many and important reasons, the field staff in our organization tend to say 'we' not when referring to themselves and their colleagues in the organization, but when referring to the people groups they serve. The summit gave us a powerful and indelible sense of belonging to one another and serving in a common task. The whole AI process—and the summit as the fulcrum at its center—gave everyone a role in mapping our future and a personal stake in pursuing it."

As the ABIM story suggests, the task of the discovery phase is to explore the organization's positive core. It is an invitation to search, with the curiosity of a wide-eyed child, for the best in oneself, in others, and in the whole system to create a foundation of confidence and broadened understanding for the tasks of dream, design, and destiny. In this chapter we walk you through day 1 of an AI Summit—the discovery process. We look at:

- Extending a warm welcome
- Setting the stage
- Presenting sponsorship statements
- Introducing appreciative inquiry
- Launching the paired appreciative interviews
- Debriefing the interviews
- Discovering and mapping the positive core
- Presenting the conceptual underpinnings of AI

We also review a list of optional activities that can be used during the discovery phase, including a continuity scan, storytelling, and "the elders speak." The chapter concludes with a description of how presummit data, such as posters with quotes, photo galleries, videos, books of stories, reports, and provocative propositions from previous summits, can be integrated into an AI Summit agenda. Exhibit 7.1 offers an overview of a typical day of discovery. This is only one of many possibilities. We encourage you to experiment with others.

Exhibit 7.1

Overview of a Typical Day of Discovery

Time	Activity
Morning	**Key tasks: Getting started, introducing AI, building relationships, beginning to discover the positive core through paired appreciative interviews**
8:30–9:00	Participants arrive and are invited to engage in some sort of pre-start activity, such as listing high-point events in the history of the organization, the industry, and the world on pre-constructed wall timelines (optional)
9:00–9:15	Welcome, sponsorship statements (why we are here, what we hope to accomplish, etc.)
9:15–9:45	Introduction to AI, 4-D cycle, overview of the week
9:45–10:00	Introduction to paired appreciative interviews
10:00–11:45	Paired appreciative interviews are conducted (includes break)
11:45–12:00	Process-level debriefing of the paired interviews
12:00–12:30	Overview: Conceptual underpinnings of AI
12:30–1:30	Lunch
Afternoon	**Key tasks: Small-group team building, discovering and mapping the organization's positive core, beginning to gain a sense of the whole**
1:30–2:45	In table groups, share stories from the interviews and discover the positive core (forces and factors that allow the organization to be at its best)
2:45–3:15	Table groups report out to the large group
3:15–3:45	Break
3:45–4:45	Positive core is mapped in a plenary session to highlight the most important, life-giving aspects of the organization's past and present.
4:45–5:00	Review of the day and preview of the next three days

SETTING THE STAGE

The early moments and experiences of any new situation send signals to participants about what they can anticipate. They are an opportunity to set the stage for healthy relationships and high expectations. Stage-setting opportunities can be found in how participants are welcomed, the selection of activities prior to the official start of the morning, the tone of sponsor statements, and the way AI is introduced.

Extending a Warm Welcome

A welcoming beginning goes a long way toward setting the tone for safe, open, and inclusive participation. We provide three kinds of greetings. First, it is helpful to have people stationed in the parking lot, at the front door, and in hallways to welcome people, give directions, and guide participants to the meeting room. We generally have members of the logistics team serve in this capacity. Second, it is important to have a well-organized and easily accessible registration area where people can check in, get name tags, and be directed to their seats. Again, this is a role for the logistics team. Third, it builds relationships when summit facilitators informally greet people as they enter the room. We walk around the room, introduce ourselves to people, and get to know them briefly by name. This gives summit participants a sense of connection with us right from the start. It also enables us to get a feel for the room—how friendly people are, how excited or anxious they are, and how much they know about the summit process.

Getting an Active Start

It can be useful to get people going on a simple self-managed activity prior to the formal start of the summit. This seems to help alleviate the inevitable anxiety that comes from being in an unfamiliar situation as well as making productive use of the time before the formal session starts. Examples of such activities include creating a timeline of high-point moments in the organization's history or posting and reading data collected from other members of the organization prior to the summit. Both of these optional activities are described later. The overall goal at this point is to create a sense of safety and to set a norm of productive, participative action.

Sponsorship Statements

At the beginning of a summit, people want a statement from their organizational leaders—the sponsors—about the purpose and importance of the meeting. A hopeful, encouraging message helps to focus people on the summit task and communicates that the process is seen as important and will be taken seriously. The opening sponsor statements can also provide the organization's leaders an opportunity to humbly (and without finger pointing) acknowledge any current difficulties while inviting everyone to participate in the cocreation of a better future.

Tom Morrill, principal of Fairview Elementary School, began an AI Summit in just such a way. He spoke with heart and compassion about the feelings of alienation, disenfranchisement, and loss of community that he knew were present in the room as a result of the forced merger of three small schools into one larger institution. He publicly acknowledged what everyone knew at one level——that it was highly unlikely that this decision would be reversed. And then he spoke of the opportunity he saw for the future—the opportunity to discover and bring forward the very best of each culture from the three merged schools. He held out a vision of a school in which children would experience the best the faculty and staff had to offer and in which people felt connected and valued for their contributions. He finished by inviting people to bring forward the very best parts of the three cultures they represented and asking them if they wanted to participate in creating the new school based on the best of their past. Every single hand in the room went up.

INTRODUCING APPRECIATIVE INQUIRY

In order for participants to easily move into discovery, they need to know (1) what appreciative inquiry is and why it is being used, (2) what the 4-D cycle is and how it will serve as the outline for their discussions, (3) why we invite stories in the interviews and how they will be used throughout the summit, and (4) what is unique about an appreciative interview and how to conduct it. We generally spend about a half hour presenting this introductory information before we ask participants to engage in appreciative interviews.

Although this presentation varies, we typically cover much of the material that is contained in Chapter 1 of this book. We provide some background on AI, present AI as a powerful approach to organization development and change, introduce the concept of the positive core, and talk about the AI 4-D cycle. At times, we also briefly introduce the five principles of AI.[1] Then we go on to explain how AI and the 4-D cycle will be used to guide the flow and activities of the summit. At the very end of this introduction, we go over the specific purpose and agenda of the summit. We find that introducing AI before talking about the purpose and agenda creates a high level of energy and excitement for getting started.

LAUNCHING THE PAIRED APPRECIATIVE INTERVIEWS

The appreciative interview is at the heart of the overall process. Its functions include not only the obvious one of making tacit knowledge available to the whole system, but also the appreciative dislodgment of certainty and the building of new relationships. The appreciative dislodgment of certainty creates openings from which innovations and future possibilities emerge, and the formation of new relationships creates the energy and connections needed to turn those possibilities into practical action.

Our experience suggests that a period of forty-five minutes to an hour per person is needed to accomplish the interviews well. It helps to provide the participants with a time slot of one and a half to two hours that incorporates a self-managed coffee break. This allows slower interviewers to take their time and those who are faster to take a longer break.

Getting all participants into interview pairs sometimes takes a bit of attention. We have found it useful to make it a two-step process. We make sure everyone has a partner first, and then we give directions for the process of conducting interviews. This seems to help the shy participants to make a connection.

In launching the appreciative interview, we often talk about it as a unique opportunity to get to know someone with a different view of the world. The directions we give for choosing an interview partner are:

- Choose someone you do not know or know very little.
- Choose someone who works in a different department, function, or organization than you.
- Choose someone who is different from you in age, race, or gender.

It is really fun for us when, after following these directions, people come back from their interviews exclaiming, "We discovered we have so much in common!"

In addition to setting up interview partners, it is important to give clear directions for how to conduct the interviews. The guidance we give is simple:

- Each person will conduct an interview and be interviewed.
- Follow the questions on the interview guide, being certain to cover all of the questions within the allotted time.
- Use the interview guide only as a guide, allowing the interview to follow its own pace and direction. If your partner doesn't have an answer for one of the questions, go on to the next one.
- Seek stories by asking who, what, when, why, and how as probes to your partner's answers.
- If your partner veers from the positive questions, allow him or her to talk for a short while, while you listen with care, and then redirect attention back to the interview questions in the interview guide.
- Conduct your interview as a young child might, with curiosity and wonder, seeking to discover what matters most to your partner.
- Take notes of the stories you hear so you will be able to introduce your partner and share his or her ideas with your group later.

Be sure to give a clear time frame that includes the amount of time to be taken for each interview and the time to reconvene in the whole group. In addition, let participants know where to conduct their interviews. If you want them to stay in the large meeting room, say so. If they are free to find a space outdoors or in another room or sitting area, let them know that also. Clear directions on all relevant details help the process move along smoothly.

Our oral instructions are almost always complemented by a short set of written instructions contained in the participant workbook. See the Appendix, "Activity 1," for an example of these instructions and for an example of an appreciative inquiry interview guide.

It always takes people five minutes or so to make the transition into the interview process. We usually give people about fifteen minutes to get fully into the flow, and then we walk around just in case anyone has any questions. We don't interrupt; we just circulate and make ourselves available.

DEBRIEFING THE INTERVIEWS

Appreciative interviews are a high-energy activity. When participants return, they are generally lively and ready to share what they have learned. But before unpacking the interviews in small groups, we always take about fifteen minutes as a large group to debrief the interview process—not the content, the process. We ask people to share any words or thoughts about what the interview was like for them. Invariably they say that they loved the positive energy; that they made a new friend; that they discovered much in common with their partner; that they learned a lot about their own strengths, their partner's strengths, and the strengths of the organization; that it was exciting, inspiring, uplifting, and fun. This debriefing activity is important because it allows people to hear from others, connect with a sense of the whole, and begin to feel the power of the appreciative process.

DISCOVERING THE POSITIVE CORE

After the debrief, it is time to direct people to their small groups to introduce their partners and begin sharing what they have learned. We call this activity "discovering the positive core" because it allows people to reveal all of the hidden strengths that have allowed the organization to function at its best. It is always delightful to see people connect strength with strength, hope with hope, joy with joy, and watch as their capacity expands with each new story that is told. This activity invites people into a new relationship with their organizational history—not one that problematizes the past, but one that learns and leverages its best examples to create new possibilities for the future. It sets the tone for the entire summit by building an environment of collective confidence.

As with most appreciative inquiry activities, there are as many ways to discover the positive core as there are people to discover it. Next we share two approaches that have worked well for us.

Revealing Root Causes of Success

Root causes of success are the forces and factors that cause, create, or support success. These factors can be at the individual level, work unit level, or organizational level. To reveal root causes of success, we walk people through two steps. First, we invite them to go around their table and introduce their partner by sharing stories and highlights from the "opening" and "closing" sections of their interview (see Chapter 6 for an explanation of the opening, middle, and closing sections of an interview guide). These are usually questions about what attracted them to the organization, high-point experiences, what they value most, and their images of the future.

We call this first step "discovering the resources in our community" because it allows people to appreciate the experiences, gifts, strengths, and aspirations of the others around the table. We invite people to listen for patterns or unique "ahas" as others share their partner's stories. Then, after everyone in the group has had a chance to share, the group's recorder makes two lists on flipchart paper: (1) patterns from the high-point stories and (2) emerging images of the future. See the Appendix, "Activity 2," for a sample worksheet for this activity.

For the second step, we have the groups go back around the table, and each person shares his or her partner's stories and highlights from the "middle" section of the interview guide. These are the "topical" questions that focus on the summit task (e.g., leadership, customer service, collaboration). We call this step "discovering the positive core of our organization when we are at our best" because it allows people to identify the strengths, assets, capacities, capabilities, values, traditions, practices, and other factors that drive success with regard to the summit topic.

We invite people to listen for patterns that support success and make it possible. Then we ask the recorder to draw a line down the center of a flipchart page. At the top of the page on the left side of the line they write *Stories*, and at the top of the page on the right side of the line they write *Root Causes of Success*. Finally, we ask each group to prepare a three- to four-minute presentation that includes one exemplar story and a description of their "top five" or "top ten" root causes of success. See the Appendix, "Activity 3," for a sample worksheet for this activity.

Creating a Map of the Positive Core

Once the root causes of success have been discovered in small groups, it is time to share the discoveries with the large group. This is a very important part of the summit process because it is the first time participants will be hearing from each other about the content of the summit topic at the level of the whole. Strengths, resources, and capacities get connected and amplified across all 200, 300, or 1,000 people in the room. People gain immediate access to a "logic of the whole" and are inspired by the power and potential of the whole system working in concert.

We have found that the best way to do this is to create some kind of big, bold visual display of the positive core. We call this a "map of the positive core." Visual displays are important for three reasons. First, like a great work of art, they create a spirit of inspiration in the room. When, for the rest of the summit, people can look to one end of the room and see a huge exhibition of their greatest strengths and capacities, it encourages, excites, and elevates their energies. Second, visual displays focus and draw meaning from the whole-group discussions. When people see their ideas illustrated on the walls, they gain a sense of pride and accomplishment. They see that they are making progress through the dialogue process. Finally, visual displays are excellent ways to remember and communicate what happened at the summit. They can be preserved as is, reduced to a more manageable size, or photographed and included in reports, slide shows, photo albums, posters, banners, and other media.

There are many different ways to create a positive core map. One that we are particularly fond of is to put a big 8 ft × 20 ft piece of butcher block paper on one wall of the conference room. It is ideal if the paper can be cut into the shape of something meaningful to the organization or if a picture of something meaningful can be drawn on the paper. For example, Roadway Express (a trucking company) cut the paper into the shape of a truck with two trailers. The first trailer was for all the root causes of success (discovery). The second trailer was for dreams of the future. All the data was posted on 8.5 × 11–inch colored sheets made up as lading bills. With all of these elements of the positive core "on board," the company was "rolling down the road to success." The summit concluded with everyone signing their names on the truck cab.

We generally provide each table with ten large pieces of colorful construction paper. Just before it is time for people to report their story and root causes of success, we ask them to cut the pieces of construction paper into a certain shape that is meaningful to the organization. For example, at the Santa Ana Star Hotel and Casino summit, they cut the pieces of paper into the shape of a star (see next page). Other organizations have used diamonds, circles, triangles, and other shapes. Then we ask the tables to write each of their root causes of success on a separate piece of construction paper. When they get up to present, they go over to the positive core map on the wall, and while one person presents, the others post their root causes of success on the map. After all the table groups have presented, the whole group gathers around the positive core map and reflects on what patterns, highlights, and surprises they see.

Identifying Life-Giving Themes and Creating a Scattergram

A second approach to discovering and mapping the positive core is to share stories with a focus on locating the "themes" that are present when they and the organization are most alive. Themes can come from any of the questions in the interview protocol. They provide a link between the past and the images of the future that will be created in the dream and design phases. They are the basis for collectively imagining what the organization would be like if the exceptional moments uncovered in the interviews became the norm in the organization.

Exhibit 7.2 contains examples of themes—life-giving forces—that people have identified from interviews done in their organizations.

Exhibit 7.2

Examples of Themes

Themes from interviews with a group of professional socio-technical systems consultants on the interview query "Tell me about a time when you felt most alive as a practitioner."

- Working with people's core values
- Putting integrity into practice
- Recognizing the "footprints" of our work long after we are gone
- Being real and authentic
- Designing organizations that create more humanity than they consume

---

Themes from interviews with a group of line managers in a social service agency telling stories about their working lives:

- Doing things collectively

(continues)

Exhibit 7.2 *(continued)*

- Removing barriers to unity
- Ownership, support, commitment to common good
- Commitment to appreciating each other
- Getting together, sharing information, and socializing
- Transitioning from prosperity to austerity can lead to innovation and creativity

Examples of Themes

Themes from interviews with a group of line managers in a national bank inquiring into their culture at its best:

- Being the best
- Shared ownership
- Cooperation
- Integrity
- Empowering people

There is no prescription for a theme. It is entirely up to the group to decide upon the life-giving forces of their own system. The challenge for the AI facilitator is to let the groups go where they need to go with as little constraining structure as possible while still getting the work done. Exhibit 7.3 contains instructions for a theme identification exercise.

Exhibit 7.3

Instructions for Theme Identification Exercise

1) *Choose a work group:* Take your interview partner and join three other interview pairs, forming a group of eight.

2) *In your group:*

- Choose (1) a discussion leader, (2) a timekeeper, (3) a recorder, and (4) a reporter.

- At your table, each person (briefly) shares one or two of the best stories told by his or her interview partner. After hearing each other's stories, create a brainstormed list of the themes that were present in the stories— about high points, life-giving forces, ideas that "grabbed" you—thoughts

Exhibit 7.3 *(continued)*

about what life is like when things are at their best. From your group's "brainstormed" list, agree on and select three to five topics for your group and put them on a flipchart. Post the sheets.

[*Note:* If you have several topics (i.e., strong leadership, congenial work environment, etc.), each covered by a separate question, you can use this exercise for each separate topic.]

Instructions for Theme Identification Exercise

3) *Themes:* A theme is an idea or concept about what is present in the stories when people are reporting the times of greatest excitement, creativity, and reward. For example, you may hear stories in which people report "a feeling of success," "clarity about purpose," or "fun and excitement." These phrases are themes. In your brainstormed list, include all of these kinds of phrases that people can identify. Then select three to five themes that the whole group feels are important and that you would all like to have in your ideal work environment and organization.

4) *Prepare the following chart to be posted on the wall:* [*Note:* For this exercise, we recommend that you suggest three to five as an approximate number of themes, but make it clear to participants that you do not want them to be constrained by those numbers. The idea here is to capture the ideas that are most important to people. Also, do not give in to the inclination to put together similar themes or to combine charts in any way. Leave them exactly as they are. Step 6 allows people to highlight similar themes.]

Themes	Dots
1)	
2)	
3)	
4)	
5)	

5) *Creating a scattergram:* Each table group answers any clarifying questions about the themes they have listed on the chart.

- Each person has three or four Avery dots. Working alone, each person decides of all the themes on the wall which are most important and should be included in the dream organization of the future.

(continues)

Exhibit 7.3 *(continued)*

- Take up to five minutes to decide and place the dots. Please use each dot on a separate theme.

[*Note:* You can use markers instead of Avery dots. The scattergram is more vivid if you use all one color.]

Instructions for Theme Identification Exercise

6) Making sense of the scattergram: What do you notice about the charts? What themes are most important to this group?

[*Note:* At this point the group will often notice similar themes and remark on that. Try to reinforce the idea that every theme on the wall is important to at least one group in the room. The scattergram is intended to give a visual image of the whole group's energy and to facilitate everyone's actively engaging with everyone else's ideas. It is not designed to be a decision-making tool. Do not count and put numbers by the dot clusters. This is not a prioritization exercise. It is an opportunity for the group to see what is important to them as a whole. We rarely put any order to the themes, which allows the next step—shared images of a preferred future—to use all of the theme data as the basis for their images.]

Within an AI context, something can be a root cause of success, life-giving force, or element of the positive core even if it is mentioned in only one story. These are what we call "unique ahas"—things that people respond to with an exclamatory "yes!!" This is different from the traditional approach, governed by scientific ideas about statistical validity, where something has to be mentioned a certain number of times before it can legitimately be "on the list." In AI, if just one person identifies a theme that strikes a chord with others, then it is most likely that it is a life-giving force for the system. Of course, we also consider something a life-giving force if it is mentioned by several people. The key is to tap into the intuitive emotional abilities of the group as they decide what is a life-giving force for them.

PRESENTING THE CONCEPTUAL UNDERPINNINGS OF AI

Because the interview process is so effective at creating an appreciative dislodgment of certainty, after the interviews curiosity is high about how AI works. At this point that we review some or all of the following material in an informal thirty- to sixty-minute presentation based mainly on storytelling.

- Positive change versus a deficit theory of change[2]
- The cultural consequences of deficit discourse[3]
- The idea of the positive core and positive change[4]
- The idea of positive image leading to positive action[5]
- The power of the unconditional positive question[6]
- The importance of balancing continuity, transition, and novelty[7]

OPTIONAL ACTIVITIES THAT CAN BE USED DURING THE DISCOVERY PHASE

There are some essential activities of the discovery phase, and there are some optional activities. We consider the essential activities to be the paired interviews, the small-group discovery of the positive core, and the whole-group report-outs and mapping of the positive core. This flow allows for one-on-one intimacy, small-group learning, and whole-group integration of meaning.

Some of our favorite optional activities include a continuity scan, storytelling, and "the elders speak." Table 7.1 provides a summary of these optional activities.

WORKING WITH PRE-SUMMIT DATA

Sometimes, as was the case with ABIM, it makes sense to jumpstart the discovery process by engaging people in productive summit-related tasks before they arrive at the session itself. The pre-summit task usually involves interviews with a wide variety of key stakeholders. Quotable quotes, compelling stories, and elevating images from the interviews are then presented at the summit in the form of posters, a photo gallery, videos, books of stories, and so on. In some cases, people prepare a report or a wall display with provocative propositions from previous summits.

When the Upstream Technology Group (UTG) of BP wanted to increase the overall productivity of their roughly 700 researchers and scientists, they began by developing a customized interview guide that was sent to about one-third of their employees. The interviews were conducted and summaries sent electronically to a central location where

Table 7.1

Optional Discovery Activities

Activity	Description	Purpose
Continuity scan	Timelines are created by posting flipcharts (or foam boards) across one wall of the summit plenary room and drawing one to three horizontal lines representing the organizational, industry, and global histories. Three or four time eras, such as *Before the 80s, The 80s,* and *The 90s to now* (or some uniquely relevant alternative) are posted along the timelines. People are then invited to list key events in order to identify factors that have sustained the organization overtime and are desirable in the future. Once participants have listed key events on the timeline, the continuity scan questions for discussion include: • What are all the qualities of your organization, the processes, systems, products, services, or general ways of doing things, that have contributed to your organization's success in the past? • Of these, which do you want to maintain to ensure continued success as we move forward into a new era of doing business? These questions are discussed at table groups once everyone has had a chance to review the content of the timelines. We have found that these discussions can be enriched significantly by inviting either table-based or whole-system storytelling	To provide a vivid picture of the organization's strengths and historical core capabilities. Excitement is generated as people make connections about the organization's history. As history is brought into focus and becomes meaningful, people are more able to imagine possibilities for their collective future. The continuity scan: Serves to jog the organization's memory and helps members recall long-forgotten successes, strengths, and dreams. • Allows an organization to honor its elders, the successes of the past, and to build upon a foundation of positive potential. • When dreams and designs for the future are grounded in stories of past successes, energy and enthusiasm open for cooperation, change, and continued success.

Table 7.1 *(continued)*

Optional Discovery Activities

Activity	Description	Purpose
Storytelling	Often connected with the timeline and continuity scan exercise, whole-system or table-based storytelling is an invitation for people to share, through the use of narrative, an event or time period that captures some important moment or transition in the organization's history. Instructions for this task can be "As you look at what people have listed as key events in the history of our organization and its relationship to the outside world, what stories spring to mind that capture any of these key moments?" Summit participants are invited to attend to "rapport talk" rather than "report talk." and to listen for stories told by others that best highlight their hopes and dreams.	Storytelling is a vehicle for making meaning among a large group of people. Since meaning is made among people, not among facts and data, stories provoke the collective imagination and liberate people to choicefully create the future. Storytelling allows values to be expressed, explored, and adapted. Stories ignite the human spirit of curiosity and creativity. They contain seeds of wisdom grounded in experience. Through public storytelling summit participants become familiar with a means of expressing ideas and interests substantially richer in meaning than a lists of facts and information, data presentations, and descriptions. Great stories make impossible actions seem possible and provide impetus for change.
The elders speak	This is a form of invited storytelling that provides special time and space for the organization's elders. Either in conjunction with the continuity scan or as a stand-alone activity, the organization's elders are invited to tell their stories of how the organization has evolved, how it has used its strengths and capacities to overcome challenges and grow, or just moments when they as elders felt most alive and engaged.	The very act of conducting a continuity scan allows an organization to honor its elders. By inviting the elders to speak from the perspective of history, the role of elders is again revered in stories and in action. As a result there is an increased understanding of the significance of intergenerational relationships.

a book of responses was compiled, indexed both by question and by interviewee category. The purpose of indexing by interviewee category was to see the differences between people within UTG and their clients.

Once the summit began, the participants conducted one-on-one interviews with each other and spent time in small groups discovering their root causes of success. Then they turned their attention to the book of interview data. The tables received different but overlapping sets of pages from the book. People spent time individually reading the pages and circling key stories, words, and images. Then, back in their table groups, they shared the most powerful quotes, stories, and images and identified the root causes of success contained in them. Finally, they combined the root causes of success from the pre-summit interviews with the root causes from their own interviews and, as a large group, created a map of the positive core.

In another example, the Canadian Department of National Defense held two summits one year apart. The second summit was focused on evaluating the progress that had been made since the first. Attendees were asked to interview five people (colleagues, clients, and stakeholders) and to bring the results of those interviews to the summit. Upon arrival, they sat around a huge fireplace and shared their best stories in a large circle. The next day they posted on the walls some 300 typed success stories and categorized them into themes. They also posted the provocative propositions that were created at the first summit.

After they had completed their on-site paired interviews, they reviewed the success stories and provocative propositions on the walls and circled the phrases and words that had meaning for them. Finally, with the stories, provocative propositions, and paired interviews as background, they conducted a continuity scan, which allowed them to create a large vivid illustration of the organization's positive core.

BUILDING MOMENTUM TO DREAM

Day 1 is complete, and there is a buzz in the room. Some people are heading home, but others are staying behind to continue conversations with their colleagues. They have learned about appreciative inquiry, established new relationships, gained a sense of the whole organization, and amplified their strengths. They have discovered potentials and possibilities that they never dreamed of before, and they can't stop talking about them. There is a sense of excitement and anticipation for the next three days.

This is common at the end of the first day of an AI Summit. The one-on-one appreciative interviews have created a context of safe, open, inclusive participation and have allowed each participant to establish a deep appreciative relationship with at least one other person in the room. The process of discovering the positive core in small groups has begun to build a sense of community and has created a fusion of strengths among diverse participants. And the creation of the positive core map has allowed people to begin to develop a sense of the "whole system" and has given people a glimpse of the power that is possible if the entire organization were to mobilize their energies in a common direction. The discovery phase of an AI Summit enlarges a sense of possibility and builds momentum to dream.

CHAPTER 8

DREAM

In this chapter we take you through the dream phase of an Appreciative Inquiry Summit. We begin by sharing some theoretical perspectives on the power of bold dreaming and possibility-focused visioning that have influenced the way we design our summits. We then offer specific designs for the dream phase, walk through some important choice points, and highlight keys to success.

THE POWER OF POSITIVE IMAGES OF THE FUTURE

The purpose of the dream phase is to engage the whole system in moving beyond the status quo to envision valued and vital futures. It is an invitation to people to lift their sights, exercise their imagination, and dream about what their organization could look like if it were fully aligned around its strengths and aspirations. This is based in part on the work of Fred Polak[1] and other pioneers in the field of image theory. In the 1960s, Polak was the Director of Planning for Royal Dutch Shell and, later, for the Dutch government. Struck by how societies and corporations seemed to gravitate in the direction of their images of the future, he launched a sweeping study of Western civilization to see if his observation held true across countries and epochs.

What he found confirmed his suspicions: The rise and fall of images of the future preceded or accompanied the rise and fall of cultures.

Whenever a society's image was positive and flourishing, "the flower of culture [was] in full bloom." New advances in art, architecture, music, commerce, science, and politics burst forth, and there was a palpable vibrancy to civic life. Once the image began to decay and lose its vitality, however, "the culture [did] not long survive."[2]

This same dynamic, observed Polak, holds true for collectivities of all sizes, and it is due to the "activation effect" of positive images. When a team, department, or organization holds a clear and compelling image of where it wants to go, the image "activates" the conversations, choices, commitments, and behaviors necessary to get there. People become inventive about accomplishing their hopes and dreams. They develop strategies, attract resources, build products, launch initiatives, and draw on personal ingenuity to get things done. Positive images of the future literally become self-fulfilling, self-propelling engines for change.

Think, urged Polak, of modern management practices, full employment, social security, the length of the work week, and profit sharing. They were all once figments of someone's imagination. But over time, as these images gained focus, depth, richness, and clarity, they attracted support and mobilized action to bring them to fruition. Polak's conclusion is that for any collectivity, its image of the future is not only an indicator of where it is going, but also a "force for action" that powerfully promotes certain choices and puts them to work in determining the future.

INTERNAL DIALOGUE THAT INSPIRES

If powerful guiding images of the future are so important, the question must be asked: Where do they come from? How do organization-wide images get created and sustained? An intriguing answer is provided by psychologist Robert Schwartz.[3] He claims that an image of the future is essentially a pattern of "internal dialogue" within a group or organization. As organizational members go about their day-to-day business, they are continuously engaged in a process of "self-talk" about what kind of organization they are, where they are going, and how they are going to get there. For example, these days Southwest Airlines' internal dialogue is about being the industry leader by pursuing a strategy of low-cost, customer-friendly service. This internal dialogue provides an image of the future for Southwest that mobilizes energy and guides action.

But, claims Schwartz, not all internal dialogue leads to high performance. In research he did during the 1980s, he found that high- and low-performing groups had a distinct difference in their patterns of self-talk. Healthy, high-functioning groups had a positive to negative dialogue ratio of 2:1 or higher, whereas unhealthy, dysfunctional groups had a ratio of 1:1 or lower. This suggests that more than any other factor, it may be the stories organizational members tell themselves about themselves, particularly with regard to their capacity to accomplish valued goals, that determine their eventual prospects for success.

If the organizational self-talk carried out around the water cooler, in meetings, on the telephone, via e-mail, and even outside "the office" is negative or lacking in vitality, the organization will tend to fall into dysfunction. If, on the other hand, it is positive and focused on a truly desired future, it holds the potential to be the organization's most powerful ally for promoting high performance and constructive organization change.

DARING TO DREAM

The dream phase of an Appreciative Inquiry Summit, then, is an invitation to the entire organization to shift its internal dialogue. Its purpose is to engage everyone in a spirited conversation about their organization's greatest potential. By doing this, the organization as a whole creates for itself positive guiding images of the future that expand the realm of the possible. For many organizational members, this is the first time they are invited to think "great" thoughts and create "prodigious" possibilities for their organization. The process is both personally and organizationally healthy and inspiring.

In this chapter we walk you through day two of an AI Summit—the dream process. We look at:

- The dream phase in action
- Alternative approaches to dreaming
- Creative dreaming
- Opportunity mapping
- Consensus visioning

We also review of list of optional activities that can be used during the dream phase, including pictures, drawings, and metaphors; a guided-image exercise; and a dream book. Exhibit 8.1 offers an overview of a typical day of dreaming.

Exhibit 8.1

Overview of A Typical Day of Dreaming

Time	Activity
Morning	**Key tasks: Reflecting on learnings from the previous day, understanding the positive image–positive action relationship, envisioning the future of the organization**
8:30–9:00	Welcome, getting started, overview of the day
9:00–10:00	The positive image–positive action relationship
10:00–11:30	Envisioning the future (includes a self-managed break)
11:30–12:30	Write dream statements
12:30–1:30	Lunch
Afternoon	**Key tasks: Enacting and enriching the dreams**
1:30–2:00	Preparing creative presentations of the dream
2:00–3:00	Presenting creative presentations
3:00–3:30	Break
3:30–4:45	Enriching the dreams
4:45–5:00	Review of the day and preview of next day

THE DREAM PHASE IN ACTION

Our 4 × 4 design calls for dedicating the second day to dreaming. This is normally done in the same mixed groups as the day before, when people were working on the discovery phase. We like to keep them in the same groups for three reasons. First, as we enter the dream phase, we often invite participants to refer back to their interviews from the day before. For this reason, it is important that interview pairs stick together.

Second, we find that over the course of a summit, people like some continuity and some change. In days 3 and 4, people usually get their fair share of change. Depending on the agenda, they may spend time in stakeholder groups, design groups, and cross-functional action teams. Days 1 and 2 counterbalance days 3 and 4 by providing an initial foundation of continuity.

Third, we find that after people have spent a day in the discovery phase valuing each other, sharing stories, and mapping their positive core, they are eager to stay together and hear one another's hopes and dreams. Because of the relational bonding they have done, they are able to support each other in dreaming bolder dreams and connecting those dreams to the "stories of strength" they heard the day before.

Getting Started

We like to start the day with something light or creative that elevates positive energy and allows all participants to bring their attention into the room. In our work with the United Religions Initiative, we commonly started with a moment of silence or prayer led by people of different faiths. In the work with CRWRC in East Africa, a handful of participants would arrive in the conference room a little early and begin singing, clapping softly, and swaying to the music. As people gathered, the group grew until we became a mighty chorus of about 200 people. After a couple more songs, people gave each other a handshake, a hug, or a pat on the back and then got to work. At another summit, facilitators Tom Osborn and Sallie Lee read a few headlines from the morning newspaper and then invited participants to talk briefly at their tables to come up with a headline that captured their excitements about the day before and hopes for the day to come. There are many other ways to do this, but all of these activities have in common that they bring people into the room, build connections, and start things off on a positive note.

The Positive Image– Positive Action Relationship

After the opening activity, housekeeping items are reviewed, and then we give an overview of the day. Following that, we set up the dream phase by discussing the positive image–positive action relationship. This is usually a very interactive and engaging session. People seem to connect immediately with the logic, and they almost always have many examples from their personal and professional lives that they are eager to share. This process of sharing ideas and stories invariably builds momentum for the task ahead.

Three Keys to Dreaming

After the positive image–positive action conversation, we transition into providing the purpose and guidelines for the dreaming exercise. Typically we stress three key points:

- **Build on the positive core.** One aspect that differentiates appreciative inquiry from other visioning or planning methodologies is that images of the future emerge out of grounded examples from the most positive past; they are compelling possibilities precisely because they are based on extraordinary moments from an organization's history. In this sense, the dream phase is both practical, in that it is grounded in the organization's history, and generative, in that it seeks to expand the organization's potential.
- **Aim higher.** Henry Ford once said, "If you think you can or you think you can't, you're right." All too often organizations settle for mediocrity because they don't believe in their own capacity for greatness. They lack confidence and set their sights low. The dream phase of an AI Summit is an opportunity to get beyond business as usual by aiming higher. It calls for passionate dialogue about high ideals that organizational members desire and toward which they are willing to commit their energies.
- **Think like an artist.** In the dream phase, the point is to use people's stories of the past and hopes for the future just as an artist uses materials to create a portrait of possibility. The stories and hopes provide the palette of colors—reds, yellows, greens, blues—that allow organizational members to paint vivid, compelling pictures of what the future could look like if their best ideas were brought forward into practice.

ALTERNATIVE
APPROACHES TO DREAMING

Over the years we and our colleagues around the world have experimented with many different designs for dreaming. Just about all of them, if handled with care and sincerity, can work. We would like to share three alternative approaches that we have found to be most useful.

One alternative is what we call *creative dreaming*. Creative dreaming is appropriate when the organization wants to mobilize energy and action around a new strategic direction or set of organizational priorities but does not need to come to consensus on the precise wording of a particular purpose or vision statement. This process allows people to share their aspirations with the rest of the organization and to look for points of common interest and excitement, but does not bog things down by trying to force false consensus. The purpose of creative dreaming is to allow people to create a set of new possibilities that attract and inspire them.

A second alternative is called *opportunity mapping*. With this approach, participants create an opportunity map that allows them to identify specific areas of focus before the dreaming begins. Once they have completed the opportunity map, they follow a process similar to creative dreaming. This seems to work especially well with groups who do more "hands-on" work and feel less of a passionate connection to the "big picture" of the organization.

A third option is called *consensus visioning*. We use this option sparingly, only when the organization expresses a firm desire to draft a common purpose or vision statement. For us, the point of dreaming is to open up creativity and to expand possibilities, not to converge and narrow down the possibilities. However, on those periodic occasions when a division or organization really needs to craft a common purpose or vision statement, we use the consensus visioning process to generate the images and then to analyze them and come to consensus. See Table 8.1 for an explanation of the steps for each alternative.

Table 8.1

Three Alternatives for Dreaming

Creative Dreaming	Opportunity Mapping	Consensus Visioning
Purpose: To create a new set of possibilities that attract and inspire organizational action.	Purpose: To mobilize action around a specific set of key opportunities.	Purpose: To come to consensus on a purpose, mission, or vision statement for the whole organization.
1. As a small group, envision the future by sharing each person's dreams for the organization (from interview guide).	1. As a whole group, create an opportunity map and form groups around the different opportunities.	1. As a small group, envision the future by sharing each person's dreams for the organization (from interview guide).

(continues)

Table 8.1 *(continued)*

Three Alternatives for Dreaming

Creative Dreaming	Opportunity Mapping	Consensus Visioning
2. As a small group, write a "dream statement" that captures the best of your collective dreams.	2. As a small (opportunity) group, envision the future by sharing each person's dreams for the specific opportunity.	2. As a small group, write a "dream statement" that captures the best of your collective dreams.
3. As a small group, prepare and perform a creative presentation of your dream as if it were happening now.	3. As a small group, write a "dream statement" that captures the best of your collective dreams.	3. As a small group, prepare and perform a creative presentation of your dream as if it were happening now.
4. After all the presentations are complete, the large group enriches the dreams by sharing thoughts, highlights, excitements from the presentations.	4. As a small group, prepare and perform a creative presentation of your dream as if it were happening now.	4. After all the presentations are complete, the large group enriches the dreams by sharing thoughts, highlights, excitements from the presentations.
	5. After all the presentations are complete, the large group enriches the dreams by sharing thoughts, highlights, excitements with each opportunity group.	5. After the large-group discussion, include a process for coming to consensus on a single purpose, mission, or vision statement.

CREATIVE DREAMING

Once we have finished reviewing the purpose and guidelines for dreaming, we invite people to launch into the dreaming activities. If we are following the format for creative dreaming, we typically give people the rest of the morning, including a mid-morning break, to envision the future and craft their dream statements. This usually takes about two to two and a half hours. Then, in the afternoon, we invite participants to prepare and perform creative presentations of their dreams and to enrich the dreams through dialogue.

We will use the work we did with the Illinois Credit Union League (ICUL) to illustrate this process.

Step 1: Envisioning the Future

The dream phase of an appreciative inquiry process begins with the future-focused questions in the interview protocol. This means that already during the discovery process people have begun to think and talk with each other about their hopes and aspirations for the future. By now, fresh combinations of images, ideas, and possibilities are beginning to emerge. With this in mind, we begin dreaming by envisioning the future based on the dream questions from the paired AI interviews.

First, the group chooses a discussion leader, timekeeper, recorder, and reporter (see guideline 1 in the accompanying box). We encourage people to switch roles from the day before. This allows each person to experiment with different responsibilities. It also allows new dynamics and patterns of conversation to emerge in the group.

Second, participants share their partners' responses to the dream questions from the day before (see guideline 2). This is a very important part of the process. It allows each person a chance to share his or her partner's full response before opening things up to general discussion. This ensures that the distinctive voice of each person is heard before the group begins to move in the direction of searching for commonalities. It also ensures that the group does not get swept away by the ideas of one or two people before everyone's ideas get out on the table.

Third, participants begin adding texture, richness, and depth to their dreams (see guideline 3). They are invited to explore their images of the future in detail, including topics of purpose, relationships, strategies, initiatives, impact, and so on. This is important because it gives additional definition to the dream. It helps the group move beyond the simplistic cliches of "motherhood and apple pie" to offer a vision that is as complex and dynamic as the real world in which they live and work.

Fourth, the small groups begin to weave the threads of individual dreams into a collective tapestry (see guideline 4). An important theme here is inclusion. Rather than pushing for premature consensus or agreement, it is important for the group to look for ways to get the perspective and ideas of each group member into the collective dream. If after good, rich discussion this does not happen naturally, the discussion leader or the recorder can go around the table and ask each person to share one idea or image that he or she wants to make sure is a part of the group dream. The recorder can capture these on a flipchart page so they do not get lost. From there the group can add, revise, rearrange, augment, and expand the list of ideas in any way it wishes as it follows its conversational course; but no matter what else happens, the voice of each member is affirmed and valued.

Fifth, key elements of the group's collective dream are listed on a flipchart page (see guideline 5).

Envisioning the Future

Purpose: To imagine a future for the ICUL that you want to work toward.

Guidelines

1) Select a discussion leader, timekeeper, recorder, and reporter.
2) At your tables, have each person share highlights from interview questions 7–9.
3) As a group, put yourselves in the year 2005. Visualize your organization the way you really want it as if it exists now. Imagine the organization's positive core is fully alive! What is it like? As you create your image of the future, consider possible reference to some of the following areas (but you choose—these are only examples):

- ICUL's higher purpose
- Organizational culture, quality of work life
- Nature of leadership (visionary, empowering, servant, etc.)
- Nature of external relations between ICUL and others (e.g., the chapters, the credit unions, banks, local, state and federal governments, national associations and lobbying groups, etc.)
- Nature of internal relationships—with senior leadership, between the "home office" and the "field," between colleagues at all levels
- Organizational practices and structures creating an empowered culture
- Decision making and planning processes
- Collaboration and teamwork
- Attraction and retention of members
- HR practices (e.g., performance appraisals)
- Use of technology, networks, e-learning, and sharing of information

---

- Excellence in training, learning, and development
- Image and reputation you want—what makes ICUL a magnet for good people
- Change readiness and methods for increasing change capacity
- Communications practices
- Most exciting and promising strategies and directions being pursued
- Positive impact and results
- Other desirable feature (you choose!)

4) Spend enough time talking as a group to imagine the ICUL of the future. This is an exercise in creative dreaming—of the kind of organization you want to work toward.

5) List on a flipchart the key elements of your collective dream.

Step 2: Writing Dream Statements

After giving the small groups ample time to dream, we invite them to write a dream statement that reflects their image of the future. The purpose of this dream statement is to put the key elements of their collective dream into words. Writing a statement in prose is much more powerful than just a laundry list of ideas. It provides a way for people to talk through what they really mean and to create a powerful guiding image.

For example, a couple of years ago one of the key elements of the dream for staffing and retention for McDonald's regional managers was to be a "people-first organization." Simply to list "people-first organization" among a dozen others ideas on a flipchart page had relatively little meaning. But the idea sprung to life as a guiding image when one group took the time to talk through what it meant and wrote this dream statement:

> McDonald's is truly a "people-first" organization. The environment is filled with people who care, have an ear to listen, a hand to help, and a smile that brightens the day. The culture is characterized by dignity, respect, trust, and kept promises. People are given freedom, autonomy, and encouragement to make important decisions and be creative with their work. People are regularly praising, recognizing, and valuing one another for their contributions. This encouragement and affirmation creates a positive revolution within the company. Self-respect, self-esteem, pride, and fulfillment are the norm, and members treat each other and the customer like

gold. As a result, customers come to McDonald's restaurants for an uplifting experience, and employees come to McDonald's to engage in life-changing and life-enhancing experiences. At McDonald's, PEOPLE is our way of doing business.

To write a dream statement as eloquent as this one takes time and the inspired participation of everyone in the small group. Our experience is that writing a good dream statement takes a minimum of an hour and can easily take longer.

We separate step 1 and step 2 of the creative dreaming process for two reasons. First, we find that the "performance pressure" of writing a dream statement for public consumption often stifles good conversation about the dreams themselves. People get focused on how they are going to craft the statement before they take the time to share, discuss, and explore deeply one another's dreams. When this happens, it curtails the power and richness of the dreaming process.

Second, when we shift from step 1 to step 2, people usually take a short break. Even if the break is just a pause and stretch right at their tables, it allows group members to integrate their thinking and to approach the task of writing with a fresh perspective. The following box shows an "activity brief" for writing a dream statement.

Dream Statement

Purpose: To capture on paper your dream for the ICUL.

Guidelines

1) Assign a discussion leader, timekeeper, recorder, and reporter.
2) Capture your group's dream in a five-year dream statement written on a flipchart page:

> *"In 2005 the Illinois Credit Union League is . . . [your image of the ideal as if it is happening right now]"*

3) Make sure that your statement is:

- *Desired.* Does it reflect what you really want? If you got it, would you want it?
- *Bold, provocative.* Is it a stretch that will attract others?
- *Affirmative.* Is it stated as if it is happening now?
- *Grounded.* Are there examples that illustrate your dream as a real possibility?

Step 3: Preparing and Performing Creative Presentations

After the dream statement is written, we invite people to prepare a creative presentation of the dream. We agree with Marv Weisbord and Sandra Janoff[4] about the importance of these creative presentations for anchoring the group's hopes and dreams in their bodies and psyches. We believe there are at least three reasons for this. First, the presentations require that people act out their dream. This grounds the dream by having people consider at a concrete, hands-on, day-to-day level what it actually means to put the dream into practice.

Second, the presentations tap into the imagination, and as Polak says, it is often this creative, artistic, imaginative dimension that gives the guiding image of the future its gripping appeal. The creative presentations allow people to "see" the dreams and develop an emotional connection with them.

Finally, the presentations almost always bring with them a healthy dose of humor, which connects people and creates a new level of positive affect in the group. People crack jokes, blurt out unrehearsed lines, and act in ways that are delightfully unexpected and pleasantly surprising. We have found over the years that these dream presentations are often one of the most fondly remembered parts of the AI Summit experience. People may not recall all the elements of their positive core or the exact wording of another group's dream statement, but they do remember highlights from the creative presentations.

Over the years there have been many times when people (executives, members of summit planning teams, and others) have told us that their organization does not "do" creative presentations. They claim that their culture is too macho, or that their senior executives do not like "process," or that there is not enough trust in the organization to allow people to open up and be that vulnerable. We don't buy this, and there are three things we say in response.

First, there are many ways to do a creative presentation. It does not have to be as outgoing as a skit or a song. It can be a drawing, a news report, an employment interview, a new process flow, or whatever the small group decides. No one has to do anything he or she doesn't want to do.

Second, by the time people get to the afternoon of the second day, they are in a completely new place relationally from where they were when they arrived at the summit. By talking as equals across the table, interacting at breaks, appreciating the best in each other, and dreaming about a common future, people build whole new levels of trust and relatedness that allow them to work together energetically on creative presentations.

Finally, we have never yet had a group of people who, once into the flow of the summit, did not want to do the creative presentations. In fact, the preparation and delivery of the creative presentations invariably prove to be a highlight for people, both during and after the summit. This holds true for frontline employees as well as senior executives.

A final thought on creative presentations has to do with the question of how many presentations to do. Clearly, thirty or forty presentations is a lot to sit through. We feel that after about eight to ten, the law of diminishing returns begins to kick in. People have laughed so hard and expended so much emotional energy during the first eight or ten presentations that after this time the energy begins to wane. On the other hand, there have been times when groups of fifteen to twenty tables insisted that they all present, and it went well. We have experimented with:

- Breaking into three rooms with ten simultaneous presentations in each
- Having ten groups volunteer to present while the rest draw pictures of their dreams
- Doing half of the presentations before lunch and half after
- Combining two or more table groups per presentation
- Limiting the presentations to three minutes in length

All of these alternatives have advantages and disadvantages, and each of us prefers a different one, so we would encourage you to continue to experiment. We do, however, strongly recommend creative presentations. They are a powerful medium for bringing the dreams to life. Following is an "activity brief" for preparing creative presentations.

Creative Presentation of Your Dream

Choose a creative way to present your collective vision as if it is happening now (e.g., a TV special, magazine cover story, skit or drama, "a day in the life," a work of art, other): **5–7-minute presentation**

Step 4: Enriching the Dreams

After the creative presentations have been given, it is time to reflect as a whole organization on the images of the future that have been offered. The purpose of this activity is to help the group generate a sense of excitement around common guiding images of the future. It is important to link this activity back to image theory and the philosophy underlying appreciative inquiry. The point here is not to come to consensus. It is not even to insist that everyone agree on a common image of the future. The point is to allow people to talk about the images that make them feel most inspired—the images they feel are most compelling for the future of the organization.

This is also a time to refine images of the future. After the creative presentations, there are usually so many images swirling around that people need a little time to pause, reflect, and sort out their deeper aspirations from the euphoria of the moment. This is a very important process because it allows people to sort out what they really want and what they are truly committed to work on in the design and destiny phases. To skim over this step can leave people feeling empty, with only a half-hearted desire to move forward.

The approach we use most is simple, quick, and direct. We ask each small group to make two flipcharts. One contains the images they feel hold the most promise for the future of the organization, and the other contains thoughts about what these images mean for how we organize as we enter the design phase of the AI 4-D cycle. When they have finished their lists, we invite people to share ideas from their group discussion with the whole group. We conclude by asking the groups to post their flipcharts on the wall under the two headings and encourage them to begin the next day by visiting and reflecting on the charts. See the Appendix, Activities 4, 5, and 6, for a complete set of dream worksheets.

OPPORTUNITY MAPPING[5]

As mentioned earlier, the purpose of the "opportunity map" is to allow the group to begin to develop a positive guiding image of the future by identifying the most important opportunities toward which it wants to move. This works well in groups in which the majority of the people work more at a tactical rather than a strategic level. For example, in our work with John Deere, many of the people at the summit worked at a particular station on an assembly line. They cared about each other and about the product they produced, but they felt less energized when dreaming about the future of the whole header section. They loved the practicality of the opportunity map.

To conduct the opportunity mapping, we begin by linking to the interviews from the day before. The dream and "three wishes" questions provide ideas and images for the opportunity map. For example, in work our with John Deere the following questions were in the interview guide:

> **Question 3:** Image of the Future. *Imagine that tonight you fall into deep sleep, and when you awake three years from now, things have changed radically at the Header Manufacturing Section. You have extended your lead in the marketplace. Corporate is buzzing over the dramatic success of your plant. An article in Fast Company magazine describes how the header section —by tapping into the pride and involvement of its employees—has dramatically reduced costs, increased quality, and sped up product cycle time. Innovation is happening at every level, your processes are becoming more and more agile, and you are enjoying unparalleled levels of customer service and employee satisfaction. Customers demand John Deere products, and won't buy anything else. Employees feel respected, empowered, and full of pride in what they do. They wouldn't consider working for any other company!*
>
> *What happened to allow for this kind of success?*
>
> *What part did you play in this success?*
>
> **Question 4:** *What three wishes, in order of priority, do you have to help the header section reach and sustain its future success?*

Step 1: Brainstorming Key Opportunities

With the responses to the dream and three wishes questions in mind, we invite people to brainstorm and prioritize a list of opportunities to advance their summit topic (see the accompanying John Deere worksheet).

The Future of the
Header Manufacturing Section

Moving From Discovery to Dream:
Mapping Opportunities for Success

Self-manage: Select a discussion leader, timekeeper, recorder, and reporter.

Purpose: To begin to build a future you want—a header section that from top to bottom is truly dedicated to outstanding speed, quality, and cost competitiveness.

1) Share your wishes and dreams from the interviews you did yesterday morning (questions 3 and 4). Add in any ideas or thoughts about changes or improvements that you think will have a major impact on increasing quality, reducing costs, and improving product cycle time.

2) Brainstorm a list of opportunities to increase quality, reduce costs, and improve product cycle time at the header section.

3) As a group, choose the three to five opportunities you all believe will have the greatest impact on cost, quality, and cycle time, and write them on a flip chart.

Step 2: Creating the Opportunity Map

Once the small groups have prioritized their opportunities, we invite the whole group to move to one wall of the room on which is posted a large piece of white butcher block paper. For a small group of, say, 30 to 60, a 6 ft. × 6 ft. sheet of white paper will suffice. For 60 to 150, we prefer a 6 ft. × 12 ft. sheet. Once you get above 150, it works better to create multiple maps.

In the center of the paper is a circle with the topic of the summit or words such as *Sustaining Our Success* or *Key Opportunities* written inside. The facilitator then asks the participants to call out the opportunities they consider most strategic in the next three to five years. As each opportunity is stated, the facilitator draws a line out from the center circle and writes the opportunity on that line. As additional opportunities are shared, the facilitator asks, "Is this a new opportunity, or is it related to one we already have on the map?" If it is new, a new line is drawn out from the center and the opportunity is written on that line. If it is related to an opportunity already on the map, a line is attached to the existing line and the idea is written on the new line.

After about forty-five minutes, the process draws to a natural conclusion when all the key opportunities have been listed. As a final act, each participant is given seven Avery dots and invited to vote for the opportunities they think are most crucial to the sustained success of the organization (see example below).

The mapping is useful because it allows everyone to talk at once as they stand in front of the wall, and yet it still gets their ideas out in an organized way and allows the group to set priorities in the context of the whole. It is an effective way to focus the wide-ranging activity and thinking of the group into a common set of opportunities. Because the map is framed in a positive way, searching for opportunities rather than problems, it allows the group to develop a sense of energy and optimism about the future. The voting with Avery dots is useful because it allows the people to see the energy and interests of the whole group.

Although for some this may seem chaotic because people are moving around and at times talking over each other, the group self-regulates and order emerges. At times, several conversations occur at once; at other times, the group stops, listens to one person, and responds accordingly.

Step 3: From Opportunity Map to Bold Dream

After a break, the entire group regathers around the opportunity map to take a fresh look at their work and to identify the most important opportunities displayed on the map. Once they are identified, small groups self-select around these opportunities and then follow a process similar to that of creative dreaming (see the accompanying John Deere worksheet).

The Future of the Header Section

Ideal Future Scenarios: **Dreaming the Future We Want**

Self-manage: Select a discussion leader, timekeeper, recorder, and reporter.

Purpose: To imagine and define the future you want to work toward: a header section that from top to bottom is truly dedicated to outstanding speed, quality, and cost-competitiveness.

1) Put yourselves three years into the future. Imagine the header section you really want, from the perspective of the opportunity area you have chosen.

- What is happening?
- How did this come about; what helped it happen?
- What are the things that support this vision (leadership, structures, training, procedures, etc.)?
- What makes this vision exciting to you?
- How does this vision maximize speed, quality, and cost-competitiveness?

2) Capture this dream in a dream statement. Draft on flipchart paper (see examples from BP ProCare below).

- Use vivid language.
- Be positive.
- Be bold, provocative; make it a stretch that will attract others.

3) Choose a creative way to present your vision to the rest of us in a five-minute presentation as if it existed now; use as many members of your group as possible in the presentation.
Examples: A TV news report, skit, hiring interview, song or poem, "day in the life,"

Example Dream Statements
Opportunity Area 1: Learning and Development

> *We are a learning organization. We challenge ourselves to step out of our comfort zone, think in new ways, and expand our capacity*

---

to create the kind of organization that we desire. We have an ongoing commitment to education and development for all members, including formal and nonformal education and training and on-the-job learning through interaction with each other and with people from other organizations. We will give special attention to four core competencies that are crucial to the success of our business: quality and customer service, cooperation and group process, business management, and technical automotive repair skills.

Opportunity Area 2: Continuous Improvement

We are committed to continuous improvement in all areas of the organization. This requires that each member is always on the lookout for ways to improve the business and that we take time for regular team meetings in which we can evaluate our performance, make adjustments, set new goals, and commit ourselves to new ways of doing things. It also includes stretching the organization to new levels of excellence by searching our profitable business opportunities, obtaining resources, and engaging in growth-oriented, risk-taking behavior.

Step 4: Supplementing the Dreams

At this point, there is an important difference to highlight between creative dreaming and opportunity mapping. When the small groups present their dream statements in the process of creative dreaming, those statements are literally left hanging on the walls. They serve as background to the work that is to come in the design and destiny phases but do not need to be further refined, voted on, or ratified in any way.

In contrast, when the small groups present their dream statements in the process of opportunity mapping, those statements become the working vision statements for the small (opportunity) groups as they transition into their design and destiny work. Thus, it is important for the other teams to be able to give input into the dream statements. To accomplish this, we post the statements of each of the groups around the room in the form of an art gallery. Participants are then invited to circulate around the room, writing their comments on blank sheets of flipchart paper posted under the statements.

The purpose of this "gallery walk" activity is to allow each member of the organization to have input into all of the strategic dream statements. This process is extremely important. By writing the dream statements, presenting them, and then allowing each individual to offer input, the organization fosters voice in everyone and yet focuses its attention and harnesses its energy in specific directions.

CONSENSUS VISIONING

The purpose of consensus visioning is to come to agreement on a common vision statement for the whole organization. There are many ways to do this. One way is simply to vote once the dream statements have been written and enacted. Each person gets one vote, and the statement with the largest number of votes wins. Voting can also be done in a couple of rounds. The statements with the highest number of votes (say, the top five) in the first round go on to the second round, in which there is a runoff for the winner. We tend to avoid the voting approach as much as possible, however. Although it is simple, it is also reductionistic and less generative than other options. There is little opportunity for dialogue and therefore little possibility for creating a blend of multiple dream statements or a completely new innovation. Furthermore, the fact that a statement gets the most votes does not mean that the majority of the people in the room connect with it or even support it.

A second option is to name a subgroup to work on a common vision statement during the evening and then report back to the group in the morning. This group can include a representative from each table. All participants can be given an opportunity to circulate around the room, writing comments on each statement highlighting the things they like and things they would like to add. This input then goes to the subgroup, so that the vision statement they create represents as best as possible the sentiments of the group. A third option is to have a subgroup work on the vision statement on the third morning of the summit while others go on to design activities.

OPTIONAL ACTIVITIES THAT CAN BE USED DURING THE DREAM PHASE

So far in this chapter we have illustrated our favorite ways of engaging groups in the dreaming process, but there are other, equally good alternatives.

Pictures, Drawings, Metaphors

In our work with CRWRC we invited organizations to draw and describe their images of the future in metaphorical terms. A group from Honduras imagined its ideal organization as a winding river carrying with it nutrients of all kinds, bringing life and vitality to an entire region. In West Africa, the participants described their organizations as fruit trees deeply rooted in the soil of African culture and tradition. They identified eight essential capacities that serve as "water, fertilizer, and sunlight" to support the healthy development of their organizations in the unique cultural contexts of West Africa—servant leadership, participatory management, organizational development, resource development, community empowerment, technical expertise, networking and partnership, and spiritual resilience.

Another nice example of a metaphor comes from Eileen Conlon, organization development consultant and OD/HR manager for Bob's Clam Hut in Kittery, Maine.[6] She led the staff of the Clam Hut in building a "family tree" to provide a visual image of "the best of Bob's," attributes that they wanted to amplify in the future. She hung a huge tree drawn on cloth, and employees came forward and added leaves that represented the key elements that were crucial to Bob's positive future. A staff member then drew a picture of the tree, framed it, and hung it in the dining area so that customers could see where the Clam Hut was headed. The leaves of the tree were also used by employees in daily "spot" meetings as reminders of what was important to them.

Guided-Image Exercise[7]

One process that can be done with a limited amount of time is a guided-image exercise. Someone, a facilitator or volunteer from the group, reads the following directions or creates his or her own. Pause a bit between sentences to give people time to imagine.

> *"Get comfortable, close your eyes if you like, and bring one of the interview topics we have chosen into your mind. Imagine that topic has been implemented fully in your everyday life and work. Imagine that it is your first day back at work, and you are excited because you know that you'll find a workplace that has more of that topic present. Wander around your workplace. As you meet people in the course of the day, what pictures emerge that are life giving and energizing? What are you feeling? What*

are people doing differently? As you head home from the day, what is life like and how has it changed? What conversations do you have with those at home? What do you tell them about the changes at work? Congratulate yourself for being part of such a healthy and meaningful change in your work and in your life. Open your eyes and return to this room at your own speed. When ready, share a few words describing your experience."

Dream Book with Personal Messages and Drawings

On several occasions we have facilitated multiple summits within the same organization or community. The United Religions Initiative (URI) opted not to hold one global summit but rather to hold regional summits in six areas of the world. The first was a five-day summit in North America. As we designed the summit, one of our considerations was how to create continuity and connection across the six summits. Along with inviting participants from all regions to attend, we created a dream activity that could move from summit to summit.

We developed a dream book. At the first summit each small group was given a page of large artist-quality paper on which to draw their dream. On the back of the page each member of the group was invited to write a message of hope to summit participants in other parts of the world. All of the pages were then compiled within a magnificent wooden cover carved by a New Zealand artist as a gift to the United Religions Initiative. The book, along with enough blank pages for all of the following summits, was hand-carried to Africa one month later by representatives from North America attending the African regional summit. The process continued until the book was filled with dreams crafted by participants at all six regional conferences.

GIVING FORM TO THE DREAM

The dream phase of an AI Summit is highly imaginative. It invites people to ascend to the level of their highest aspirations, and it inspires excitement about what could be. The next phase, design, gives form to the dream by embedding it in the systems, structures, and practices of the organization. It takes people's highest aspirations and begins to make them real.

CHAPTER 9

DESIGN

The Vice President of Operations stood up in front of sixty employees, about 10 percent of the workforce, and announced with pride, "We have achieved our stretch target goal. We have met 'the 25-cent challenge' for this quarter, to reduce the cost of production per pound by 25 cents through process excellence. We have tried to reduce the cost of production for ten years. This is the first year we have achieved it. And we got there by involving all of you!"

This announcement was made at the second of three AI Summits conducted at the headquarters of the Green Mountain Coffee Roasters in Waterbury, Vermont. The process, led by AI consultant Ilene Wasserman,[1] began six months earlier, when the president and CEO, Bob Stiller, expressed his desire to launch an appreciative inquiry into "Enhancing Profitability through Business Process Excellence," a task that left little ambiguity about its purpose.

The first step was to create a broadly representational planning team, called the "dream team." They selected sixty formal and informal leaders from multiple levels and prepared them to go out and interview every member of the organization, plus a wide range of stakeholders. At the summit, the sixty leaders analyzed the stories they collected in the interviews, interviewed each other, and dreamed: "If we could imagine these stories being *everyday and ordinary,* what would our processes look like?"

When they got to the design phase, they identified five core business processes that, in their view, held the keys to their success:

- Market to Sell: Everyday Customer Amazement
- Procure to Pay: Faster, Better, Cheaper
- Products and Promotions: Brilliant Process Management
- Order to Cash: Customized Relationships
- Plan to Produce: Excellence in Execution

They wrote provocative propositions about what each of these processes would look like if they were perfectly designed to actualize their dreams. They drew process maps to create vivid pictures of the ideal designs. Then all sixty participants wandered around from station to station asking questions, providing input, and integrating the designs. On the final day of the summit—the destiny phase—each team crafted a plan of action to implement what they had designed.

Three months later, Bob Stiller, the VP of Operations, and many others began to use AI as the basis for their biannual company-wide meetings, leadership meetings, process team meetings, sales meetings, hiring process, new employee orientation, and performance review process.

OVERVIEW OF THE DESIGN PHASE AND A GENERIC AGENDA

As the Green Mountain Coffee Roasters case illustrates, the design phase of an AI Summit is, in many ways, like building a house. First you explore the best features of other houses, including those from your own past. Next you dream about what the ideal location, size, design, and layout might look like. Then it is time to sit down with an architect and begin designing.

The design phase of an AI Summit involves creating the "social architecture" of the organization in a way that builds on the positive core and makes possible the fulfillment of the organization's dreams. When we talk about social architecture, we mean the organizational systems, structures, strategies, processes, procedures, job descriptions, workflows, task groupings, strategic alliances, preferred practices, and so on. In short, we mean all of the ongoing commitments and approaches that define an organization's identity, culture, values, and potential. Vibrant social architecture creates an enabling environment that propels people forward in a healthy, high-performance way.

In this chapter we walk you through day 3 of an AI Summit—the design process. We look at:

- The concept of design and its importance to the AI Summit
- Getting started
- Creating a design possibilities map
- Selecting high-impact organization design elements
- Crafting provocative propositions
- Enriching the provocative propositions

We conclude with a brief discussion of how to continue design activities after an AI Summit. Exhibit 9.1 provides an overview of a typical day of design.

Exhibit 9.1

Overview of a Typical Day of Design

Time	Activity
Morning	**Key tasks: Reflecting on dreams from the previous day, understanding the importance of values-based organization design, identifying high-potential design possibilities, selecting high-impact design elements, crafting provocative propositions**
8:30–9:00	During this informal "getting started" period, participants are invited to walk around the plenary room and reconnect with the dream statements and images from the preceding day
9:00–9:15	Review of the day's focus and agenda
9:15–9:30	Short input on how the design of an organization can be reinvented to enliven organizational values and dreams
9:30–11:00	Small groups create customized design possibilities maps, whole group "votes" (includes break)
11:00–11:30	Set up the writing of provocative propositions
11:30–12:30	Small groups craft first draft of provocative propositions
12:30–1:30	Lunch

(continues)

Exhibit 9.1 *(continued)*
Overview of a Typical Day of Design

Time	Activity
Afternoon	**Key tasks: Enriching, integrating, and building commitment for the provocative propositions**
1:30–2:15	Small groups present the first draft of provocative propositions to large group
2:15–3:30	Whole-system dialogue to enrich, integrate, and build commitment for the provocative propositions (includes break)
3:30–4:00	Small groups craft final version of provocative propositions
4:00–4:45	Small groups present final version of provocative propositions, large group gives appreciative feedback
4:45–5:00	Preview of next day and wrap-up

THE CONCEPT OF DESIGN AND THE IMPORTANCE OF THIS PHASE

Winston Churchill is rumored to have said, "First we shape our structures and then our structures shape us." We believe this is very much the case in organizations. Virtually everything in organizational life is influenced by design choices made in the past. How much time you spend in the office; how hard you work; with whom you interact; how closely you collaborate; how free you are to innovate; how much you grow and develop; how fulfilled you feel at work; the performance of your work group and of the larger organization—all of these factors are directly shaped by the design of your organization's social architecture.

The design of an organization's social architecture is also a key ingredient in the sustainability of large-scale change. We are firm supporters of the idea that passionate action on an individual basis is essential to organization change, but we are equally convinced that organizational transformation is much more than the cumulative mass of personal transformations. It requires changes in the very fabric of the organization. In fact, time and again, when we have returned to client organizations three, five, and even ten years after the initial AI work, they have identified deep change in the social architecture of the organization as a primary factor in their sustained success.

And yet it seems as though organization design is to people what water is to fish. It has a profound influence on their performance and well-being, but they rarely pay attention to it, much less take steps to change it. In an AI Summit, it is just the opposite. We see every element of an organization's social architecture as a human creation open to reinvention and "redesign." We believe that changes in social architecture represent powerful leverage points for moving an organization toward its dreams. As a result, we create conscious conversations about how organizations can design themselves to heighten their health and performance. We persistently ask the question: What forms of organizing can bring out the best in people, liberate cooperation, and give form to our highest values and ideals?

Finding answers to this question is clearly an ongoing quest, but our experience is that there are four essential ingredients for appreciative organization design:

- Make it values-based.
- Develop designs that liberate human creativity.
- Involve the whole system.
- Embrace perpetual designing.

The Power of Values-Based Organization Design

Sociologist Kenneth Boulding writes that when human communities take time to imagine the future, they gravitate in the direction of "the most highly valued part of the field."[2] Organizations take action around the possibilities that offer the most promise for realizing their values and aspirations. The task in the design phase, then, is to invite conversations around organization design elements that powerfully embody the values of organizational members.

Consider the following example from the McDonald's summit on global staffing and retention. When they asked the question "What forms of organizing will bring out the best in our people . . . ?" they settled on nine organization design elements. One of them concerns their commitment to invest in the communities in which their restaurants are located. They crafted the following proposition, which reflects their most deeply held values and has clear implications for their corporate strategy, policy, programs, and procedures:

> McDonald's is known and admired as the world's most socially responsible business. People understand that McDonald's is more than just a restaurant; it is an organization giving back to each community in ways that transform lives. The organization is so respected in local communities that people see it as their first choice to begin and advance their careers. McDonald's commitment also includes strong and dynamic relationships with educational institutions, many of whom send their top students to McDonald's for career experiences. Positive involvement in the community fills the entire McDonald's family with a profound sense of pride and joy.

In the process of appreciative organization design, propositions like this one, a bold yet actionable image of what the organization aspires to become, shape the organization's social architecture.

Creating Organization Designs That Liberate

Dee Hock, founder and CEO emeritus of the VISA Corporation, makes a compelling case that in today's highly diverse, complex, and rapidly changing environment, more self-organizing, innovative, and liberating organizational forms are needed.[3] He points our that command-and-control institutions are failing everywhere. They are unable to achieve the purposes for which they were created, and their very nature alienates and disheartens the people caught up in them. He calls for organizations designed around such a compelling purpose and set of principles that they free people to organize in any manner, at any scale, in any area, and around any priority that is relevant to and consistent with the purpose and principles.

The design phase of an AI Summit is structured with this very idea in mind. It invites people to clarify their shared purpose and craft a set of design propositions that are so compelling that they empower the entire organization to act in a dynamic, self-organizing way to build the future

Involving the Whole System

Organization designs that liberate cannot be devised by leaders alone and imposed on an organization. They must arise from the dialogue among members of the organization. They are not frozen mandates to be obeyed under threat of punishment. They are a living set of commitments capable of developing with the participation and consent of the community. Properly done, they are always in the process of creative evolution. For example, although the preceding McDonald's proposition is crystal clear, it does not dictate a particular practice or method. It is highly desired by the members of the organization, and they will find infinite ways to accomplish it.

The Joy of Perpetual Designing

When people dare to dream of the positive contributions they and their organizations can make in the world, no existing organization design is perfectly suited to the realization of their dreams. Each new hope, aspiration, or strategic direction requires a new social architecture to support it. Organizations must continuously renew themselves to sustain high performance. In this sense it is sometimes better to think of organization design as a verb—designing—rather than a noun. It becomes a continuous and dynamic inquiry into the new organizational forms that will most powerfully propel the organization toward its emerging dreams and aspirations.

GETTING STARTED

To begin design activities, we often find it useful to do a little teaching piece that introduces the concepts of organization design and of social architecture. We draw on some of the preceding ideas and make analogies to the design of a new product, the design of a house, or the writing of a constitution for a country. We point out how every aspect of the product, the home, or the country's government has to be designed—consciously selected and articulated to reflect its values and dreams.

CREATING A DESIGN POSSIBILITIES MAP

After introducing the concepts of organizational design, we launch into the creation of design possibilities maps. In our early work with appreciative inquiry, when we got to this point we asked people to select from a variety of existing frameworks of organization design. These included the McKinsey 7-S model,[4] the Galbraith Star model,[5] the Nadler-Tushman Congruency model,[6] and the Weisbord 6-Box model.[7] Even though all of these frameworks were nonprescriptive in that they did not require any particular design choices, we found that our clients struggled with the categories used in them. They felt like a forced fit. These frameworks were someone else's—not theirs.

While searching for alternatives, we came across an approach developed by our colleagues David Cooperrider and Jane Watkins that invited people to create a "home-grown" set of design elements. The approach allowed people to use their own language and concepts of organizing. We adapted their model into what we now call the Design Possibilities Framework. It is a process that involves everybody in the system in identifying and mapping the design elements that they believe have the highest potential to accomplish their dreams. The process includes the following steps:

Step 1. On a flipchart, draw an empty "design possibilities map," using as much of the flipchart as possible. Place in the inner circle of the map a statement that represents the dream for the organization created on the previous day. See Exhibit 9.2 for an example of a blank design possibilities map.

Step 2. Have people brainstorm all of the key relationships, both within and outside the organization, that will impact or be impacted by the dream if it is accomplished. Write these in the second circle of the design possibilities map.

Step 3. Have people brainstorm all the formal organization design elements that will influence the accomplishment of their dreams. Write these in the outer circle of the design possibilities map. It is always useful to provide a few examples of "formal organization design elements" (see Table 9.1).

Table 9.1

Examples of Formal Organization Design Elements

- Job descriptions
- Education, training, and leadership development processes
- The organization's policies on social responsibility
- Key organizational strategies

Table 9.1 *(continued)*

Examples of Formal Organization Design Elements

- Compensation and reward systems
- Planning processes
- Communication systems
- Decision-making approaches
- Organization, unit, and individual goals
- Measurement systems
- The performance review process
- Strategies for attracting and retaining talent
- Competencies
- Core business processes and work flows
- Management practices
- The organization's mission, vision, and values statements
- Organizational structures
- Customer relations policies and practices
- Stakeholder relations policies and practices

It is important to remind participants that these categories are merely examples. When they fill out their design possibilities maps, they should use categories and language that make sense to them.

Exhibit 9.3 shows a customized design possibilities map for the BP Upstream Technologies Group. Exhibit 9.4 shows a map for the Canadian Broadcasting Corporation (CBC). You will notice on the CBC map that the formal organization design elements are in the second circle and the key stakeholder relationships in the outer circle, a variation on what we recommend above. Either way works. Our rationale for putting key relationships first is (1) we believe that human relatedness is at the heart of the organizing process, and (2) our experience is that most people can identify key relationships more quickly than they can formal design elements. Placing relationships first facilitates an easy start to the activity. But in cases like the CBC, when people want to put the formal design elements first, it can work just as well. See the Appendix, Activity 7, for a complete set of worksheets for the design possibilities process.

Exhibit 9.2

Example of a Blank Design Possibilities Map

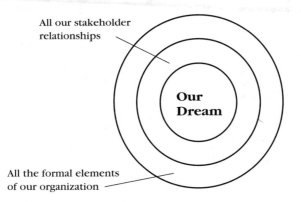

All our stakeholder relationships

Our Dream

All the formal elements of our organization

SELECTING HIGH-IMPACT ORGANIZATION DESIGN ELEMENTS

Once the design possibilities maps have been developed, people proceed to select high-impact organization design elements they want to work on. In identifying these high-impact design elements, it is essential to balance individual passion with a sense of what is important for the whole summit community. To achieve this we use a two-step process.

First we invite each participant to grab a marking pen and visit three other tables. At each table, they are asked to vote for the three design elements with the greatest potential for bringing their dreams alive. During this selection process, one person from each table "stays home" to answer the questions of visitors.

Once all the votes are cast, people are invited to visit at least three additional tables to see how others have voted. Then people are asked to return to their seats, and we take about fifteen minutes in the large group to hear people's impressions and excitements about what they saw as they toured the various design possibilities maps. The purpose is not to rank-order or prioritize design elements; it is simply to give people a visual sense of what is important to the whole group and to hear people's perspectives.

Exhibit 9.3

Customized Design Possibilities Map for BP's Upstream Technology Group

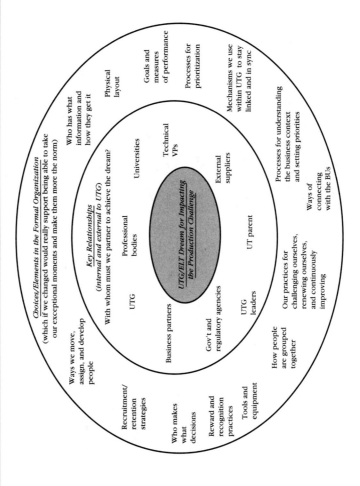

Exhibit 9.4

Customized Design Possibilities Map for the Canadian Broadcasting Corporation

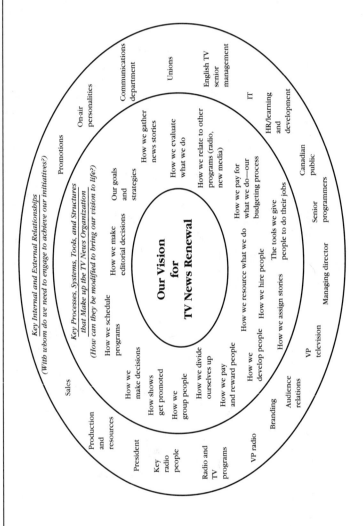

Once the voting and debrief are completed, the next step is to invite people to group themselves into design teams according to their interests. The process includes the following steps:

Step 1. We tell people that they will be leaving their "max-mix" groups and forming new "design teams" to create the ideal future for a design element of their choice. We tell them that they will spend the rest of the day in the design teams.

Step 2. We announce that anyone who is passionate about a particular high-impact design element can write their interest on a flipchart page, bring it to the front of the room, present it to the whole group, and invite others to work on it with them. That person will then be the convener for that design element. We clarify that to be a convener simply means to lead a conversation resulting in a provocative proposition for that topic. It does not necessarily mean leading action on the design element during the destiny phase or after the summit.

Step 3. As conveners step forward, they present their interest and answer any questions of clarification. Then they are assigned a meeting room or meeting space within the conference room.

Step 4. Remaining summit participants are then invited to go to the design conversation in which they have the most interest.

This simple process results in everyone being given equal voice in the selection of those design elements for which there is the most passion. Because we do not limit the announcement of design conversation topics to those that have been previously identified, we also ensure that any emergent idea or energy has a place to go.

CRAFTING PROVOCATIVE PROPOSITIONS

Once people are in their new groups and have had a chance to introduce themselves, it is time to begin the crafting of provocative propositions. Each group crafts a provocative proposition for the design element(s) on which it is working. These propositions are expansive statements of how organizational members plan to organize themselves in pursuit of their dreams. They are a set of principles and commitments about how people want to work together. They are provocative in the sense that they describe the ideal organization. They stretch the status quo, challenge common assumptions and routines, and suggest real possibilities for change.

At the same time, provocative propositions are not "pie in the sky." Because they are built on the organization's positive core, they are grounded in real examples of success from the past. They are statements that bridge the best of "what is" with aspirations for "what could be." They are meant to answer the question: What would our organization look like if it were designed in every way to expand our positive potential and unleash ever-higher levels of performance?

The Process of Writing Provocative Propositions

There are many ways to begin to write a provocative proposition. Some groups start immediately to write ideas on a flipchart page. Others talk for a good forty-five minutes before jotting down a single word. In some groups, everyone wants to contribute to the precise wording. In others, this task gets delegated to one or two people and is later ratified by the others. Any of these approaches can work. There are a couple of ideas, however, that we recommend.

- First, begin with an appreciative inquiry! People are in new groups. They are focusing on a new topic. The most enlivening thing they can do is share stories about when and why their particular design element was at its best. For example, if a group is working on the design element of leadership development, there is no better way to start than by inquiring into people's most fulfilling experiences of professional growth and development, or asking about the characteristics of the best leaders people have ever worked with, and so on. To cycle forward into a new appreciative inquiry adds depth, richness, and insight to the provocative proposition process.

- Second, dream bold dreams! Provocative propositions are meant to challenge common assumptions and stretch the status quo. If the people at Green Mountain Coffee Roasters had written propositions that were weak, conservative, and "business as usual," it is doubtful they would have sparked the dramatic turnaround that they did. Encourage people to propose the extraordinary.

- Third, on a more practical level, if after a period of time a group is having difficulty with the writing, encourage them to brainstorm to get a bunch of their best ideas up on a flipchart page. Then they can begin to weave those ideas into a series of sentences that make up the proposition. Finally, they can reflect on what they have written and refine it if necessary.

- Finally, it enhances the power of a proposition enormously to write it in prose. To get something down in prose (instead of a list of bullet points) requires people to talk through what they really mean and to sift through the shades of meaning before coming to a joint resolution. It elevates the level of dialogue. It also has a longer-lasting impact. The provocative propositions written by American Baptist International Ministries have become a statement of purpose and principles that will guide the organization and promote its identity to the external world for years, if not decades, to come.

Criteria for Good Provocative Propositions

A provocative proposition is a statement of what an organization aspires to be and to do to accomplish its dream. It is an ideal that guides and gives direction to decisions, actions, and results. A proposition is always filled with both high ethical and moral content and practical, actionable ideas. Yet it never prescribes the ideal; it only describes it.

Whenever we ask people to write provocative propositions, we share with them our formula for a good proposition. It includes four guidelines:

- Is it provocative—does it stretch, challenge, or interrupt the status quo?
- Is it grounded—are there examples from your stories that illustrate the ideal as a real possibility?
- Is it desired—if it could be fully actualized, would you and would your organization really want it? Does it truly lead to your dream?
- Is it stated in affirmative and bold terms as if it is happening now?

For a complete worksheet on creating provocative propositions, see the Appendix, Activity 8.

Three Examples of Provocative Propositions

Following are three examples of provocative propositions from different organizations in different industries.[8]

- An example from a consumer products company of a proposition for their ideal strategy development process:

  Our company accelerates its learning through an annual strategic planning conference that involves all 500 people in the firm as well as key partners and stakeholders. As a setting for strategic learning,

teams present their benchmarking studies of the best five other organizations, deemed leaders in their class. Other teams present an
annual appreciative analysis of our company, and together these
databases of success stories (internal and external) help set the
stage for our company' strategic planning.

- An example from a high-technology company of a proposition for
their ideal HR-line relationship:

Human Resource staff regularly sit in as full partners with their line
clients during key strategy sessions. Line managers receive such
timely, rapid, and on-target support that they invite input from
their HR consultants, not only on HR issues, but on a wide range
of general management concerns. Articles are written about this
exemplary partnership.

- An example from a manufacturing company of a proposition for
their ideal work environment:

Our organization has an environment that attends to the physical,
mental, and spiritual health of employees. Equipment for physical
workouts and for swimming is available to all. The cafeteria offers
healthy food and a pleasant atmosphere. Employees are given
"mental health" days off along with the usual time for sick leave.

ENRICHING THE
PROVOCATIVE PROPOSITIONS

Once the provocative propositions are written, they are shared with
the large group and opened to a process of appreciative dialogue to
enrich them and to integrate them with other propositions. This
process is essential for three important reasons. First, it promotes
learning and produces a deeper level of "collective intelligence" on
the part of the whole system. People are informed about new directions. They see connections they didn't see before. They are drawn
to surprising new possibilities. And they gain a more comprehensive
sense of the direction of the whole.

Second, it promotes social bonding. As groups share their work,
it is inevitable that one proposition will be in creative tension with
another. Paradoxes and unresolved questions are inevitable characteristics of dynamic organizations. But where differences exist, more
appreciative dialogue is called for. This leads to interest, curiosity,

deeper exploration, passionate engagement, laugher, joy, and spirited conversation. As these connections multiply, new levels of understanding emerge and the relational bonds of the organization are strengthened.

Finally, dialogue produces commitment to support the propositions on the part of the whole system. When people have an opportunity to give input and have influence, they immediately become more invested in the result. This is particularly true when they see their input reflected in the final draft of the proposition.

To enrich the provocative propositions, we ask people to go through four steps:

Step 1. Each small group gets up in front of the room, introduces itself, and reads its proposition. Usually the groups will also provide a brief overview of their topic and the process they used to create the proposition. In most cases, they are legitimately proud of their work. For each proposition, we invite two or three quick words of appreciation that responds to the question: What do you like most about this proposition and the image that it holds for the organization? We keep these comments very brief. Time for deeper dialogue comes later. Then we ask for a round of applause and move to the next one.

Step 2. After all the groups have presented, we give everybody a pack of 3 × 5 Post-it notes and ask them to circulate around the room providing "appreciative feedback" to as many groups as they can. We define appreciative feedback as comments that (1) highlight the strengths, (2) offer hopes, or (3) provide integration and elevate the sense of the whole. We ask that at least two group members stay at each table on a rotating basis to be available to answer questions and engage visitors in dialogue. We encourage people to provide both written and verbal input so that their ideas can be documented and incorporated into the revised version of the propositions. This is always a very rich and engaging period of dialogue as people stretch one another's thinking and together search for higher ground.

Step 3. Once all the appreciative dialogue has taken place, we give the design teams about a half hour to revise their propositions. This is usually plenty of time because they have been revising already as a part of the dialogue process. More than anything else, the half hour is spent getting things in final form.

Step 4. As a concluding act, the design teams present their final versions of the provocative propositions. After all the propositions have been presented, the floor is opened for comments about what the propositions are calling the organization to be and to do as participants move into the final day of the summit.

It is not necessary to perfect the provocative propositions. It is necessary only to gain agreement that the current expression of them is good enough to move the organization resolutely toward its dream. Each proposition will influence and refine every other proposition in a dynamic, ongoing progression.

CONTINUING THE DESIGN PROCESS AFTER THE SUMMIT

In some cases, organizations want to spend more time deepening and refining their conversations about design. For example, the Santa Ana Star Hotel and Casino completed the final draft of its "Service Principles" one month after the last mini-summit. American Baptist International Ministries took six months to refine their statement of purpose and principles. The United Religions Initiative took three years to finish its organizational charter. Whenever a design process is carried forward from a summit, it is important to ensure frequent opportunities for the whole system to give input on all revisions.

CONCLUSION

One of the things we learned early on in our work with the AI Summit methodology is that if discovery, dream, and design are done well, destiny almost takes care of itself. People have a new level of confidence in their capacities, a clear image of their purpose and direction, and a powerful set of provocative propositions that give guidelines for action. This comprehensive vision of the future, filled with values and commitments and hopes and aspirations, energizes and informs a wide range of action initiatives. It unleashes a virtual explosion of purposeful activity. In the next chapter, we explore this dynamic by walking you through the destiny phase of an AI Summit.

CHAPTER 10

DESTINY

Over a five-year period, the size of the Human Resources community at the Department of National Defense (DND), Canada, was cut back dramatically. Workload stayed essentially the same. Turnover shot up, morale plummeted, and historic divisions between civilian and military personnel grew deeper. Monique Boudrias, Assistant Deputy Minister, Civilian Human Resources, became determined to do something of substance to create a positive and sustainable change in her organization. Robert LeGris, the DND's Director of Organization Development, saw in this difficult situation an opportunity to initiate a large-scale cultural change. He had read enough about appreciative inquiry to imagine the possibilities. The two of them, along with two senior OD consultants at the DND, formed a representative fifteen-person planning group and designed an AI Summit process focused on the topic of "Service without Borders: An Invitation to Excellence."

Within ninety days Madame Boudrias welcomed some 300 participants—including HR advisors (military and civilian), their clients, union leaders, and other key stakeholders—to the organization's first AI Summit. During the next three days they identified the community's positive core; expressed their dreams for what they could become; designed ways that their work practices, systems, and structures might be modified; and planned for "back-home" improvisational action.

During the following year, hundreds of small and large changes were implemented, and a second summit was planned to discover what had been achieved, why, and how they could build on that. There was a strong desire on the part of participants to broaden and deepen the impact of the first summit by dedicating significant time in the second summit to the destiny phase.

Participants arrived at the second summit having each conducted five interviews among colleagues and clients to ascertain what was working in the change process. The meeting began with the posting of 300 success stories! It was apparent that the organization had achieved a great deal and had changed significantly. During the discovery, dream, and design phases, the group used these stories to expand the organization's positive core, refresh its vision, and renew its social architecture.

At the end of each day participants sent their new ideas and propositions via e-mail to colleagues who were not at the summit, asking them for their reactions and input. They began each morning by reading the return e-mails that had come in overnight from across the country and around the world. Dozens of recommended action initiatives came flooding in. Summit participants discussed these recommendations and proposed many more of their own. By the time they got to the destiny phase, the growing sense of "wholeness" was palpable.

Once they launched into the destiny phase, participants broke into action teams and planned a series of initiatives that would help them to achieve their collective image of the ideal organization. They then spent a full day creating a "roadmap to the future" that allowed them to sequence and integrate their many action ideas. This created a process of focused dialogue about who was planning to do what and how these initiatives would build on each other.

In the following year, the DND reported significant changes in the organization and in the ways people began to think about change. Appreciative inquiry is increasingly becoming the DND's orientation for organization development, executive team building, leadership development, instructional design, and operational improvement.

As was the case with the DND, one task of the destiny phase is to unleash and encourage individual passion for action in service of the whole. A unique feature of the appreciative approach is its commitment to liberate the creative energy for excellence in all people. But it is much more than that. It is also about identifying and mobilizing key strategic action initiatives that will move the whole organization quickly and directly toward its ideal image of the future. If done well, the destiny phase can support both small- and large-scale change at every level of the organization.

In this chapter we walk you through day 4 of an AI Summit—the destiny process. We look at:

- The power of inspired action
- Getting started
- Formation of innovation teams
- Innovation teams get to work
- Creating a roadmap of the future
- Practical tactical planning
- Back-home groups
- Great endings

We also review a list of optional activities that can be used during the destiny phase, including common-interest action planning, innovating from provocative propositions, creative planning, and stimulating "back-home" improvisation. See Exhibit 10.1 for an overview of a typical day of destiny.

Exhibit 10.1

Overview of a Typical Day of Destiny

Time	Activity
Morning	**Key tasks: Reflecting on learnings from the previous day, understanding the importance of inspired action, formation of innovation teams**
8:30–9:00	Welcome, getting started, overview of the day
9:00–10:00	Overview of self-organizing process, formation of innovation teams
10:00–10:30	Break
10:30–12:00	Innovation teams meet, get to know one another, focus initiatives, select team leaders, create plans for working together
12:00–12:30	Innovation teams post their initiatives on a roadmap
12:30–1:30	Lunch
Afternoon	**Key tasks: Integrating innovation team work, fostering improvisation, determining back-home next steps, summit closing**
1:30–2:30	Presentation of roadmap with plenary dialogue
2:30–3:00	Plans for after the summit: fostering improvisational change

(continues)

Exhibit 10.1 *(continued)*

Overview of a Typical Day of Destiny

Time	Activity
3:00–3:30	Break
3:30–4:30	Back-home groups
4:30–5:00	Summit closing

THE POWER OF INSPIRED ACTION

We define inspired action as action on behalf of the whole that is energized by a deep encounter with the positive core. As people connect with their strengths, dream bold dreams, and organize to fulfill their highest aspirations, they act spontaneously with vision and commitment.

In our experience, a great deal of change occurs at each phase of the 4-D cycle. The process evokes change all along the way, not just at the end. As people who didn't know one another meet, conduct appreciative interviews, share dreams, and work on provocative propositions, many subtle and not-so-subtle changes occur, and unexpected action is unleashed.

An example of inspired action from the discovery phase comes from the McDonald's global staffing and retention summit. At the summit an owner-operator from San Antonio, Texas, shared a story about a program he had started to provide free tutoring for his high school–age employees. The employees came to work, clocked in, and for the first hour of their shift, they were paid while they did their homework with the help of a tutor (if desired). The students loved it, the tutors loved it, parents loved it, teachers and administrators loved it, and the restaurant owner benefited from attracting and retaining top talent. After learning about this best practice, several other McDonald's restaurants adopted similar programs.

An example of inspired action from the dream phase comes from the Santa Ana Star Hotel and Casino. One group's dream was simply to remove all the broken machines from the casino floor. In their skit, they enacted a slow work day in which everyone worked together to get rid of broken machines and to rearrange the floor. They portrayed what it would look and feel like without all the customer complaints about broken machines. On the last day of the summit, a cross-functional, cross-departmental team went to work on the complex task of assessing and removing broken machines.

An example from the design phase comes from American Baptist International Ministries. One of their propositions was to become a "flexible, team-based organization." During the destiny phase, an action team formed and launched a six-month organization redesign and training process to implement the "team-based" vision articulated in the proposition.

Inspired Action Supports Positive Self-Organizing

During the destiny phase of the summit the whole group discusses ideas and potential projects that have been sparked over the course of the week. Then individuals are asked to step forward with their proposals for action. Others of like mind and interest join them, and action teams are formed to carry on work in the service of the whole. Enthusiasm runs high as people give voice to their commitment to the organization's future. Whatever is offered up determines what will be done. It is an emergent, self-organizing process for setting the organization's action agenda for going forward.

Inspired Action Is Tailored to the Dreams of the Organization

Because they are chosen and carried out by participants, the actions that emerge from an AI Summit are tailor made to the unique needs of the organization. For example, during the United Religions Initiative global summit participants discovered roots of cooperation within their own traditions, dreamed of possibilities for a United Religions Organization, and took the first steps toward designing a charter. The question for action was: What research and development needs to occur, in the coming year, to be able to draft a full charter for the United Religions? Participants then identified R&D areas, self-selected into R&D groups, and organized for a year of research, inquiry, and experimentation.

Inspired Action Aligns
Discovery, Dream, Design, and Destiny

When ideas for action initiatives bubble up during the first three days of a summit, we do not inhibit these conversations. We simply ask that people keep them alive and hold them for in-depth discussion on the last day. In this way, actions that are selected are better informed by the wisdom and knowledge accrued in discovery, dream, and design.

Consider the case of Hunter Douglas Window Fashions Division. During their appreciative interview process it became evident that education was one of their cornerstones of success. Over and again stories were told of employees who valued and benefited by both job training and personal training such as "toastmasters." During the dream activities, images abounded of an expanded training curriculum, employee mentors, and even a building dedicated as a learning center. They produced provocative propositions that outlined this in vivid detail. Then, during the destiny phase, people self-organized into groups to (1) create a mentoring program; (2) redesign the employee orientation; (3) establish a Hunter Douglas University; (4) educate employees throughout the organization in AI; (5) maintain communication among all levels, shifts, and departments; and (6) conduct a high-involvement strategic planning process. Not surprisingly, many of the self-organized teams focused on the organization's core value of educational excellence.

Inspired Action Balances
Planning and Improvisational Change

The inspired action that gets sparked at an AI Summit is like a two-sided coin. On one side is improvisation—the unplanned emergence of initiatives within and across departments and functions that support the realization of the organization's dreams and design. On the other side is strategic change—the formation of innovation teams focused on specific projects to achieve specific results. Innovation teams get started at the summit. Improvisational initiatives spring up both during and after the summit. It is essential for each organization to find the right balance of strategic initiatives and emergent, improvisational activities.

In the section that follows we go through a series of activities designed to launch innovation teams and encourage "random acts" of transformation following the summit.

GETTING STARTED WITH THE DESTINY PHASE

We begin this last day of the summit by summing up what has been done over the prior three days. We encourage a sense of celebration about what has been accomplished and a sense of anticipation about what is yet to come. We include a reference to the summit task and its relevance to the organization's ongoing success. And we foreshadow the day as one of self-organizing for action after the summit.

FORMATION OF INNOVATION TEAMS

In most cases we facilitate the formation of self-organized teams. We generally call them innovation teams to keep the focus on innovation. They may also be called action teams or project teams. Whatever their name, they are groups of highly committed people who volunteer to achieve a specific goal or result on behalf of the organization. They are usually cross-functional, cross-level, and cross-departmental. On occasion, customers or other stakeholders have volunteered to serve as innovation team members.

For the formation of innovation teams we use a self-organizing process similar to that of Open Space Technology.[1] The process works like this:

1) We review the positive core map, the dream, and the provocative propositions and ask people to think about, make note of, and discuss with two or three other people the things they believe would most significantly move the organization toward the dream and provocative propositions.

2) We outline the conditions for convening an innovation team: You must believe this is important to the organization, and you must be willing and able to make it happen. We are very clear that people should only initiate actions that they are willing to carry to fruition. This is not a time for recommendations. It is a call for people to commit to specific actions and results.

3) We ask anyone who is willing to convene a team to write their innovation—idea, project, or initiative—on a piece of construction paper and to prepare a ten-second announcement and call for others to join them.

4) We have conveners line up, and one by one announce what they hope to see happen and ask others to join their innovation team. As conveners are making announcements, we hang their ideas on the wall so they are readily visible to the entire group.

5) We reduce the number of potential innovations by condensing overlapping ideas. In general, all the ideas proposed are of value. In some cases, however, the organization has decided to limit the number of projects. When this is so, we ask for a show of hands indicating how many people are planning to join each team. In this way we can determine which ideas hold the greatest interest for participants. Ideas with no interest are eliminated.

6) On occasion, but not often, we will have the large group vote on the top five or six innovations.

7) Then we ask people to circulate around the room and join the innovation teams of their choice. We acknowledge that they may join the team for the summit only or for the duration of the project. We encourage them to commit as fully as they can to support the innovation's becoming reality.

8) We suggest that the newly formed teams begin with introductions and, if time permits, even a brief appreciative interview—one question related to the innovation at hand.

INNOVATION TEAMS GET TO WORK

We then give the innovation teams time—anywhere from one hour to four hours—to meet and plan. At the end of the designated time, each team presents to the whole group. We encourage the teams' presentations to be informative and to solicit any help or resources they need from the whole group. Because this is the last day of the summit, we want everyone to be as well informed about what will happen after the summit as possible. We also want to optimize the time the whole system is together by ensuring that people know how they can provide ongoing support for the innovation teams.

Support for Innovation Team Planning

There are times when we provide the innovation teams with a planning template. This serves both to support the teams' planning and to educate participants about planning. In many organizations, when people from all departments and all levels attend the summit, the expertise about how to get things done in the organization varies. We find that teams appreciate a template. It may be as simple as the following:

- Who are your team members, and what is their contact information?
- How will you as a team stay in communication with one another?
- What is your goal?
- How does it support the dream and/or design?
- What additional information do you need to achieve this goal?
- Who else should be on your team? Who will invite them?
- What are the actions you need to take to achieve your goal?
- Who will do what by when? What is your timeline for completion?
- What additional resources will you need? How will you get them?
- When will you meet next?

We emphasize to a team that all the actions in their plan must be actions that someone in their team will take. This is their project, and they are responsible to ensure it is successful, whatever it takes. Because the mix of people at the summit is so diverse in terms of functions, departments, and levels, each innovation team becomes a powerful microcosm of the whole organization.

Once, in a moment of "facilitator lack of faith," we noticed a team planning a process that would require employees each to be paid a day of overtime. Concerned about the cost of the innovation, we asked the senior vice president to listen in on the team's plan. His response reinforced the benefit of having the whole system in the room. He said, "Yes, I know what they are doing, I am on that team." See the Appendix, Activity 9, for a sample worksheet for this activity.

Establishing Innovation Team Leadership

We also support innovation team success by asking members to select a team leader and coordinator. The team leader is often, but not always, the person who initially proposed the innovation or activity and who will facilitate meetings and involvement. The coordinator's role is to manage logistics, documentation, and communication among team members.

Serving in a leadership role for an innovation team has proven to be a great developmental activity for many people. Innovation team leaders and coordinators are often frontline employees with little or no formal leadership experience. We have been delighted over the years as we watched a shy receptionist lead a meeting, a determined technical service representative convince his manager to support his innovation team's effort, and a team of frontline employees transform the company's image in the eyes of vendors. As a result of the visibility, learning, and relationships they gain in the process, innovation team leaders are often promoted.

After the summit, it is the job of the advisory team to follow up and provide ongoing support to the innovation teams (see Chapter 12 for more on this). It is important during the summit for the advisory team and the innovation teams to talk about how they will relate after the summit.

CREATING THE
ROADMAP TO THE FUTURE

While the innovation teams are meeting in the morning, we create a curved roadway (imagine the Yellow Brick Road) on the floor of the plenary room. It is usually made out of strips of bright plastic tape and is about 3 feet wide. We also tape a straight timeline, marked in months or quarters, on the floor alongside the roadway. The roadmap winds up looking something like Exhibit 10.2.

Exhibit 10.2

Roadmap to the Future

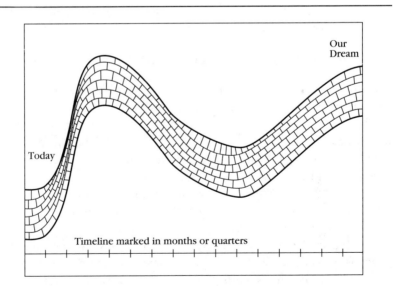

Locating the Action Plans on the Roadmap

Before the teams break for lunch, we ask that the team leaders join us for a meeting. Then while the rest of the group is having lunch, we ask them to place a cone containing the team's plan on the spot on the roadmap where the most intense aspect of the team's work is expected to take place. We have used both official traffic cones borrowed from the local highway department and Styrofoam triangles (16" base, 2' high) cut from sheets of Styrofoam 4 feet by 8 feet by 6 inches thick.

Whole-System Roadmap Dialogue

After people come back from lunch, they see for the first time all the plans mapped onto the metaphorical roadmap to the future. The energy is very high as team presenters, roughly in the order of the timeline, step forward with their innovation team behind them and describe their innovation and their plans for realizing it. We have found that their reports combined with the physical display of the cones provides a strong sense of confidence to the summit community that "we really will make this happen."

The other major advantage of this roadmap activity lies in its ability to help people see possibilities for mutual support and logical sequencing of actions. The whole group dialogue that follows the reports from the innovation teams is a lively exchange of information and support for the innovation teams. One of the things that makes this whole-system planning dialogue work is the physical movement and placement of cones along the roadmap. In a very kinesthetic way this allows the energy to stay high as the summit begins to come to an end.

PRACTICAL TACTICAL PLANNING[2]

An alternative approach to planning action initiatives comes from the work we did with John Deere. They used the following format in their summit to reduce costs, increase quality, and improve product cycle time.

Day 1: Discovery. Participants conducted paired appreciative interviews and discovered and mapped the positive core.

Day 2: Dream. Participants selected key opportunities and created dream statements for each.

Day 3: Design. The first thing in the morning, the group prioritized the opportunities based on how critical they were to the future of the business. After voting, they narrowed it down to ten key design initiatives focused on different aspects of the organization's social architecture. Participants were then invited to work on the initiative of their choice. They worked all day on designing the initiatives using a "business case approach." In addition to crafting a provocative proposition, each group was asked to demonstrate how it would exceed a certain hurdle rate for return on investment (ROI). Each group presented its initiative and ROI to the rest of the participants and asked for feedback. This allowed the whole group to understand, give input, and support the rest of the projects.

Days 4 and 5: Destiny. Both days were spent on practical tactical planning on the initiatives. Participants acknowledged that when they returned to the plant it would be difficult to find the focused time. The participants were committed to making as much progress as possible. They coordinated and collaborated among groups, bounced ideas off each other, integrated and blended projects, and contacted stakeholders to gain additional information, influence, and resources.

The last half of day 5 was spent debriefing, working on communications planning, and acknowledging the group's remarkable accomplishments for the week.

POST-SUMMIT PREPARATION

It is now time, on the afternoon of the last day, to talk about what will happen after the summit. We talk about communicating the results of the summit, supporting the ongoing work of the innovation teams, and fostering improvisational change throughout the organization.

Plans for communicating summit results are shared and discussed by the whole group. Very often new ideas for communication are generated during this discussion. Hunter Douglas created a newsletter, *The Focus 2000 Inquirer,* to keep all employees up to date on appreciative inquiry activities. British Airways inaugurated "Banners on the Run" so that all of the best-practices banners could be viewed by employees at all twenty BA stations in North America. Each banner was given an itinerary—a schedule for its rotation through all of the stations. Each month the banners were taken off the wall and sent on to the next station on the itinerary. In this way the banners were able to visit all BA locations within twenty months, and all employees were able to learn about the business and best practices of the entire North America customer service organization. Other organizations have created posters, videos, and brown bag discussions to share the outcomes of their summits. For more on communication strategies, see Chapters 6 and 12.

Fostering Improvisational Change

We often take time to talk about how change happens with the whole group. We emphasize that goals and plans will be carried out with much greater success if we can approach the post-summit period with a spirit of improvisation. We stress that clear goals and roles are essential to any large-system change process, *and* that the world seldom plays out exactly as we imagined, planned, or decided. Although chance does favor the prepared, new opportunities arise and unforeseen events require change in even the best-laid plans and well-developed strategies. And sometimes we find that our own best efforts have consequences that we never intended. Consequently, we need to move into the post-summit work with an understanding of the spirit of improvisation.

Frank Barrett, professor of management at the Naval Postgraduale School, writes that the best organizational change processes are not neatly engineered and packaged programs, but are more like what happens in a jazz ensemble.[3] In a jazz group the players go in with some basic understanding of each other's roles and activities—not dissimilar to a set of goals and plans. The music begins with a known refrain in which each of the players has a more or less established part. But then, as one of the players hears an "opportunity," rather than continuing with "the plan," the player seizes the opportunity and a whole new set of possibilities emerges. As first one player and then another builds on the unexpected but inevitable opportunity, the players' ability to improvise leads them beyond preestablished goals, roles, and plans.

The beauty of this approach is not only that it keeps the energy high and creates unimagined music, but that it uses mistakes as a platform for greater invention. Jazz players make mistakes in the notes they play when they are improvising. However, what sets great jazz ensembles apart is not just their skill or experience (although those matter too)—it is their commitment to each other. This commitment takes the form of working with the mistakes of others until the mistakes are transformed to the basis of great innovation—the possibility to create something that has yet to be imagined.

An AI Summit creates a flurry of improvisation. One of the key tasks toward the end of a summit is to encourage organizational members to go out and improvise. Use plans as springboards for opportunities and transform mistakes into unexpected possibilities. Another key task is to prepare leadership to provide visible and tangible support to innovators (see Chapter 12 for more on this).

BACK-HOME GROUPS

In many summits we invite participants to gather in their "back-home" groups. That is, we ask them to join with others in the same department, function, or business unit. External stakeholders are invited either to form groups of their own or to join with the departments they most closely relate to in the day-to-day operations of the business.

We do this to acknowledge that we have begun the transition from the summit back to the workplace, and to support the relationships in which people will find themselves in the next work day. The task is illustrated in Exhibit 10.3. It focuses on sharing the key ideas and information from the summit with those who did not attend.

Exhibit 10.3

Communicating with the Folks Back Home

Three Most Important Things to Communicate to the Folks Back Home	Our Best Ideas about How to Share These Ideas and Information	Our Best Ideas about Who, Where, and When to Do This
1.		
2.		
3.		

GREAT ENDINGS
SUPPORT GREAT BEGINNINGS

The ending of an AI Summit is often bittersweet. People are relieved that the four days of mindful conversation and attentiveness are over, and they are excited about what is to come. They are anxious to get back to work in new and different ways, and they wonder if it will last. The ending of the summit must give people an opportunity to express their gratitude for the process, their anxiety about the future, and their confidence in the new possibilities that are now on their roadmap.

In many cases we offer an invitation for anyone in the room to stand up and share something that has been meaningful to them in the past four days and, if they want to, to add something they are personally committing to do in the next seven to fourteen days to help them to realize their dream. Or they can bring up something they would like to offer to the group—be it time, space, access to data, introductions to key resources, finances, or whatever.

We emphasize that we are asking for what call "simple commitments" only, that is, commitments that can be carried out without negotiation, with resources under their control, and within the time available. We also clarify that this activity is purely voluntary. The value of this activity is that it gives participants yet one more chance to be heard and yet one more chance to engage and contribute in a very personal way to the future they have come together to create. The level of generosity and voluntary commitments displayed in this last stage always amazes us and creates the perfect platform for a few well-chosen words of closing from the sponsor.

The closure by the sponsor usually covers the expected ground: a review of what has been accomplished, a commitment to the future, and a call to keep the spirit of appreciative inquiry alive. Then the sponsor asks each of the following groups to stand up and receive an ovation for their work: first the planning team, then the logistics team, then the advisory team. Finally, of course, all of the participants are asked to stand and shake each other's hands. And with that the summit is over.

OPTIONAL DESTINY ACTIVITIES

With each of the 4 D's in the AI 4-D cycle, there are an unlimited number of ways to carry out the intent of the D. We have used each

of the following activities at different summits to meet the needs of
a unique organization or community.

Common-Interest Action Process

There are times when it is much better to form teams around common interests rather than have individuals declare their intention
and seek others to join them as described earlier. When this is the
case, we suggest a variation on the following activity. Give each participant at the summit a piece of flipchart paper and a marker. Ask
the person to make a hole in the paper big enough to put his or her
head through. Then ask the person to write the one thing that most
interests him ot her on the paper in big, bold letters and to put the
paper over his or her head with the interest printed on the front.

Then direct everyone to interact with others and form interest
groups. When we did this at a United Religions Initiative summit, it
was dubbed the "Toilet Seat Activity!" Interest groups formed on
topics such as Women and Spirituality, Interfaith Education, Earth-
Based Spirituality, Peace Building among Religions, and India-
Pakistan Relations. After groups have formed, give them time to
meet one another; to discuss their interests, concerns, and hopes for
the future; and to decide if they want to carry out a project or not.

This is a very energizing and validating activity for a large group
of people. It is a way for people to continue to meet new people even
on the last day of the summit, and for people to self-organize for
continued sharing and working after the summit.

From Provocative Propositions to Innovations

There are times when organizations want to make a direct correla-
tion between their provocative propositions and whatever actions
will occur. When this is the case, we ask people to self-organize first
into provocative proposition groups. Then we have them brainstorm all the creative things that might be done to realize their chosen provocative proposition. We encourage this list to be truly an
out-of-the-box brainstorm, based on the best ideas heard during discovery and dream discussions.

Once the lists are made, the groups decide what they will do and
how they will organize to do it. At British Airways Customer
Service North America, the original interview topics served as the
framework for provocative propositions and innovation teams.

Creative Planning

It is possible to write planning poems, draw maps to the goal, or otherwise creatively express the intention of the innovation teams after the summit. Although most organizations want specific plans to guide their post-summit work, some are content with creative expressions. Indeed, in Nepal, where paper and markers are scarce resources, colleague Mac Odell has on many occasions had groups draw pictures in the dirt and then go out and immediately—before tea—take action to realize their picture plans.

Stimulating Back-Home Improvisation

There are many ways to stimulate improvisation back home after the summit. Frank Barrett,[4] in keeping with his jazz metaphor, poses the following questions to summit participants as a way to getting them to think about what they might do differently after the summit:

- What small thing could make a big difference?
- What unlikely connections can you make or facilitate?
- Whose voices do you need to listen to?
- Who might you hang out with, and from whom might you borrow ideas?
- What minimal forms would enable maximum possibilities?
- What would it mean for you to solo, and when might you need to support others?

FINAL DESTINY:
SUSTAINING POSITIVE CHANGE

Destiny is a time for integration, commitment, and focused action. It is a time for agreeing on how we will take the work of the earlier phases and move it forward at a practical level, and how we will support each other in that process. But it is more than that. It is also a time for seeding the organizational ground of transformation so that it can continue to grow new inquiries and lead to more discovery, learning, and sharing of knowledge, wisdom, and best practices. The fourth day is in that sense both a day of closure for the summit and the start of the rest of the organization's life. Successful destiny activities set the stage for ongoing positive change.

CHAPTER 11

FACILITATING AN AI SUMMIT

A s with all else in an appreciative inquiry process, appreciative facilitation is inquiry based, affirmative, empowering, and full voice. It seeks to draw out the best of people in ways that give them the opportunity to express their thoughts and feelings. The purpose of appreciative facilitation is to guide a group of people, large or small, through a 4-D cycle—focused on a meaningful change agenda. Sounds simple, and in many ways it is.

The art of appreciative facilitation lies in being a great social architect, not a change agent in the traditional sense of the word. Appreciative facilitation is not about trying to change anybody or anything. It is not about getting a group of people to achieve a predesignated goal or set of objectives. It is about helping people organize their dialogues, interactions, and activities so they can collectively discover and create the future they want for their organization or community. At its best, appreciative facilitation gives people a real-time experience of the future they most desire. This allows people to see that their hopes and dreams are genuinely possible and can be realized on a day-to-day basis.

This chapter explores the practice of appreciative facilitation and its application to the AI Summit. We discuss what it takes to be a good appreciative facilitator; how to create a safe, inviting, and generative environment; how to invite meaningful dialogue and skillful sense making; how to manage time and energy; how to foster high-level involvement and participation; how to support self-management; and how to guide a group through each phase of the 4-D cycle.

SO YOU WANT TO BE AN
APPRECIATIVE FACILITATOR

Within the appreciative inquiry community it is well understood that you cannot do appreciative inquiry without being appreciative inquiry. The best AI practitioners are those who live and work by the principles of appreciative inquiry.[1] They "live in the question" and see the "glass half full." Just as it is not possible to lead people through an inquiry without being curious and willing to learn, you cannot facilitate an AI Summit without being a model of AI yourself. The following questions can help you check your level of AI-self-readiness.

Are You Glad to Be Here?

It is absolutely essential that you find joy in AI and in facilitating an AI Summit. If you are glad to be working with a particular organization or community, and glad to be facilitating their summit, you will enjoy yourself and so will the summit participants. Your attitude plants the seeds for the summit experience for all who attend. In addition, a joyful attitude will give you the strength and energy you need to serve the large group of participants without getting tired and worn down by the process.

The reasons AI facilitators answer yes to the question "Are you glad to be here?" include:

- "I believe in what the organization is doing and I want to help. They are on a mission that matters, and I have the opportunity to make a difference."
- "It is an opportunity for me to learn—about a new business, organization, industry, and myself."
- "It is an opportunity to do something new or to apply AI in a different way."
- "I really like the people involved."
- "I believe my strengths are just what is needed to help the organization succeed."

Interesting people, the promise of results, being able to make a difference, and learning are all things that keep AI facilitators "glad to be here" and able to set a tone of positive anticipation for summit participants.

If you answer no to the question "Are you glad to be here?" get out. Don't attempt to do an AI Summit if your own inner dialogue tells you not to. You won't be very effective, it won't help the organization, and you might get sick. Remember, positive images lead to positive action.[2] Without images of positive possibility, your actions are not likely to support the organization's or community's success.

Are You Curious about the Purpose?

Facilitating an AI Summit requires an unwavering focus on the purpose of the summit. You must be familiar with the purpose and why it is important to the organization and to the industry at large. At the same time, you must be curious about the purpose and what the participants know about it.

The more interested in and curious you are about the purpose, the better. Your interest and curiosity will be contagious. Facilitating an AI Summit requires a great deal of positive energy, enthusiasm, and inspiration. Curiosity unleashes energy, whereas having answers restrains energy. Curiosity also helps you build a strong collaborative relationship with summit participants. When they see your genuine desire to join them as an equal and to help them make progress toward their valued goals, it creates a spirit of cooperation and positive exploration that reverberates throughout the summit.

Are Your Appreciative Eyes in Focus?

Perhaps the single most important capacity of an appreciative facilitator is the capacity to see with "appreciative eyes," that is, to see the best in people, their intentions, and their actions. How do you know when your appreciative eyes are in focus? You see merit in all ideas and comments; you are able to demonstrate unconditional acceptance of thoughts and feelings; and you value even seemingly disruptive, contentious, or conflicting ideas and actions. You are able to see dreams underlying cynicism and ideals concealed within critique. And of course, you seek to discover and mobilize the positive core of people, teams, and organizations.

Your capacity to see the strengths in people, to see the glass as half full even in the midst of adversity and despair, not only models AI for summit participants. It also serves as a harbinger of hope.

CREATING A SAFE, INVITING, AND GENERATIVE ENVIRONMENT

The ideal summit environment is an emotionally safe space where a highly diverse group of people feel invited to express themselves, and their most cared about and creative ideas. It evokes participation, creativity, and respect for diversity among participants. And it varies from organization to organization, community to community, and situation to situation. For example, what created a safe, inviting, and generative environment for a U.S. Navy summit was very different from what produced such a climate for a child welfare summit or an interfaith summit.

To equalize the impressions of power and give a clear message that everyone's ideas mattered, uniforms were banned from the Navy summit. All participants, officers, and enlisted people wore street clothes. To ensure that youth were comfortable and felt included at a child welfare summit, cookies and soda pop, Tinkertoys, and pipe cleaners were in full supply. And to support comfortable relationship building among 250 diverse interfaith participants at the URI's first summit, photos were taken of everyone upon arrival and hung on a large map in the dining hall, connecting names, faces, and homelands.

Levels of Engagement

Noted architect Frank Lloyd Wright said, "God is in the details." Paying attention to all of the logistical fine points mentioned in Chapter 6 and extending a warm welcome as described in Chapter 7 can go a long way toward creating a safe, inviting, and generative summit environment, but honoring differing levels of engagement is also essential.

At an AI Summit people are invited to participate at multiple levels. Each summit begins with a one-on-one interview experience that gives participants a chance to meet and learn about one other person in depth and to express themselves in an intimate dialogue. Later, each participant sits at a table of eight people and has the opportunity to engage at the small-group level. And finally, there are often open plenary sessions where people are able to speak to the entire large group. No one must speak to the large group who doesn't want to, but the opportunity is available. Having access to multiple levels of engagement creates both a sense of safety and an invitation to participate.

WHAT ARE WE FACILITATING?

Appreciative facilitation is unique in several key ways. Grounded in social construction theory[3] and built on the principles of appreciative inquiry, it focuses on conversation, relationships, and meaning making. The facilitation of an AI Summit makes it possible for people who don't usually interact and talk with one another to come together to build their common future.

Meaning Making

Appreciative facilitation is about helping people make meaning through relational interaction. As facilitators, our attention is on conversational processes such as inquiry and dialogue, and the meaning that emerges. It is not on human behaviors. Our focal point for organizational transformation is relationship building, not human behavior change. We seek to foster "relationship-enhancing" conversations—those through which people come to know and respect one another.

Discovery

Without discovery, learning, and sharing of knowledge, wisdom, and best practices there is no appreciative inquiry. Inherent in the process of AI is a search, an exploration, and a discovery. The facilitation of an AI Summit seeks to elevate discovery from an activity to a way of knowing, learning, and organizing. It aims to enhance participants' curiosity and capacity to wonder in order to elicit new possibilities. It aims to uncover stories of the past that, when remembered and retold, can bring to light potential for innovation and excellence.

Appreciative facilitation focuses on the art of asking unconditionally positive questions—those asked during the initial appreciative interview; those that guide discovery, dream, design, and destiny activities; and those that emerge during the summit. Questions are held in high regard. They are discussed as a source of positive, life-giving potential, an opportunity for discovery and learning. Appreciative facilitators don't offer answers as much as they invite questions that help uncover the most positive possibilities and potential for action.

With a focus on discovery, the outcomes of a summit are uncertain. As new ideas and information surface, collective meaning shifts. As high-point stories, dreams, and designs are shared, collective meaning takes form. Appreciative facilitation helps participants "live in the questions" and be comfortable with uncertainty throughout the process.

Storytelling

As mentioned earlier, appreciative inquiry aims to create a narrative-rich environment, an organization or community where people tell stories as a way of developing relationships and sharing best practices. During an AI Summit we invite people to share their ideas in the form of stories, to tell stories about high-point experiences, exemplary organizations, and dreams.

Stories invite interest and curiosity. As a result, they help people get to know one another in very purposeful ways. Stories also carry a great deal of information and can be analyzed to understand the root cause of organizational success. In general, stories do not evoke arguments; instead they create a safe, collaborative environment.

MOVEMENT THROUGH THE 4-D CYCLE

The 4-D cycle is to an AI Summit what the skeleton is to a body: It provides the frame and the structure. It allows for movement and stability. In its simplest form, the facilitation of an AI Summit is about bringing the 4-D cycle to life and giving participants clear directions for discovery, dream, design, and destiny activities. It requires a careful sense of timing so that groups have enough time, but not too much, to complete the activities.

The facilitation of an AI Summit is not open ended. It is focused on a clear purpose and a coherent process. The art of appreciative facilitation is to design activities in advance of the summit and adapt them during the summit as needed. Most of the adaptation occurs in how the 4-D's are carried out, not in their purpose. For example, for a series of four summits with one organization, we planned that dreams would be acted out as skits. At the second of the four summits we were tight on time, and we asked half the groups to act out their dreams and the other half to draw their dreams. It turned out that the drawings were richer representations of the dreams than the skits and were favored by the participants. At the third and fourth summits we asked all of the groups to draw their dreams. The drawing process fit better into the culture of the organization and into the schedule. After the summits, the drawings were photographed and put into the company newsletter.

Variety as the Source of Innovation

General system theorists such as von Bertalanffy[4] have long recognized the relationship between variety and innovation. The more variety there is in a system, the more likely is innovation. This simple principle applies to AI Summits. The more variety in the room in terms of roles, ages, ethnic backgrounds, work and life experiences, and ways of expressing ideas, the more creative and innovative the collective wisdom can be.

Consequently, appreciative facilitation encourages variety, diversity, and the valuing of differences. All stakeholders are invited to the summit. A wide variety of methods are used to foster participation and expression. And whenever possible, AI Summits are multimedia events that may include verbal discussions, video presentations, music, graphic facilitation, and even "outdoor experiential" activities.

From Conflict to Collaboration

Early on in our work with AI Summits we made an interesting discovery: The more we asked people to discuss their differences, the more they discovered what they had in common. We have also observed the reverse: The more we ask people to seek common ground, the more they see the need to differentiate themselves. And so the process of AI starts with people getting to know one another through their high-point experiences and hopes for the future. No attempt is made to create a collective idea or image until the dream phase. AI goes from the individual to shared dreams to collective designs to inspired action. In this way the process takes people from their own perspectives toward the whole. It starts by affirming uniqueness and then moves toward spirited collaboration and focused action.

At times, the reason for an AI Summit is to build bridges among conflicting groups of people. When this is the case, a clear, compelling, and transcendent purpose is essential. In other words, we do not directly focus on the relationships among conflicting groups; rather, we bring them together to work jointly on a purpose that is meaningful to everyone. When all the stakeholders are in the room to discuss and resolve a higher-order purpose, small conflicts fall aside. For more on the use of AI in conflictful situations, we suggest you read *Positive Approaches to Peacebuilding*.[5]

MANAGING TIME AND ENERGY

With 200 to 500 or more people in the room, the management of time and energy is crucial to success. A summit agenda is usually chock full, so time is of the essence. It is important to be clear about start and stop times for the entire process, all activities and breaks. We ask people in the beginning of a summit to self-manage to observe the time frames we set. We announce times, we post them on flipcharts or screens around the room, and we stick to them. If the whole group seems to be taking too long for a particular activity, we ask to see a show of hands of groups that need more time. In this way we can get a quick read of the need for additional time. If more groups need time than don't, we will extend an activity by three or five minutes. Seldom will we extend it much longer, because the groups who are ready to go will get bored and feel penalized for following the time frame established.

As people get involved and become busy with an activity, the noise level in the room goes up. As groups complete their task, energy drops and people begin wandering in and out of the room. Managing time well keeps energy and enthusiasm up and it demonstrates respect for people who keep track of their group's time.

There are a lot of ways to signal participants that time is up. Some facilitators use bells, others use music, and still other simply resume the working session. One approach that works especially well is a digital slide show. Have someone take pictures throughout the session and then run them on a continuous loop about five minutes before the end of the break. People love to see the photos and will develop the habit of getting back from break in time to see them.

One important reminder about managing time in a large group setting: No matter how behind you are, do not tell participants that you are cutting things out of the process, or push them to do it all faster. Just make changes to your agenda and introduce the time for the activities as if this is what you intended to do from the start. Feeling behind time or not having enough time to do a good job will create anxiety and drain the energy from the group. As a facilitator your job is to help them feel as if they always have enough time to do what needs to be done. In some situations you must manage the perception of time more than the actual time.

FOSTERING PARTICIPATION

The AI Summit is a high-participation process. It works best when everyone who has a stake in the purpose shows up and has an opportunity to participate while feeling safe. We seek to foster participation by giving very clear directions, giving people time to make note of their own ideas before sharing in their groups, and offering a variety of visual as well as verbal activities. In our experience some people are highly verbal, whereas others can write poetry or draw pictures. Offering all of these as vehicles for expression ensures optimal participation.

Multilingual Summits

Fostering multilingual participation at a summit requires a bit of extra attention. It is extremely useful to have all summit materials translated into all of the languages represented. In addition, translators may be needed for some people. And where possible, have facilitators who speak the languages of the people present. In some cases, such as our work with the United Religions Initiative, it is important for people to meet across languages in the same groups. In such situations, translators must be assigned to individuals and accompany them throughout the process. In other cases, as in our work with the Santa Ana Star Hotel and Casino, language-specific groups can be formed and one translator assigned to serve the entire group.

Here are a few tips for facilitating multilingual summits:

- Tell the whole group up front that the summit will take place in multiple languages.
- Take time to repeat directions in multiple languages so everyone knows what is expected and everyone experiences the multilingual environment.
- Give people time to talk in their own language, even if they are working in English or some other common language. Make time for "mother language" meaning making.
- Allow participants to make presentations in their "first" languages so everyone can gain appreciation for the multilingual nature of their organization or community.

Involvement in a multilingual summit is a rich and rewarding experience for participants and facilitators alike. There is much to be shared and learned across cultures and languages. Energy and enthusiasm soar when songs are sung, skits performed, and presentations made in multiple languages. The spirit of inquiry comes vitally alive when people engage in multilingual dialogue.

SUPPORTING SELF-MANAGEMENT

Above all else, appreciative facilitation aims to treat participants as adults and to foster self-management. The facilitation team for an AI Summit is generally small. As a rule of thumb we estimate two facilitators for every 100 people attending the summit. With so few facilitators, self-management must prevail. Here's what we do to support self-management.

Give Clear Directions

In working with a large group of people, there is little tolerance for fuzzy directions or mixed messages. Whatever is said at the front of the room starts a "whisper down the lane" of communication. To keep all the groups working on the same activity, directions must be given verbally and visually. We find it very helpful for a group to hear the directions presented by a facilitator, to see them on a flipchart or projected slide, to see them in their workbook, and then to have the opportunity to ask questions of a facilitator who walks around the room checking in with the groups. The principle of campaign communication, "same message, multiple channels," applies here too.

Designate Small-Group Roles

When the directions are clear, the majority of groups at a summit will get right to work. We have found it very helpful, however, for groups to begin by designating the following roles:

- Discussion leader: The person who ensures that conversations stay on track and that everyone has a turn to talk
- Timekeeper: The person who keeps track of the group's time and suggests when to move on to the next step in the process
- Recorder: The person who records key ideas and prepares the written presentation on a flipchart if needed
- Reporter: The person who makes the group's presentation to the whole

We suggest that groups assign roles before they begin working on each activity, and we encourage them to rotate the roles from activity to activity. We also point out that these roles can be very useful in daily staff meetings, project meetings, and team meetings of any kind.

Use Worksheets as Activity Guides

The agenda for an AI Summit is carefully thought out and structured in advance. Participants receive an agenda and a book of worksheets that describe each activity in the summit in detail. For each activity or task the groups are asked to do, the following information is provided on a worksheet:

- Title of the activity or task
- The purpose of the task
- The steps the group should take to do the task
- What deliverables are expected
- The time allotted for the task

Clearly structured activities allow groups to work efficiently and creatively. When all persons in a group have the same set of directions in their workbooks, confusion is minimized. We find that a good summit workbook not only supports self-management but also aids in keeping the entire large group focused. A sample participant workbook is provided in the Appendix.

FACILITATING THE 4-D CYCLE

In general, facilitating the 4-D cycle requires that you give clear directions, step back and let the groups do their work, and then facilitate their presentations to the whole group. While groups are working, we suggest you walk around the room and check in with them to answer any questions they may have. We recommend that you sit in with two or three of them to get a feel for what they are talking about and how the process is going. Be careful, however, not to steal too much air time or serve as the group's facilitator, even if they are struggling. Promote self-management and the emergence of informal leadership by allowing groups to find their own rhythm and their own answers.

Because the nature of the task is different in each phase in the 4-D cycle, each requires a slightly different kind of facilitation. What follows is a brief overview of the spirit called for in each of the four phases.

Facilitating Discovery

The task of the discovery phase is to help people feel safe, comfortable, and energized about the potential of their next four days together. It is about giving people an opportunity to establish new relationships, get to know each other at a deep appreciative level, and begin to develop a sense of identity for the group as a whole. And finally, it is about a broad exploration of the organization's positive core to build confidence and understanding for the tasks of dream, design, and destiny. All in all, discovery is about searching, exploring, and learning. Anything you do to facilitate participants' openness to explore the best of what has been and what is in their lives and their organizations will aid the discovery process.

Facilitating Dream

The energy of the dream phase is quite different from that of discovery. It is a time to move from what is known to what can be imagined. Your role is to encourage people be creative and to dream bold dreams. Successful facilitation in the dream phase requires that you invite creativity in as many ways as possible. Dream is about lifting up images of possibility and life-giving potential. It is about giving voice to courageous hopes for a better world. As a facilitator your job is to invite the expression of quiet hopes to become amplified and shared, to support people personally and collectively to remember and say what they have always wished could be, and to elevate imagination as the most direct path to a positive reality.

Facilitating Design

The facilitation of design again requires a shift of energy in the group—a shift from imagination to dialogue and commitment making. Whereas dream is about big, out-of-the-box images for the future, design is about what the group is willing to commit to as their collective future. Whereas dream is about what is possible, design is about the kind of organization, structure, systems, and processes that are needed to realize the possibilities.

In facilitating design it is important to keep participants energized and hopeful by giving them opportunities to present their provocative propositions and to get appreciative feedback. Stretching to create radically new designs that translate dreams into reality and coming to agreement on provocative propositions that compel can be absorbing work. It is important for groups to know that others in the whole group support their statements of the ideal organization. After all, at this point, each small group is indeed working on behalf and in support of the whole. Anything you can do as a facilitator to get the whole group to support and build on what is being written will help to promote deep organizational transformation.

Facilitating Destiny

Destiny is a time for action. As such, it too is marked by a distinctive energy. The goal during destiny is threefold. First, it is to facilitate individual passion for action in service of the whole. It is about helping people to identify what they really want to work on and then getting them connected with others who share the same passion. Second, the goal is to build commitment to support success. No initiative will be successful if it is abandoned. All projects need the support of others in terms of time, money, people, visibility, and so on. The destiny phase is a time to build that support. Finally, the goal of destiny is to establish next steps, new targets, and future events to build momentum for positive change. Be sure, toward the end of every summit, to leave time for discussion and commitment making about what comes next—for individuals, for the action teams, and for the organization as a whole.

BEING APPRECIATIVE INQUIRY

Facilitating an AI Summit requires a willingness to learn as well as a willingness to assist others in their process of learning and co-creating. It requires a willingness to be AI, not just do AI. Being appreciative inquiry involves all of the following qualities:

Be an inquirer, learn, and change. Appreciative inquiry facilitators are students of organization life. They are curious and open to new insights and understandings about human systems, individuals, and organizations. They work from the assumption that life is mysterious, uncertain, and ever changing—that there is always something new to be discovered. They understand that learning brings change. Each new Appreciative Inquiry Summit is an opportunity to learn, grow, and renew.

Seek what is energizing, for self and others. Appreciative inquiry facilitators attend to what breeds success, what makes people happy and enthusiastic, and what creates healthy, irresistible conversations and commitments. They balance work, play, and renewal. They have fun and are committed to searching for positive possibilities in all that they do. They work in the service of the triple bottom line: social, financial, and environmental well-being.

Work relationally, trusting in cooperation. Appreciative inquiry facilitators work as a community of practice, partnering with one another and clients to bring out the best. They value open and inclusive dialogue, democratic processes, and emergent organizing that foster co-creativity.

Challenge institutional forms of discrimination and injustice. Appreciative inquiry practitioners understand that discrimination is institutionalized in the cultures and structures of organizations. They design dialogues, processes, and organizations that offer opportunities for all voices to be heard, understood, and respected.

Focus on meaning, not methodology. Appreciative inquiry facilitators seek to contribute value and integrity in all they do. Recognizing that there is no right or wrong way of doing appreciative inquiry, no absolute set of practices, and no one perfect methodology, they continually innovate to meet the needs of clients. They work from principles and philosophy to create practices meaningful to the situation.

Reframe deficit dialogue into affirmative possibilities. Appreciative inquiry facilitators focus on positive potential. They validate and affirm what is, while at the same time draw out possibilities for the future. They mind their own language and choice of words, and whenever possible speak in words that honor reality, give hope, and bring out the best of people, relationships, and situations.

Organize around values and generative, life-giving factors. Appreciative inquiry facilitators organize time, attention, relationships, and work to be congruent with their highest values and with healthy, sustainable organizational life.

Methodologies and tools are little more than reflections of the intention, awareness, and presence of their users. This holds true as well for the methodology and practice known as the Appreciative Inquiry Summit. Leaders and consultants who engage in appreciative inquiry to satisfy their own ego needs will experience no more or no less success with AI than with any other organization change methodology. But those who see the potential of appreciative inquiry to cultivate excellence, to learn what is truly life giving for themselves and others, and to lift up life-centered organizations will experience the enjoyment that comes from being appreciative inquiry.

PART IV

AFTER
THE SUMMIT

Every ending brings forth a new beginning. And so it is with an AI Summit. What ends is the static way in which conversations, relational practices, and working interactions are viewed and experienced. Conversations now focus on identifying, sustaining, and strengthening the affirming qualities of the organization—its positive core. Relational practices now focus on deeper levels of understanding and cooperation by inquiring into and embracing diverse points of view. Working interactions now focus on recognizing and understanding patterns and interrelationships, and learning how to structure them in more effective and efficient ways to better achieve the organization's hopes and dreams.

In many ways, the period after the summit is the time to reap the benefits of all that has been done before and during the summit. It is also the time to sow the seeds of sustainability—to reinvent processes, procedures, systems, and structures and bring them into alignment with the dream and designs expressed at the summit. Post-summit activities fall into two broad categories:

- *Summit follow-up*—those things that are logical extensions of the summit, such as communication, and support for innovation teams and summit initiatives
- *Building an appreciative organization*—those things that will further the organization's capacity to work from its positive core and to realize the hopes and aspirations of its members individually and collectively

The materials in this section are intended to give you a sense of what can occur after a summit. It is not intended to give you a formula for what you must do. It is full of stories about organizations and what they have done after their summits. Recognizing that all summits are different, we encourage you to use this section selectively. We hope that by learning what other organizations have done you will be better able to meet the unique needs of your organization as they emerge after the summit.

CHAPTER 12

SUMMIT FOLLOW-UP

Summit follow-up activities flow from and vary with the summit task. Each organization sets out to accomplish something unique and important to its business when it decides to sponsor an AI Summit. The organization's unique change agenda and its summit task determine the nature and scope of follow-up activities.

Consider the case of a large manufacturer of electrical equipment in the United States. When a new sales manager came on board, he inherited a team in rapid decline. The team of thirty sales men and women from across the country was suffering from three years of decreasing sales, increasing turnover, and plummeting morale. The manager described the situation to us, saying, "I have a team in a vicious cycle of failure. The team has a negative reputation in the organization. That erodes their confidence and self-esteem, which undermines their performance, which in turn further destroys their reputation." To reverse the team's slide and break the cycle of failure, the manager decided to hold a three-day AI Summit focused on the topic of Team Growth.

The planning team invited a range of stakeholders from the corporate offices, from various departments throughout the company, and from their customer base to improve understanding and support at all levels. Together they established a new vision and set of values for the team; formed four "innovation task forces" to drive key business results in the areas of sales, marketing, quotations, and product procurement; and launched a comprehensive Appreciative Leadership Development (ALD) program.

Summit follow-up included support for the four innovation teams focused on business development and the ALD program. ALD included an appreciative performance appraisal process, a mentorship program, a series of training programs, and enhanced promotion opportunities. Summit follow-up activities involved the sales team as well as people from the human resources, marketing, and product development departments.

Over the course of the next two years, this same sales team rallied to produce remarkable results. It outpaced the organizational averages in almost every category, including sales, profitability, morale, turnover, promotions, leadership competency scores, team diversity, and budget allocation. Three months after the summit the manager commented:

> The AI Summit was very important for us. It allowed us to discover our collective strengths and resources with the whole system in the room, and then to develop a vision and plan to leverage those resources much more effectively. It completely shifted the momentum of the team, both internally and externally. We began to believe in ourselves, and the rest of the organization moved from seeing us as second-class citizens to organizational superstars!

We can again see the link between the summit task and summit follow-up activities in another, equally successful and yet strikingly different case. As we described earlier, the Santa Ana Star Hotel and Casino used a series of mini-summits to fruitfully elevate customer service, employee awareness, and performance. The summits were a wonderful opportunity for all 850 employees to share stories of superior customer service, to imagine what superior customer service at Santa Ana could be, and then to draft both a service mission and set of service principles.

Each of the five summits resulted in a draft service mission and set of principles. After the summits, a small team compiled the work that had been done by summit participants. They narrowed the mission and principles down by selecting two service mission statements and three principles in each of ten service areas. They then created a voting process so that all employees could have a voice in determining the organization's final service mission and principles.

In this way, discussions about superior customer service continued for several weeks after the summits. Over time the discussions changed from "what are our principles?" to "how do we live them, recognize them, and reward them?" These discussions led to the creation of a new recognition and reward system organized around the service principles, several new customer initiatives, and an appreciative performance review process. The ultimate measure of success was the increase in customer satisfaction and retention.

FIVE AREAS FOR SUMMIT FOLLOW-UP

Although each summit leads to a unique set of follow-up activities, there are five areas that frequently emerge as relevant following an AI Summit. They are listed in Table 12.1 and described in this chapter.

Table 12.1

Six Areas for AI Summit Follow-up

- Communicating outcomes
- Supporting innovation teams
- Supporting improvisational initiatives
- Recognizing people working in new ways
- Furthering the use of appreciative inquiry

The most important thing to remember as you embark on follow-up activities after your summit is that successful follow-up activities must be exemplary of new ways of doing things. They must be congruent with summit outcomes. They must not be business as usual. They must be demonstrable enactments of the dreams and designs expressed during the summit.

COMMUNICATING OUTCOMES

A great deal happens during an AI Summit, making communication one of the essential follow-up activities. For those who attended the summit, follow-up communication will serve as a reminder of both the experience and the outcomes. For those who did not attend, it will foster their understanding of the event and its outcomes.

It is important, then, to communicate the memorable stories, activities, and visions of a better future after the summit as a way of sustaining the momentum and reinforcing expectations established during the summit.

Keeping in mind the need to make follow-up communication congruent with what was learned and committed to during their summit, the British Airways advisory team launched a number of highly creative communication vehicles. Recognizing that not all employees had direct access to e-mail at work or always read the internal newsletter, the new communication process included the following features:

- The book of inspiring stories collected during the pre-summit interview process was sent to all employees.
- Quotes collected during the summit were turned into a set of posters and hung in meeting rooms and conference rooms.
- News posters full of pictures and personal information as well as business information were hung in break rooms and cafeterias.
- Announcements on colorful paper were attached to paychecks.
- E-mail notices were sent to supervisors reminding them to print out and post or distribute important information, as well as to announce it at staff meetings.
- A plan was established to ultimately get all employees access to e-mail at work.
- Employee input was solicited to make the internal newsletter more meaningful and interesting.

There are many creative ways to communicate the outcomes of an AI Summit. Table 12.2 outlines some of the most effective communication vehicles to keep people informed and to keep the momentum moving forward.

Table 12.2

Follow-up Communication Vehicles

Communication Vehicle	Benefits
Videos with talking points	• Provides a visual experience of the summit activities • Communicates a lot of information quickly and easily • Gives summit perspective to organization members not in attendance • Cost effective

Table 12.2 *(continued)*

Follow-up Communication Vehicles

Communication Vehicle	Benefits
Newsletters/e-mail documents	• Provides clear, concise, and speedy dissemination • Wide diffusion throughout the organization • Can be used to communicate progress of change effort • Cost effective
Face-to-face follow-up meetings after the summit • Large groups • Small groups • Individual meetings with supervisor/manager • Department/team meetings with managers • Leadership presentations to employees	• Builds higher trust and durability of message • Ensures continuity of message and eliminates incoherence • Easier to customize message to particular audience • Builds higher commitment levels for the change • Provides an opportunity for immediate feedback • Can be used to communicate progress of change effort • Provides opportunity for those not in attendance to join innovation teams
Summit proceedings	• Documents summit activities start to finish • Provides a permanent record of what transpired • Serves as a communication tool for those who attended • Documents plans and actions
Story books	• Communicates the summit outcomes in story fashion with pictures and quotes • Fosters creativity in communicating the summit message
Progress maps	• Visibly records the progress of each innovation team • Serves as a vehicle to track and celebrate success • Serves as a self-management/motivation tool for all innovation teams
Website	• Easy access and availability • Provides clear, concise, and speedy dissemination

SUPPORTING INNOVATION TEAMS

Providing the necessary follow-up support to innovation teams formed in the summit is absolutely critical to achieving success for their initiatives. Follow-up support comes in many forms (e.g., time, people, funding resources, coaching from senior executives, meeting management facilitation, and recognition), and providing it is ultimately the responsibility of the advisory team.

The advisory team plays several important roles after the summit. They include, but are not limited to, being positive champions or advocates for the work of the innovation teams, integrating across teams to ensure that summit activities are effectively and widely diffused throughout the organization, and providing resources to ensure continuous and sustained progress.

We often encourage advisory teams to meet monthly to review and coordinate the activities of all of the innovation teams. In many cases advisory team members are also members of the innovation teams and can serve as liaisons between the two teams. When this is not the case, we ask members of the advisory team to volunteer to be point persons for each of the innovation teams. Their role is to keep the advisory team informed of how the innovation team is doing and to ensure that the innovation team gets the support it needs to succeed.

Being Positive Champions

Advisory team members serve as coaches, exemplars, and advocates for the work of the innovation teams. We view this role as that of an *affirmative builder* who positively and passionately encourages the innovation teams to self-manage and hold themselves accountable for their own success. This includes:

- Encouraging innovation teams to seek greater levels of involvement and input from other stakeholders in the organization
- Encouraging teams to seek greater knowledge and awareness about what is happening and how things work in the organization
- Encouraging teams to think big (creatively with an eye toward the future) and take strategic risks to bring about the desired future

For many organizations the AI Summit and the formation of innovation teams represent the first real effort to establish a high-involvement, non-authoritarian culture. Consequently, both innovation team members and the advisory team may have the tendency to revert to their old ways of doing things. It is important for the advisory team to be coaches and not approval givers. It is also important that they empower the innovation teams in all of their interactions.

When one of the British Airways innovation teams asked for a meeting with the advisory team, it seemed that they wanted approval for what they were doing. The advisory team agreed to the meeting and decided to do whatever they could to "level the playing field." The meeting room was set up with tables and chairs in a circle. There was no special, separate place for the advisory team. The advisory team showed up in casual clothes and sat all around the room. The innovation team presented their ideas complete with PowerPoint slides and a prototype of what they were proposing. For several of them, this was their first formal presentation ever. They did a great job, and their project ideas were fantastic and provocative. Together the innovation team and the advisory team refined the prototype and agreed to a timeline and budget. The collaboration paid off in results as well as in lessons about how to truly foster employee initiative and accountability.

Integrating across Teams

Effective implementation of summit initiatives by innovation teams requires large amounts of interaction and support across traditional organizational boundaries. These interactions (interdependencies), both horizontal and vertical, must be managed if the changes identified are to be sensibly diffused throughout the organization. Advisory team members who participate on innovation teams can often perform this integration role themselves. In other situations, an integration team may be formed. A good way to do this is to have members of the innovation teams serve on or rotate into the integration team.

Green Mountain Coffee Roasters created a unique method for integrating the work of their innovation teams. They set up an information center. It was a room that was open to all the teams to use for meetings, to post plans and progress reports, and to share successes. By keeping their work on display, the teams were able to stay informed about one another's efforts and to coordinate activities. In addition, they could schedule joint meetings when they saw the need. Other people and groups in the organization could visit the information center to learn about what the teams were doing and how things were going. This greatly aided the integration of the innovation teams' work with the ongoing work of the organization.

Providing Resources

Providing support in the form of adequate resources is critical if innovation team initiatives are to be successful. Resources identified by innovation teams usually include such things as skills, tools, space, people, knowledge and information, time, technology, and equipment.

Many organizations find it useful to give innovation team members a designated amount of overtime to use for their initiative. This allows teams to set their own times for meeting and gives individuals the freedom to volunteer to work beyond their usual jobs. This, of course, requires careful coordination among innovation team members, their supervisors, and the advisory team.

Because the AI Summit brings together the whole system and innovation teams are made up of people from all functions and levels of the organization, very often they are able to self-resource. That is, they have access to all the information, people, and financial support they need to achieve their goals. What teams like this need most is encouragement to do what they believe is good for the organization. They need to be entrusted to create projects, practices, and programs based on their collective awareness of the organization.

SUPPORTING
IMPROVISATIONAL INITIATIVES

Many of the positive results from an AI Summit are unplanned. They are improvisational and emerge from unexpected connections. For example, people meet for the first time and learn something new, ideas heard during a discussion are transferred from one department to another, a new dream is born, or a group pieces together information in a new and unique way. Such "improvisational initiatives" are the norm when it comes to follow-up to an AI Summit.

The best way to support such efforts is to invite them. They are more likely to happen when everyone at the summit is encouraged to go back to work after the summit and to do things differently, to work in alignment with the hopes and dreams expressed during the summit. Such was the call issued by the general manager of Hunter Douglas Window Fashions Division at their first summit. Numerous improvisational initiatives were spawned following the summit, many of which required support. After conducting interviews in another business unit, a frontline employee declared to his supervisor that he could rebuild their $100,000 printing press to "print double"—that is, print two rolls of fabric at the same time. The supervisor said, "That's not possible." The employee said, "I know it is because I've seen it done in the other business unit. And furthermore, I've been to appreciative inquiry and you are supposed to let me try new things. All I need is a few weekends of overtime." The supervisor gave in and handed him the overtime box. Within two weekends the printing presses were printing double, and the company saved $200,000 as they canceled plans to buy two new presses.

In another, equally dramatic improvisational initiative, an employee decided to offer classes in English as a second language to Laotian employees working the night shift. When the Human Resources Director heard about it, he offered her a job coordinating the program. She got a promotion, the company got an ESL program, and dozens of employees improved their English and were also able to get better jobs.

RECOGNIZING PEOPLE WORKING IN NEW WAYS

Without a doubt, one of the most important summit follow-up activities is the recognition and reward of people and teams who are working in new ways. There is no better way to highlight the importance of what was discussed and decided on during the summit than to significantly reward people who work in alignment with the dreams and designs expressed there.

In one company a reward program was created that was directly linked to the company's values. In another, a reward and recognition program was designed to reinforce practices associated with each of the principles articulated during the summit. In still another, a second round of appreciative inquiry focused on collecting stories of best practices of outstanding teamwork. The teams featured were recognized and rewarded.

Linking recognition with communication can be especially effective. After the summit many organizations commit to communicating the "good news"—stories about employees going above and beyond to achieve the goals of the organization and to serve customers. Public recognition goes a long way to communicate, reinforce, and teach about the outcomes of the summit.

FURTHERING THE USE
OF APPRECIATIVE INQUIRY

Few organizations set out to become "appreciative organizations," yet many do. After involving the whole system in an AI Summit and experiencing the many positive benefits and changes that emerge, most organizations decide to expand their use of appreciative inquiry. Some launch a second wave of inquiry, others change their measurement systems to be consistent with an appreciative approach, and still others spread the word by teaching appreciative inquiry to frontline employees as well as to managers and supervisors.

Deepening the Inquiry

During an AI Summit people develop many different ways to use appreciative inquiry in their work. As they experience the benefits of the summit firsthand, they imagine using it to improve everything from teamwork to customer relations to financial viability. They often ask questions about the use of AI for individual issues such as coaching, leadership development, and recruitment. We encourage it all.

Each time an organization conducts an inquiry, the knowledge, understanding, and opportunities for innovation increase. It's like learning to ride a bike. At first you are a little wobbly, but soon you are racing all over town. And once you learn to ride a bike, you never forget! Similarly, in every round of inquiry new questions are raised, and when those questions are pursued, a richer and more comprehensive understanding emerges—from which yet deeper inquiries and more creative innovations result. There is no limit to the depth, breadth, and number of topics that can be explored with appreciative inquiry.

For example, an R&D organization that wanted to improve the productivity of its 700 scientists and engineers conducted a first round of inquiry into "R&D Productivity." From that round of inquiry they discovered that the three critical success factors influencing productivity were partnership, connectivity, and knowledge transfer. Although they were able to initiate some very useful actions based on this first wave of inquiry, it wasn't until the second round, designed to discover the deeper meaning and conditions supporting partnership, connectivity, and knowledge transfer, that they made quantum progress in their goal of contributing to the organization's overall capacity.

Hunter Douglas Window Fashions Division has engaged its workforce in three waves of inquiry. The first, called Focus 2000, was aimed at organization culture transformation. The second was for strategic planning and resulted in a new strategic vision and product line. The third focused on process improvement and quality. In addition, AI has been used for dozens of other organizational initiatives from customer service, to rewards and recognition, to employee orientation.

Taking an Appreciative Approach to Measurement

Time and again an AI Summit serves as a wake-up call for people managing various measurement systems in the organization. Once they understand the implications of the statement "human systems—organizations, communities, teams, and people—move in the direction of what they study," they question the measurement systems they use. All systems from employee surveys to customer satisfaction measures to productivity reporting to quality indicators are challenged and often revised. They are transformed from deficit measures, which report what's wrong, to affirmative measures that build the organization's capacity.

Several years ago we were approached by a transnational pharmaceutical firm that asked if we would determine whether a multimillion-dollar training program had been successful. What they really wanted to know was whether there had been a transfer of learning from the classroom to the workplace. We suggested that together we conduct an inquiry and ask participants to provide us with stories of how they had applied what they learned in the workplace. They responded by noting that we were asking biased questions—to which our answer was: "If they don't have any stories of learning transfer, then that will be powerful data; and if they do have stories of learning transfer, the very act of telling them will amplify the learning, and we will find out more about how the learning is actually being used."

When all of the interviews were completed and the all the stories captured and reviewed, the client system expressed delight at hearing about the unexpected ways trainees had used what they had learned. The "data" created through this appreciative inquiry evaluation process was judged by the client to be much more useful for future program development than any of the more traditional assessments they had previously conducted. It provided a deepening of the lessons learned in the training.

In another example, a large national staff organization had completed the first year of a planned multi-year culture change process, and they wanted to know whether the change process had been successful or had failed. After some intense debate on both sides of that question, it became obvious to everyone in the room that the common area of agreement was that some things, not all things, had gone as planned. They now faced a choice. They could judge the project dichotomously—as a success or failure—or they could "measure" what had gone well (and why) and what positive surprises had occurred (and why), and then decide whether and how to proceed.

They decided to hold a second summit focused on evaluating (measuring) the success of the past year. They intended to base the next stage of their culture change process on the results of the first year. Their evaluation summit started off with stories of success—many of which were a total surprise to the sponsors. This led to a new understanding of how change occurred within their organization. The added benefit was that the organization began to see itself as competent at cultural change, which was a significant new, and very helpful, self-image for the organization at the time.

Teaching Appreciative Inquiry

Often organizations embark on an AI Summit with minimal knowledge of appreciative inquiry. In the beginning they know enough to understand how it works and the benefits they might accrue by using it. In the course of planning and preparing for the summit, a few people become quite knowledgeable on the subject of AI. During the summit, however, people from all levels and functions become curious and want to learn more about AI. They want to use it at work, at home, with their religious communities, with their children's schools, with volunteer efforts, and so on. It is quite common for an organization to embark on a major AI training program after its first AI Summit.

We have developed AI training programs for frontline employees, for managers, for executives, for city government, for community development workers, and for many others. In some cases it amounts to a straight training in the principles and practice of AI with the charge to participants to go back and use AI on the job. In other instances we have created AI training programs for intact work teams, process improvement teams, or business development teams. These teams were trained in AI in order for them to conduct an inquiry into their work. The training was part classroom and part field work.

Other organizations have offered an internal appreciative leadership program that enables the ideas and practices that people learn to translate directly to their unique culture. It was with this in mind that we took a phone call from a multinational natural resources company asking if we could develop a customized leadership program for their top seventy managers. We tactfully explained that we did not consider ourselves experts in the field of leadership for natural resource companies, but we wondered if they thought there were any moments of great leadership in the total history of their seventy top managers. They acknowledged that in fact they could easily think of a half dozen or more such instances. This opened the door to a dialogue on the possibility of studying their own experiences with leadership, and in effect creating their own theory of great leadership by sharing stories about it and expanding the practice of it in their organization.

"Passionate Leadership" was the topic they chose for their leadership summit. The process of using their own history to explore, lift up, develop, and implement their own theory of leadership became so powerful for this organization that they are now using appreciative inquiry as an approach to management audits, safety, office design, strategic plan implementation, and a dozen other management issues.

Sustaining Change through Second- and Third-Wave Appreciative Inquiry

More often than not, during an AI Summit an organization decides to extend the application of appreciative inquiry. Other issues surface in the life cycle of the organization that are suited to appreciative inquiry, and second and third waves of AI are initiated.

An excellent example of this comes from World Vision, a large private voluntary organization (PVO) operating relief and development programs in over 100 countries. AI was introduced to World Vision in 1990 when then director of innovative programs, Mark Publow, invited David Cooperrider and others of us at Case Western Reserve University to help mount a response to the medical and institutional crisis of the Romanian orphanage system after the fall of the Caucesceau regime. We held a series of summits to form a complex global alliance of over 125 organizations (universities, corporations, churches, PVOs, government agencies, and associations), resulting in more than $25 million worth of direct aid, supplies, and professional services.[1]

Two years later, Publow partnered with Mike Mantel, senior director of World Vision Chicago,[2] Bud Ipema, president of the MidAmerica Leadership Foundation, and us to form Vision Chicago, a multi-organization alliance dedicated to addressing issues of housing, economic development, racial reconciliation, and education in the city. We began with a series of AI Summits that brought together a collaborative network of organizations and individuals across traditional boundaries of race, class, culture, sector, and geography. During its ten years, Vision Chicago (now called World Vision Chicago) has mobilized a network of over 1,500 organizations, resulting in more than $10 million in direct aid, $20 million in donated products, and 15,000 volunteers to invest in a positive change in Chicago and around the world. In June 1994 it was recognized by the Council of Foundations as one of eight "Models of Hope" for its pioneering work in rebuilding America's cities, and in June 1999 it won HUD's "Best Practices Award."[3]

More recently, the success of World Vision Chicago has prompted World Vision United States (WVUS) to create a "regionalization strategy" as its predominant model for action in major cities around the country, including New York, Los Angeles, Washington, Seattle, and Minneapolis/St. Paul. In many of these cities, appreciative inquiry has been used to interview a range of stakeholders to identify strengths, assets, resources, hopes, and dreams and to design an interorganizational architecture to address pressing local issues.

At the same time, AI has quickly spread to World Vision programs in Canada, Australia, Africa, Asia, and Latin America. It has been enlivened through a variety of training opportunities, field research, intervention efforts, publications, and additional organizational change efforts. See Exhibit 12.1 for an illustration of the worldwide ripple effect of AI within World Vision.

Exhibit 12.1

The Worldwide Ripple Effect of AI within World Vision

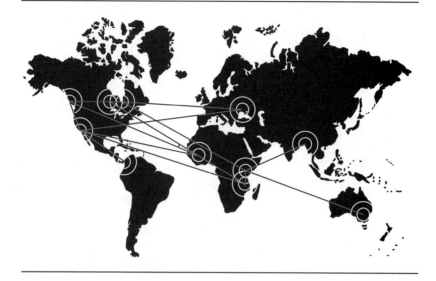

Awakening the Appreciative Organization

As seen in the World Vision example, summit follow-up is more of a beginning than an ending. For most organizations it is the awakening of their capacity as an appreciative organization. Planning for the summit signaled the beginning of something new. The AI Summit itself was something new, a first time for bringing the whole system together, a first time for relationship-enhancing communication, a first time for self-expression and self-organizing on behalf of the whole. Summit follow-up ensured the realization of the organization's destiny, the opportunity to harvest the benefits of being an appreciative organization. In the next chapter, we will explore the idea of the appreciative organization in more detail.

CHAPTER 13

THE PROMISE OF THE APPRECIATIVE ORGANIZATION

Imagine that it is 2020 and we have all just awakened from a long sleep. As you enter your place of work and look around, you notice that things are very different. Indeed, everything is as you always wished it would be. Your ideal organization has become real. What do you see that is different? What is happening? Who is there? What are they doing? What are they saying? What do you notice about the leadership, the structures, the products and services, the people, and the systems that are in place now. Who are your customers? What are your products and services? How are you organized to market, sell, distribute, or deliver them? What are you most proud of about your ideal organization?

In all of our work organizing and facilitating AI Summits, we ask questions like these. We seek to discover our colleagues' and clients' images of their ideal organization. We do this to help them recognize their ideals and to help them realize their ideals.

In this chapter we share our sense of what organizations can become when they commit to appreciative inquiry and apply it broadly, in its many forms, including the AI Summit. We describe our image of the appreciative organization. In addition, we weave the thoughts and ideas of some of our colleagues and share stories of companies that are living this ideal. The characteristics of an appreciative organization are listed in Table 13.1 and elaborated in this chapter.

Table 13.1

Characteristics of an Appreciative Organization

- Organizing from the positive core
- Nurturing appreciative learning cultures
- Sustaining positive change
- Liberating the voice and energy of people
- Cultivating appreciative leadership
- Leveraging business as an agent of world benefit

ORGANIZING FROM THE POSITIVE CORE

Appreciative organizations are strength based. Their effectiveness comes from the alignment of strengths toward a common purpose. When organizations make the shift from command-and-control to organizing from the positive core, people thrive, the business prospers, and the organization is experienced as vibrantly alive and capable of greatness.

In 2001 Chicago was one of McDonald's highest-performing regions. Under the leadership of regional manager Phil Gray, the Chicago region outpaced all other regions but one. But Phil, never at ease with the status quo, wanted more. He wanted to develop, along with restaurant owner-operators throughout the region, the next generation of innovations that would give McDonald's a quantum leap forward in attracting customers and extending market leadership. "Everyone knows the 80/20 principle," he said. "We get 80 percent of our results from 20 percent of our activity. I want to clarify what can set us apart in the marketplace—our strategic competitive advantage—and then align all of our activities around it so that we can propel ourselves forward further and faster than we've ever done before."

With this in mind, we worked with the Chicago region director of OD, Bob Roberts,[1] and a broadly representative planning team to design and implement a three-day AI Summit for McDonald's corporate staff and owner-operators in the Chicago area. The topic for the summit was "Defining Our Competitive Strategic Advantage." As a result of the summit, the Chicago region defined its competitive strategic advantage as "Back to the Basics—Quality, Service, and Cleanliness." They formed teams to focus on four business result areas—people, operations, market share, and profit—and each team developed a set of high-leverage strategies, tactics, and targets to provide an integrated plan for the region.

The results extended beyond the strategic plan to a shift in mindset. Says Bob:

> Not only did the AI Summit help us to define our strategic advantage and align our action, it created the beginnings of a culture shift in the region. We began to pay attention more to our successes and to learn from what we do right. I'm not talking here about happy talk. I'm talking about learning from when we are at out best—what does this look like—and then creating better bests over and over again until we have a culture of *instinctive excellence* where we almost don't have to think about it.

Appreciative organizations are "affirmative self-organizing systems." This means that everything about them emerges from the voluntary alignment of strengths, even their purpose. Have you ever worked with a group of people and you were the only people who could possibly do what you did? There are times when just the right people come together for just the right reason, and the reason becomes apparent because of the collective capacities of the people. Many entrepreneurial organizations start out this way: An idea draws people together, they talk about their interests and what they have to contribute, they create a common purpose, and their collective endeavor is set in motion. Sharing of interests and strengths leads to common purpose. Common purpose then charts the course of action and methods of organizing. That is the essence of affirmative self-organizing.

In an appreciative organization the positive core is kept alive through continuous inquiry and dialogue about the organization, people, and teams at their best. It is revealed and enriched through stories of best practices, exemplary actions, and hopes and dreams for the future. By raising consciousness about the positive core—over and over making it known and owned by all—an organization opens itself to its unique potential for innovation and greatness.

NURTURING APPRECIATIVE
LEARNING CULTURES

The cultures of appreciative organizations are focused on high-impact learning. They place an enormous value on learning and the benefits it can bring to an organization. The Vice President of Human Resources for a large manufacturing company once remarked that his ideal organization would be in the business of people development first and foremost. It would use the work of the business as vehicle for human learning and growth. So, he said, his manufacturing company would be in the business of developing people through manufacturing. A novel idea indeed, but one we find in the hearts and minds of many leaders of appreciative organizations—people learning and growing through business rather than simply business getting done through people.

Nurturing appreciative learning cultures requires that management practices as well as organizational processes and systems be designed to support learning. Frank Barrett, writes that appreciative learning cultures have four core competencies:

1) *Affirmative competence:* The organization draws on the human capacity to appreciate positive possibilities by selectively focusing on current and past strengths, successes, and potentials.

2) *Expansive competence:* The organization challenges habits and conventional practices, provoking members to experiment in the margins; makes expansive promises that challenge them to stretch in new directions; and evokes a set of higher values and ideals that inspire them to passionate engagement.

3) *Generative competence:* The organization constructs integrative systems that allow members to see the consequences of their actions, to recognize they are making a meaningful contribution, and to experience a sense of pride and progress.

4) *Collaborative competence:* The organization creates forums in which members engage in ongoing dialogue and exchange diverse perspectives.[2]

Sacred Heart–Griffin (SHG) High School, in Springfield, Illinois, got a good start on its journey to becoming an appreciative learning culture through the AI Summit process. SHG is a private co-ed college preparatory high school under the sponsorship of the Dominican Sisters. Sr. Marilyn Jean Runkel, president of SHG, contacted AI consultant Gina Hinrichs and asked her to design an AI

Summit process with four objectives in mind: (1) Optimize techno-logical systems in the school; (2) increase the size and scope of the guidance department; (3) make sure Campus Ministry is adequately staffed and promoted; and (4) provide state-of-the-art facilities and expanded programs in fine arts, dance, drama, music, and art.

Sr. Marilyn Jean had had been involved with OD and large-group interventions since the late 1960s and was particularly at-tracted to the AI Summit process because of its capacity to create strong community, gain broad participation and involvement of staff and other stakeholder groups, and launch "inspired" action on behalf of the whole organization. Gina and Sr. Marilyn Jean pulled together a representative design team, which met weekly to refine the summit topic, identify stakeholders, finalize the design, and arrange logistics. An invitation was sent to 100 participants: 80 faculty and staff and 20 parents, students, and community members. The three-day summit took place in a large, elegantly decorated study hall at the high school. Adjoining classrooms served as breakout rooms.

The summit schedule covered all four AI phases, with discovery on the first day, dream and design on day 2, and all of day 3 devoted to destiny. There was a heavy emphasis on the design and destiny phases because participants needed to know that action would be taken from the summit. The faculty had invested three days that they would normally use to set up their classrooms. This was valu-able time for them, and they wanted a return on the time invested. It was also critical for all participants to know that they would be part of the action to be taken. This could not be an exercise in throwing projects over the wall to leadership for implementation. Everyone would participate in constructing the future.

The results of the SHG summit process were powerful on many levels. First, faculty, staff, students, parents, and community mem-bers all gained a more holistic view of the educational community. Together they established five new strategic priorities, complete with tactical action plans, for the school. One of the most important was to engage the broader stakeholder community in identifying and ac-quiring additional sources of funding. The cooperative climate inside the school also improved. Faculty and staff built relationships across departments and generations of experience, launched initiatives to build capacity in the area of open communication and trust building, and began a shift from a tradition of command and control to a more participative environment. By emphasizing design and destiny, the summit allowed the group to move beyond the cynicism of previous failed reform efforts. The participants did not just talk about the changes but began to embed them in their organizational systems and culture.

SUSTAINING POSITIVE CHANGE

Appreciative organizations are committed to positive change— change that begins with a deep inquiry; analysis and understanding of what works well; who they are at their best; and what contributes to social, financial, and environmental well-being. They recognize that the only certainty in life is change and that sustainability requires continuous awareness, learning, and adaptability to change. Through practices of positive change, appreciative organizations create a capacity to continuously realign their strengths and redefine their business goals.

At Green Mountain Coffee Roasters (GMCR), positive change practices have become a way of doing business. These practices emerged as a result of a highly productive appreciative inquiry process focused on financial goals. According to AI consultant Ilene Wasserman, "GMCR has been able to sustain positive change through a number of practices that keep stories about what works well and the positive dialogue front and center in the organization. They are continuously collecting stories of success and distilling them to identify the principles of their success. Then they look for other ways to apply the principles. In this way they build on the positive by learning from one another and spreading it across the company."

The practices initiated at GRCR demonstrate some of the ways that appreciative inquiry can be woven into the fabric of daily work life, enhancing an organization's capacity to sustain positive change. They include:

- *Whole-company meetings.* At these biannual meetings the program begins with storytelling. The stories reinforce the shared vision and focus of the company, the passion for social responsibility that ties the organization with the global communities and the local charities they support, and the commitment of those who are innovating in these areas. Whole-company meetings are active and engaging and acknowledge the contribution of all who attend.

- *Leadership meetings.* These monthly meetings begin with some inquiry, either one-on-one or in small groups. The inquiry focuses on the topic of the meeting, serving to engage the participants, promote interactions, and stimulate thinking about the agenda.

- *Process team meetings.* These meetings continue to build on the stories that emerged from the initial AI Summit. Discussions prompt more creative, effective, and efficient business processes.

- *Sales meetings.* These biannual meetings tap the creativity of the sales force to identify what they already know about their customers and what their customers teach them about the market to improve customer intimacy and customer service.

- *Hiring process.* The inquiry process is used to identify what qualities are needed for a position and how potential candidates might fit the company.

- *New employee orientation.* Appreciative inquiry has been incorporated into the new employee orientation. A company timeline is shared along with key stories that convey the company at its best. The process has begun for new members of the senior management team.

- *Performance review process.* A process rooted in appreciative inquiry was piloted with the operations leadership team. Each member of the group crafted an interview protocol that inquired into the strengths of their particular department in relation to others. Peers, subordinates, and superiors were interviewed.

LIBERATING THE VOICE
AND ENERGY OF THE PEOPLE

Appreciative organizations are polyphonic, multi-vocal. They are rich in diversity of voice and forms of expression. Freedom of speech is operational. People are invited to speak out and they feel valued because their ideas matter. When the voice of the people is liberated, people and the organization benefit. The organization's collective knowledge and wisdom grows. And the organization comes to life with the creative energy of innovation.

Several weeks after the Focus 2000 AI Summit at Hunter Douglas, we were on site conducting AI training for frontline employees. At lunch we asked one of the employees what was different since AI had been introduced to Hunter Douglas. His response was immediate: "Let me tell you a story. Before AI if the R&D group needed a prototype run on my machine, they would go to my boss and ask him to schedule it. He would check the run schedule and tell me when to do it. Now, since AI, the R&D folks come to me directly and trust me to know when it can be done. Their trust makes me want to do a good job for them."

Appreciative organizations value the ideas of people and understand that those closest to the customer know what will delight the customer, and that those doing the job know best how to improve the job. Not only are employees motivated by being able to give their opinions and ideas, but managers are often highly energized by employees' positive contributions. Reflecting back on two years of appreciative inquiry in British Airways North America, Catherine Mascetti, Director in Customer Service, JFK, commented on the delight she experienced as employees realized they could make a difference.

> There are a lot of high points for me in the past two years. What comes to mind first is giving people opportunities and watching them as they learn to trust leadership and begin taking responsibility for co-creating the organization. When we told the forty people on the core team that we wouldn't go forward with appreciative inquiry unless they thought it was a good idea, I watched weary, jaded people turn around. They began to trust that we really were asking for their opinions, and that we really wouldn't go forward unless they thought it was a good idea, and that we couldn't create a better future without them.

Managers are all too often faced with employees who want to have a say—a negative say about all the things that are wrong and that are management's responsibility. This creates a rift between employees and managers. With appreciative inquiry, employees are invited to openly share their thoughts about the organization at its best and how they themselves might spread the success. As this happens, employees and management build positive and productive working relationships.

CULTIVATING
APPRECIATIVE LEADERSHIP

Appreciative organizations cultivate appreciative leadership. They value and develop the gifts and capacities—among managers, supervisors, and frontline employees—to engage others, to ask positive questions, to use stories, to join with others in imagining a world of

positive potential, and to build possible worlds. Management theo-
rist Peter Drucker has said that "the central task of leadership is to
create an alignment of strengths such that weaknesses are no longer
relevant."[3] An appreciative leader is able to see the best in people
and leverage their strengths to achieve significant and mutually valued goals.

Author and AI consultant Marge Schiller writes, "Something
is happening with leaders. They are changing. As our views of
how organization's work change, the models of effective leadership also change . . . information and interrelationship are the
building blocks of new organizations and the motivators for appreciative leaders."[4] Appreciative leaders are highly inclusive
and collaborative in bringing out the best of people to create a
better world.

In a recent interview, Rick Pellett, general manager of Hunter
Douglas Window Fashions Division and a person we would describe as an appreciative leader, told of the time it became clear to
him that his willingness to involve others, to share information
openly, and to ask the right questions was key not only to the organization's success but also to his own:

> At some point, a couple of years ago, I realized (or maybe I just
> remembered) that I didn't have to be the one person to "drive"
> everything that happens here. I realized and remembered that
> people are very capable, and that all I have to do is give them
> information, ask the right questions, get out of the way, and
> support them in doing great things. That one small realization
> made all the difference in the world in my performance—and in
> my comfort in my position. I have a much easier job now than
> I used to.

According to Diana Whitney and Amanda Trosten-Bloom, this
capacity to identify and bring out the best in others is deeply rooted
in a set of "humanistic social constructionist assumptions" that they
call Theory I.[5] They contrast Theory I leadership with other familiar leadership theories—Theory X, Theory Y,[6] and Theory Z[7]—and
claim that Theory I leaders are uniquely relational and appreciative
in their approach:

> Theory I leaders are drawn to organizing philosophies and prac-
> tices that are highly relational. They are attracted to approaches
> that unleash collective imagination and compel collective action.
> They are "gifted" leaders—but their gifts aren't necessarily in the

areas of raw intelligence, creativity, financial acumen, or pure business sense.

They are gifted, instead, with a certain trust . . . a certain ego strength . . . a certain willingness to stretch beyond the limits of their own capacities, and to enlist others' strengths in first imagining, then achieving, compelling goals and dreams for the future. As with all humanly endowed gifts, whether they lie dormant or blossom forth depends upon the relational ground upon which the seeds fall. The gifts of Theory I leaders come forth and are made meaningful by the many people with whom they work.

David Cooperrider has interviewed or worked with many appreciative leaders, including past president of the United States Jimmy Carter; president of Roadway Express, Jim Stanley; founder of International Physicians for Prevention of Nuclear War, Dr. Bernard Lown; founder of The Body Shop, Anita Roddick; former President of GTE Tom White; Chief Naval Officer, Admiral Clark; CEO of the Mountain Forum, Jane Pratt; and founder and CEO emeritus of Visa, Dee Hock. "What all these human beings have in common," he says, "is an uncanny capacity to see, magnify, and connect all that is good and best in people and the world around them, and to summon all that is best in life . . . a 'positive core' capable of mobilizing transformational conversation and cooperative action." He highlights three core competencies of the appreciative leader:

1) Everything the appreciative leader does conveys to others a genuine, respect-filled, positive intention to produce enduring change for world benefit. Reality, for the appreciative leader, is not a given. It is there for our active shaping in the direction of our higher purpose.

2) The appreciative leader enlarges everyone's knowledge and vision of the appreciable world—all the strengths, capacities, and potentials— by having not solid answers but expansive questions. It is precisely through inquiry itself that the appreciative leader realizes and unleashes not his or her own, but other people's genius. The art of leadership lies in the art of the positive question.

3) The appreciative leader lives with an awareness that organizations in full voice will be more creative, resilient, and knowledgeable than organizations that are in half voice; and because they hold positive assumptions about people, they as leaders are continuously expanding the web of inclusion—realizing that the best in human beings comes out when people experience the wholeness of their system.[8]

LEVERAGING BUSINESS AS AN AGENT OF WORLD BENEFIT

Appreciative organizations are agents of world benefit. They are organizations that help people create a better life, work on the boundaries between business and social good, and are able to thrive financially while doing no harm. They hold themselves accountable for a successful triple bottom line—economic, social, and environmental prosperity.

There are tens of thousands of organizations around the globe that can be considered agents of world benefit, and their stories are waiting to be told. For example, when Dr. Arnold Beckman went into his garage to invent something to help his neighbor, a citrus fruit farmer, decide when to pick his crops, he did not intend to launch a multimillion-dollar scientific technology company. He simply wanted to help a friend. He imagined that he might be able to sell 50–100 units of his invention, the pH meter. Now Beckman Instruments has grown into a Fortune 500 company that provides life-saving equipment to hospitals and research laboratories around the world.

There are many other compelling examples, such as Merck's program to provide free medicine to thousands of people in developing countries suffering from river blindness, or General Motor's efforts to develop a pollution-free hydrogen car, or Motorola's legendary commitment to integrity in the marketplace, or Ben & Jerry's commitment to leaving no environmental footprint, or the tens of thousands of global change organizations that have sprung up since World War II to create humanly and environmentally sustainable futures. Appreciative organizations join the ranks of these pioneers and strive, in all that they do, to become human communities that work in an correlated way toward a future of:

- Sustainable economic enterprise
- Human and ecological prosperity
- A global awakening of the heart that supports ways of being, relating, and doing that are themselves sources of world benefit

Today, when businesses are being called to task for unethical business practices, destroying the natural environment and indigenous cultures, and insufficiently providing for the basic needs of employees, we believe it is important to discover and learn from those that are living exemplars of best business practice. We, along with dozens of appreciative inquiry colleagues around the world, are conducting a global inquiry, and we encourage you to join in. Business as an Agent of World Benefit (BAWB)[9] is a landmark inquiry creating a typology of human *strengths* of positive business leadership at the intersection of organizations and society—and it focuses entirely on hopeful visions of the future and promising practices in the world today. As articulated in the BAWB statement of purpose, "Our belief is that business has the opportunity to aim higher and to be a creative force for good. The same inventiveness and entrepreneurial spirit used historically to create wealth *can* and *is* being applied to world issues and social change agendas."[10]

THE AI SUMMIT:
GIVING HOPE FOR THE FUTURE

The Appreciative Inquiry Summit is the most practical, the most idealistic, and the most results-oriented process for organizational change that we have ever experienced. By bringing large groups of people together to discover and discuss what they care about, it improves working relationships and the pragmatics of daily work life. By inviting participants to dream and design their ideal organization, it lifts up possibilities and liberates the potential for a better world. By asking people to take action on those things they believe will make the greatest impact, it builds sustainable organizations.

There have been people throughout history who, even in the midst of great tragedy, held on to hopeful, life-affirming images for the future. As a result, their lives have made a difference in ours. The Appreciative Inquiry Summit does this on a grand scale. As people collectively express what is in their hearts and on their minds and articulate bold, revolutionary, life-giving images for the future of their organization, they create hope for the evolution of organizations around the world that are democratically organized to realize the highest values of humanity.

PART V

APPENDIX: SAMPLE PARTICIPANT WORKBOOK

We almost always provide a participant workbook for people upon arrival at an AI Summit. These workbooks help people track the flow of events and provide most of the materials they will need over the course of the summit. There is no such thing as a "generic" workbook. Each one must be customized by the planning team for the unique situation, culture, and change agenda of the organization involved. Even when the workbook is customized, however, it is not uncommon for it to be further adapted, changed, or revised as the summit progresses.

When preparing a workbook, we usually include:

- A title page that announces the summit task, date, and location
- Purpose and objectives
- Summit agenda
- A brief introduction to AI
- What to expect
- An appreciative interview guide
- A worksheet for each summit activity
- Brief bios of the facilitators

Often, the planning team will also add things such as table assignments, a list of participants, photographs taken at work or at other summits, housekeeping details, and other information they want people to have. On the next several pages, we provide a sample workbook adapted from the one we used for the summit with the Chicago region of McDonald's, focused on the topic of "Strategic Competitive Advantage."

APPRECIATIVE INQUIRY SUMMIT
FOR
"OUR ORGANIZATION"

FOCUS 2010:
DEFINING
OUR STRATEGIC
COMPETITIVE
ADVANTAGE

Date

Location

PARTICIPANT
WORKBOOK

PURPOSE & OBJECTIVES

The purpose of the AI Summit is to define and align around a clear strategic competitive advantage for our organization.

Objectives

- To discover and build on the strengths and successes of our past
- To envision and clarify a strategic competitive advantage for our future
- To focus all our energies on gaining and growing our strategic competitive advantage through 2010 and beyond

AI SUMMIT AGENDA

DAY 1: DISCOVERY

8:00 a.m.	Continental Breakfast & Pre-start Activity (optional)
8:30 a.m.	Opening, Welcome, Sponsorship Statements
	The Power of the Positive Question: A Brief Introduction to AI
	Learning from Stories of Peak Performance: One-on-One Interviews
	Understanding How and Why AI Works
12:30 p.m.	Lunch
1:30 p.m.	Discovering the Resources in Our Community
	Discovering the Positive Core of our Strategic Competitive Advantage (SCA)
	Mapping Our Positive Core
5:00 p.m.	Adjourn

DAY 2: DREAM

8:00 a.m.	Continental Breakfast & Pre-start Activity (optional)
8:30 a.m.	Welcome, Overview of the Day
	The Positive Image–Positive Action Relationship
	Dreaming Bold Dreams: The Future of Our SCA
	Crafting Dream Statements
12:30 p.m.	Lunch
1:30 p.m.	Creative Presentations of Our Dreams
	Enriching the Dreams: Clarifying and Elevating Our SCA
5:00 p.m.	Adjourn

AGENDA (CONTINUED)

DAY 3: DESIGN

8:00 a.m.	Continental Breakfast & Pre-start Activity (optional)
8:30 a.m.	Welcome, Overview of the Day
	What Is Organization Design?
	Creating a Map of High-Potential Design Possibilities
	Selecting High-Impact Design Elements
	Provocative Propositions: Aligning Around Our SCA
12:30 p.m.	Lunch
1:30 p.m.	Coordinating to Strengthen Our Alignment and Build Commitment for It
5:00 p.m.	Adjourn

DAY 4: DESTINY

8:00 a.m.	Continental Breakfast & Pre-start Activity (optional)
8:30 a.m.	Welcome, Overview of the Day
	The Power of Inspired Action to Transform Organizations
	Formation of Innovation Teams around High-Priority Projects
12:30 p.m.	Lunch
1:30 p.m.	Building Our Roadmap to the Future
	Encouraging Improvisation and Growing Our SCA
	Planning to Go "Back Home"
5:00 p.m.	Adjourn

WHAT IS APPRECIATIVE INQUIRY?

*"Appreciative inquiry gets much better results than seeking out
and solving problems. We concentrate enormous resources
on correcting problems . . . [but] when used continually
over a long time, this approach leads to a negative culture,
a descent into a paralyzing sense of hopelessness. Don't get
me wrong. I'm not advocating mindless happy talk.
Appreciative inquiry is a complex science designed to make
things better. We can't ignore problems—we just need to
approach them from the other side."*

—Thomas H. White, President, Telephone Operations,
GTE Wireless

Appreciative inquiry is an approach to organization change
that has been used successfully in small- and large-change projects with hundreds of organizations worldwide. It is based on
the simple idea that organizations move in the direction of what
they ask questions about. For example, when groups study
human problems and conflicts, they often find that both the
number and severity of these problems grow. In the same way,
when groups study high human ideals and achievements, such
as peak experiences, best practices, and noble accomplishments, these phenomena, too, tend to flourish. Appreciative inquiry distinguishes itself from other change methodologies by
deliberately asking positive questions to ignite constructive dialogue and inspired action within organizations.

HOW TO USE
APPRECIATIVE INQUIRY

As a method of organization change, appreciative inquiry differs from traditional problem-solving approaches. The basic assumption of problem-solving is that people and organizations are fundamentally "broken" and need to be fixed. The process usually involves:

- Identifying the key problems
- Analyzing the root causes of failure
- Searching for possible solutions
- Developing an action plan

In contrast, the underlying assumption of appreciative inquiry is that people and organizations are highly generative. They are always evolving, growing, and moving toward the future. AI focuses the whole organization on identifying its "positive core"—its greatest assets, capacities, capabilities, resources, and strengths—to create new possibilities for change, action, and innovation.

The steps include:

- Discovering the organization's root causes of success
- Envisioning bold new possibilities for the future
- Designing the organization for excellence through dialogue
- Co-constructing the future.

In other words, the appreciative inquiry 4-D model includes discovery, dream, design, and destiny.

The AI "4-D" Cycle

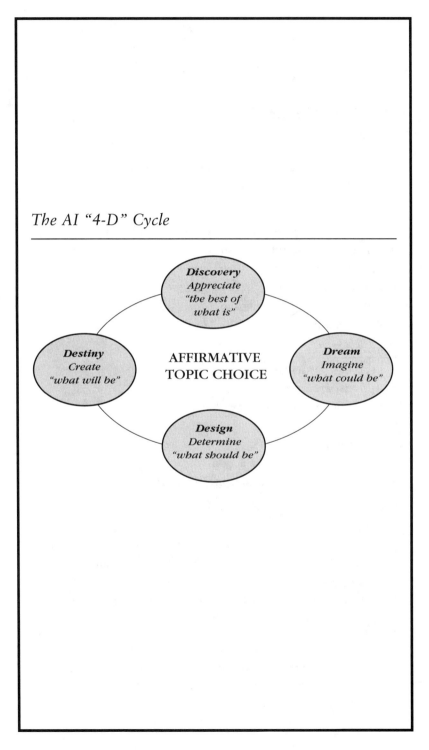

WHAT TO EXPECT
FROM THIS SUMMIT

Role of the Facilitators

- Manage the overall conference process
- Set the structure and time frames
- Explain the purpose and guidelines for the activities
- Create a constructive learning environment

Your Role

- Contribute your knowledge, experience, and ideas
- Bring out the best in those around you
- Tell lots of stories
- Analyze information and imagine new possibilities
- Self-manage your own group, time, and tasks
- Build the future you want for your organization

Ground Rules

- Everyone participates
- All ideas are valid
- Everything is written on flipcharts
- Listen, ask, and be curious
- Observe time frames
- Seek higher ground and action
- Create "relationship-enhancing" conversations

Small-Group Leadership Roles

Each small group manages its own discussion, data, time, and reports. Here are useful roles for managing this work. *Leadership roles can be rotated.* Divide up the work as you wish.

- *Discussion leader:* Ensures that each person who wants to speak is heard within the time available. Keeps group on track to finish on time.
- *Timekeeper:* Keeps group aware of time left. Monitors report-outs and signals time remaining to the person talking.
- *Recorder:* Writes group's output on flipcharts, using the speaker's words. Asks people to restate long ideas briefly.
- *Reporter:* Delivers report to large group in time allotted.

ACTIVITY #1

LEARNING FROM STORIES OF PEAK PERFORMANCE

ONE-ON-ONE INTERVIEWS: "OUR ORGANIZATION AT ITS BEST"

Purpose: To discover the forces and factors that give our organization its success and vitality when it's at its best

Guidelines:

1) Select an interview partner from your table group.

2) Interview your partner using the interview guide on the following pages. Each person will have forty-five minutes to interview his or her partner.

3) Encourage your partner to tell his or her story; draw him or her out with your positive energy and excitement.

4) Take good notes and be listening for great quotes and stories. Listen as if you had to retell the story yourself. You will share the results of your interview in the next session.

5) The information you collect in this interview will be used this week to shape the strategic future of our organization.

"OUR ORGANIZATION" INQUIRY INTO STRATEGIC COMPETITIVE ADVANTAGE

Interview Guide

(in diverse pairs: across functions *and* levels)

1. What Attracted You?

Think back to when you first decided to join our organization. What attracted you? What were your initial excitements and impressions?

2. High Point

During your entire time with our organization, I'm sure you've had some ups and downs, some peaks and valleys, some highs and lows. I'd like you to reflect for a moment on a high-point experience, a time when you felt most alive, most engaged, and most proud of yourself and of our organization. Tell the story. What happened? What was going on?

3. What Enabled Your Success?

What was it about you, others, and the organization that made your high-point experience possible?

- What were your best qualities, skills, approaches, values, and so on that made it a great experience?
- Who were significant others and what did they contribute?
- What were the most important factors in the organization that helped (e.g., strategic focus, leadership qualities, best practices, traditions, structures, processes, skills, relationships)?

Interview Guide (continued)

4. What Is Our Strategic Competitive Advantage?

A company can consistently outperform rivals only if it can establish a strategic competitive advantage—a unique value proposition that it produces better and more completely than anyone else. This kind of advantage requires the full investment of every member of the team—building on traditional strengths and discovering new capabilities that will carry the organization to higher levels of strategic excellence.

As you look at our organization from the perspective of our strengths, and as you think about the business context and opportunities, how do you define our "strategic competitive advantage"? Define it: What is the strategic competitive advantage you want and believe we have the capability to create? Right now? In the moderate time frame? Longer term?

5. Leadership for Strategic Competitive Advantage

We all pride ourselves on the things we do that add the most value to our work. Some of our activities add lots of value, and others do not. Likewise, there are some things we do as leaders—our style, our approaches to managing people—that engage everyone else in strengthening our competitive advantage. Let's reflect on some of the essential things you do that you feel add the most value to our strategic competitive advantage.

A. When you think of your precious time and how you spend it, what are the things you do that, in your view, add the most value in terms of strategic competitive advantage? Any examples?

B. In the ideal world, if you were able to recraft what you do to enhance and expand your competitive advantage, what parts of your work would you want to keep doing, let go of, or do new and differently?

- Keep doing?
- Let go of (things that are not really needed)?
- Do new or differently?

Interview Guide (continued)

C. As you reflect on *your* leadership here at our organization, you have probably had ups and downs, peaks and valleys, high points and low points. Please describe *one* achievement or situation that you are proud about—a time when you feel you had a significant impact on strengthening our strategic competitive advantage. What happened? What were the challenges? What was it about you or your leadership style? Lessons learned?

D. Let's think now about *other leaders* that you have heard about or seen here at our organization who do an outstanding job of leading us to achieve sustainable competitive advantage. Is there a story or *example that stands out* for you—something that exemplifies the kind of leadership approaches we should aim for more often? Can you describe the leadership? Insights?

6. Commitments and Practices That Support Our Strategic Advantage

Successful organizations know both how to "preserve the core" of what they do best and how to simplify by letting go of things that are no longer needed. Knowing what to preserve and what to let go of is essential.

A. As it relates to sustaining our strategic competitive advantage, what are the things we do best organizationally—for example, measurement systems, leadership approaches, ways of developing others, accountability systems, ways of delegating and building trust, technologies, etc.—things that should be preserved and strengthened even as we change in the future?

B. Assuming that no organization can do everything well, there is a need to simplify and streamline. There is a need to let go of things that, given precious time constraints, are not needed. Assuming that very few things are sacred, what things (little or large) do you feel we should consider letting go of?

7. *Imagining New Possibilities for Competitive Advantage*

If anything imaginable was possible, if there were no constraints whatsoever, what would our ideal organization look like if it were perfectly aligned to gain and grow rapidly our strategic competitive advantage? Describe, as if you had a magic wand, what we would be doing new, better, or different? Envision it happening. What do you see happening that is new, different, better ?

8. *Three Wishes*

If you had a magic wand and could change or develop anything you wanted about our organization, what three things would you do to heighten its capacity to gain and grow our strategic competitive advantage?

ACTIVITY #2

DISCOVERING THE RESOURCES IN OUR COMMUNITY

Purpose: To welcome and appreciate each other and to learn about the experiences, strengths, hopes, and resources people bring to this summit

Guidelines:

1) Select a discussion leader, timekeeper, recorder, and reporter.
2) Introduce your interview partner by sharing highlights from your interview. Focus on the stories your partner told in questions 1, 2, and 3, and his or her images of the future from question 7. Go around the table. Everyone gets introduced.
3) Listen for patterns and themes as others tell their stories.
4) *Recorder,* make two lists: (1) Themes from the High Point Stories and (2) Visions of the Future for Our Organization.
5) Prepare a two-minute report-out.

ACTIVITY #3

DISCOVERING THE POSITIVE CORE OF OUR STRATEGIC COMPETITIVE ADVANTAGE

Purpose: To share the most powerful stories and discover the forces and factors that energize our strategic competitive advantage when it is at its best

Guidelines:

1) Assign a discussion leader, timekeeper, recorder, and reporter.

2) At your tables, share stories and discoveries from questions 4, 5, and 6.

3) As stories are shared, identify all of the factors—root causes of success—that energize our strategic competitive advantage when it is at its best. Listen for all the best practices, values, commitments, leadership qualities, technologies, training, resources, structures, systems, processes, programs, relationships, and other factors that support success.

4) Create a flipchart with a line down the middle separating two headings ("Stories" and "Root Causes of Success") to capture what you are hearing about what supports our success in terms of strategic competitive advantage.

5) Prepare a three- to five-minute presentation that includes:

   • One exemplar story that powerfully illustrates our organization at its best in terms of strategic competitive advantage

   • Your top five to ten "root causes of success"

ACTIVITY #4

DREAMING BOLD DREAMS

ENVISIONING THE
FUTURE: OUR STRATEGIC
COMPETITIVE ADVANTAGE

Purpose: To imagine a future you want to work toward

Guidelines:

1) Assign a discussion leader, timekeeper, recorder, and reporter.
2) At your tables, share highlights from interview question 7.
3) As a group, put yourselves in the year 2010. Visualize your organization the way you really want it in order to maximize our strategic competitive advantage. Imagine it as if it exists today. What is it like? As you create your image of the future, consider possible reference to some of the following areas:

- The organization's purpose
- Organizational culture, quality of work life
- Nature of leadership—visionary, empowering, servant, and so on
- Nature of external relations between our organization and others
- Nature of internal relationships—with senior leadership, between the "headquarters" and the "field," between colleagues at all levels

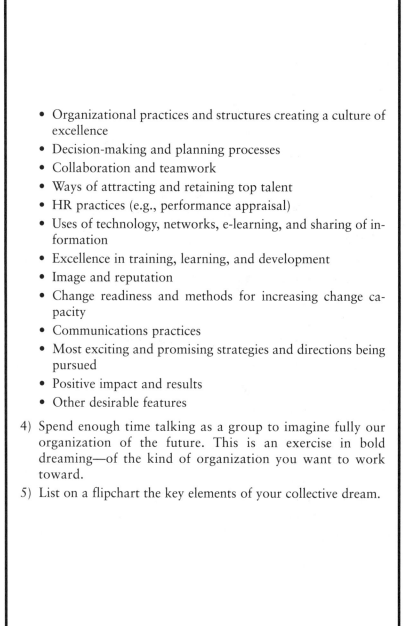

- Organizational practices and structures creating a culture of excellence
- Decision-making and planning processes
- Collaboration and teamwork
- Ways of attracting and retaining top talent
- HR practices (e.g., performance appraisal)
- Uses of technology, networks, e-learning, and sharing of information
- Excellence in training, learning, and development
- Image and reputation
- Change readiness and methods for increasing change capacity
- Communications practices
- Most exciting and promising strategies and directions being pursued
- Positive impact and results
- Other desirable features

4) Spend enough time talking as a group to imagine fully our organization of the future. This is an exercise in bold dreaming—of the kind of organization you want to work toward.

5) List on a flipchart the key elements of your collective dream.

ACTIVITY #5

CRAFTING
DREAM STATEMENTS

Purpose: To create an inspiring statement of your dream that
                 points the way to our strategic competitive advantage

Guidelines:

1) Assign a discussion leader, timekeeper, recorder, and reporter.
2) Capture your group's dream in a 2010 dream statement written on a flipchart page:

"In 2010 our organization is . . ."
[your image of the ideal as if it is happening right now]

Make sure that your statement is:

- **Desired.** Does it reflect what you really want? If you got it, would you want it?
- **Bold, provocative.** Is it a stretch that will attract others?
- **Affirmative.** Is it stated as if it is happening now?
- **Grounded.** Are there examples that illustrate your dream as real possibility?
- **Unconditionally positive.** Will it bring out the best in people, the organization, and the customers it touches?

ACTIVITY #6

CREATIVE PRESENTATION OF YOUR DREAM

Purpose: To bring your dream to life by enacting it before the large group

Guidelines: As a group, choose a creative way to present your collective vision of what the organization would look like if it were perfectly aligned to support our strategic competitive advantage (e.g., a TV special, magazine cover story, skit or drama, "a day in the life," a work of art, other). **Five-minute max. presentation.**

ACTIVITY #7

CREATING A MAP OF HIGH-POTENTIAL DESIGN POSSIBILITIES

Purpose: To create a customized map showing all the organizational elements that will help us gain and grow our strategic competitive advantage

Guidelines:

1) On a flipchart, draw a blank "design possibilities map," using as much of the flipchart as possible. Write in the inner circle of the map something that represents your dream for our organization. (See next page for an example of a blank design possibilities map.)

2) Brainstorm all of the key relationships, both within and outside the organization, that will impact or be impacted by the accomplishment of our dream. Write these in the second circle of the design possibilities map.

3) Brainstorm all the formal organization design elements that will influence the accomplishment of our dreams (see the following list of possibilities). Write these in the outer circle of the design possibilities map.

Examples of Organization Design Elements

- Job descriptions
- Education, training, and leadership development processes
- Policies on social responsibility
- Key organizational strategies
- Compensation and reward systems
- Planning processes
- Communication systems
- Decision-making approaches
- Organization, unit, and individual goals
- Measurement systems
- The performance review process
- Strategies for attracting and retaining talent
- Competencies
- Core business processes and work flows
- Management practices
- The organization's mission, vision, and values statements
- Organizational structures
- Customer relations policies and practices
- Stakeholder relations policies and practices

Example of a Blank Design Possibilities Map

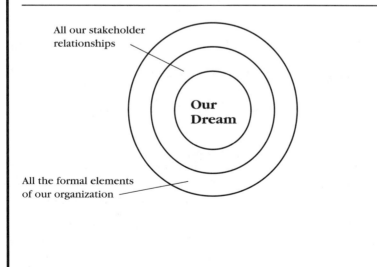

All our stakeholder relationships

Our Dream

All the formal elements of our organization

ACTIVITY #8

PROVOCATIVE PROPOSITIONS

ALIGNING AROUND OUR
STRATEGIC COMPETITIVE ADVANTAGE

Purpose: To design and align our organizational culture,
practices, structures, processes, policies, technologies, and so on to fulfill our dreams and advance
our strategic competitive advantage

Guidelines:

1) Select a discussion leader, timekeeper, recorder, and reporter.

2) At your table, review the following examples and guidelines
for provocative propositions to create a shared sense of what
your end product might look like.

3) Discuss/brainstorm the "ingredients" you would like to see
present in the ideal version of the organizational element that
your group has chosen.

4) As a group, create on your flipchart a first-draft provocative
proposition of your organizational design element—a statement of what it looks like when your design element is operating at its very best.

5) Finalize your proposition by printing a neat version on a single flipchart page.

6) Be prepared to report out **(three minutes max.).**

*"First we shape our structures and then our structures
shape us."*
—Winston Churchill

*"Most people spend 50% of their time not just doing their
job but fighting their own institutional bureaucracies."*
—Dee Hock, founder of Visa International

*"All systems are perfectly designed to achieve the results
they are currently getting."*
—Marv Weisbord, organizational consultant

GUIDELINES FOR WRITING GREAT PROVOCATIVE PROPOSITIONS

Provocative propositions are uplifting statements about how we want our organization to be designed to fulfill our dreams and grow our strategic competitive advantage.

A provocative proposition is a statement that bridges the best of "what is" with your own ideas about "what might be." It is provocative because it stretches the status quo, challenges common routines, and offers new possibilities for positive change.

Your task as a team is to create a provocative proposition about the ideal future of the organizational element (process, structure, strategy, technology, relationship, practice, etc.) you have chosen to focus on. What would your organizational element look like if it were functioning in every way, to maximize the strengths and capitalize on the opportunities discussed during the last two days?

To write a great provocative proposition, ask yourselves these questions:

- Is it provocative? Does it stretch, challenge, or interrupt the status quo?
- Is it grounded? Are there examples that illustrate the ideal as real possibility?
- Is it desired? If it could be fully actualized, would the organization want it? Do you want it as a preferred future?
- Is it stated in affirmative and bold terms?

EXAMPLES OF
PROVOCATIVE PROPOSITIONS

Work-life balance. Our organization is committed to maintaining standards and policies that reflect the work and family life balance of our employees. Alternative work opportunities attract top-quality people from inside and outside the our industry and motivate them in ways that honor employees' individual differences, needs, and aspirations.

Cooperation. We are committed to a high level of cooperation to accomplish our collective goals. We do a variety of things to promote cooperation. First, we function as a consensus-seeking group in which decisions are made through face-to-face dialogue. Second, we encourage experimentation. We maintain an environment in which failure is not punished as much as success is applauded. Third, we structure our organization with a minimum of status differences, hierarchy, and formal boundaries between functions and groups. Fourth, we offer members the opportunity to acquire the interpersonal and group skills that they need to work cooperatively. Fifth, we encourage each member of the organization to cross-train to enhance understanding and interdependence.

ACTIVITY #9

DESTINY

INNOVATION TEAM PLANNING

Purpose: To plan short- and long-term action initiatives to advance our strategic competitive advantage

Guidelines:

1) Select a discussion leader, timekeeper, recorder, and reporter.
2) Questions to consider:

- What is the purpose of this initiative? What do you hope to accomplish?
- What is your vision for the initiative? How can it promote dynamic learning and growth for the organization?
- Who else needs to be involved for it to be successful? How will you invite them?
- What are the actions you need to take to achieve your goal?
- What additional resources will you need? How will you get them?
- Who will do what by when? What is your timeline for completion?
- What is the name of your action initiative?
- Who are your team members and what is their contact information?
- How will you as a team stay in communication with one another?
- When will you meet next?

Use the planning worksheet on the next page if desired.

3) Prepare to report our on your initiative (**three minutes**).

Plan of Action for

_____

Item No.	What Will Be Done	Person Responsible	Completion Date	Help Needed from Specific Others

NOTES

PREFACE

1. A "header" is the unit on the front of a combine that cuts and collects grain. To produce an affordable premium-quality product requires an immense amount of innovation and a high degree of collaboration among all stakeholders—customers (farmers), suppliers, dealers, accounting, marketing, sales, design and engineering, production, distribution, the union, and the managers, supervisors, and wage employees who rely on each other day in and day out to manufacture the product.
2. See Chapter 1 for an explanation of the AI 4-D cycle.
3. Cooperrider, D. L., & Whitney, D. (1999). *Collaborating for change: Appreciative inquiry*. San Francisco: Berrett-Koehler, p. 10.
4. Weisbord, M. R. (1987). *Productive workplaces: Organizing and managing for dignity, meaning, and community*. San Francisco: Jossey-Bass.

CHAPTER 1

1. Schweitzer, A. (1969). *The teaching of reverence for life*. New York: Holt, Rinehart, and Winston.
2. Cooperrider, D. L., & Srivastva, S. (1987). Appreciative inquiry in organizational life. In W. A. Pasmore & R. W. Woodman (Eds.), *Research in organizational change and development* (Vol. I). Greenwich, CT: JAI Press.

3. Marjorie Schiller, Ph.D., Executive Director, Positive Change Corps, can be contacted at margeschiller@yahoo.com or at 781-749-4373.

4. Visit Imagine Chicago's website at www.imaginechicago.org.

5. Visit the Images and Voices of Hope website at www.ivofhope.org

6. Visit the BAWB website at appreciativeinquiry.cwru.edu/bawb.cfm.

7. Visit the website of the Ph.D. program in Organization Development, Benedictine University, at www.ben.edu/academics/cbtpp/od/index.html.

8. Visit the website of the Department of Organizational Behavior, Weatherhead School of Management, Case Western Reserve University at weatherhead.cwru.edu/orbh.

9. Visit the positive psychology website at www.positivepsychology.org.

10. Visit the positive organizational scholarship website at www.bus.umich.edu/positiveorganizationalscholarship.

11. Visit the website of the NTL Institute at www.ntl.org.

12. Visit the website of the Taos Institute at www.taosinstitute.net.

13. Visit the Appreciative Inquiry Consulting website at www.aiconsulting.org.

14. To subscribe to the AI Listserv, go to lists.business.utah.edu/mailman/listinfo/ailist.

15. Visit the *AI Practitioner* at www.aipractitioner.com.

16. Visit the AIR website at www.airmarket.net.

17. Visit the AI Commons website at appreciativeinquiry.cwru.edu.

18. Quinn, R. E. (2000). *Change the world: How ordinary people can achieve extraordinary results.* San Francisco: Jossey-Bass, p. 220.

19. Cooperrider, D. L., & Sekerka, L. E. (2003). Inquiry into the appreciable world: Toward a theory of positive organization change. In K. S. Cameron, J. E. Dutton, & R. E. Quinn (Eds.), *Positive organization scholarship.* San Francisco: Berrett-Koehler.

20. Cooperrider, D. L., & Whitney, D. (1999). *Collaborating for change: Appreciative inquiry.* San Francisco: Berrett-Koehler, p. 10.

21. Whitney, D., & Trosten-Bloom, A. (2003). *The power of appreciative inquiry: A practical guide to positive change.* San Francisco: Berrett-Koehler.

22. David Cooperrider and a group of colleagues at Case Western Reserve University led a one-day appreciative inquiry meeting with 3,000 members of the United Way to clarify the organization's core values. Although this meeting was not a full AI Summit, it was highly successful and offered intriguing possibilities for expanding the size of summits.

23. Provocative propositions are visionary statements written by organizational members to describe the design elements (leadership, purpose, values, strategies, systems, structures, processes, qualities of relationship, etc.) of their ideal organization. These propositions create a bridge between the best of what is and people's highest hopes for the future. They represent a "statement of intent" on the part of the organization. For more on provocative propositions, see Chapter 9, "Design."

24. Rainey, M. A. (2001). An appreciative inquiry into the factors of culture continuity during leadership transition: A case of LeadShare, Canada. In D. L. Cooperrider, P. F. Sorensen, T. F. Yaeger, and D. Whitney (Eds.), *Appreciative inquiry: An emerging direction for organization development* (pp. 205–216). Champaign, IL: Stipes.

25. E-mail from David L. Cooperrider, February 14, 2003.

26. For information about the GEM initiative, contact Ada Jo Mann at aj@aiconsulting.org.

27. Weisbord, M. R., & Janoff, S. (1995). *Future search: An action guide to finding common ground in organizations and communities.* San Francisco: Berrett-Koehler.

28. Fuller, C. S., Griffin, T. J., & Ludema, J. D. (2000). Appreciative future search: Involving the whole system in positive organization change. *Organization Development Journal,* 18(2), 29–41.

29. Johnson, S., & Ludema, J. D. (1997). *Partnering to build and measure organizational capacity: Lessons from NGOs around the world.* Grand Rapids, MI: CRC.

30. Dutton, J. E., & Heaphy, E. D. (2003). Coming to life: The power of high quality connections at work. In K. S. Cameron, J. E. Dutton, & R. E. Quinn (Eds.), *Positive organization scholarship.* San Francisco: Berrett-Koehler.

31. Visit the URI website at www.uri.org.

32. Weisbord, M. R. (1987). *Productive workplaces: Organizing and managing for dignity, meaning, and community.* San Francisco: Jossey-Bass.

33. Emery, M., & Purser, R. E. (1996). *The search conference: A powerful method for planning organizational change and community action.* San Francisco: Jossey-Bass.

34. Weisbord, M. R., & Janoff, S. (1995). *Future search: An action guide to finding common ground in organizations and communities.* San Francisco: Berrett-Koehler.

35. Owen, H. (1997). *Open space technology: A user's guide* (2nd ed.). San Francisco: Berrett-Koehler.

36. Dannemiller Tyson Associates. (2000). *Whole-scale change: Unleashing the magic in organizations.* San Francisco: Berrett-Koehler.

37. Jacobs, R. W. (1994). *Real time strategic change: How to involve an entire organization in fast and far-reaching change.* San Francisco: Berrett-Koehler.

38. Axelrod, R. H. (2000). *Terms of engagement: Changing the ways we change organizations.* San Francisco: Berrett-Koehler.

39. Bunker, B. B., & Alban, B. T. (1997). *Large group interventions: Engaging the whole system for rapid change.* San Francisco: Jossey-Bass.

40. Holman, P., & Devane, T. (Eds.). (1999). *The change handbook: Group methods for shaping the future.* San Francisco: Berrett-Koehler.

41. Hamel, G. (2002). *Leading the revolution: How to thrive in turbulent times by making innovation a way of life.* New York: Plume, p. 16.

42. Adapted from Weisbord, M. R. (1987). *Productive workplaces: Organizing and managing for dignity, meaning, and community.* San Francisco: Jossey-Bass, pp. 261–262.

43. Schindler-Rainman, E., & Lippitt, R. (1980). *Building the collaborative community: Mobilizing citizens for action.* Irvine: University of California. (Available from Energize, 215-438-8342.)

44. For more on social constructionism, see Gergen, K. J. (1999). *An invitation to social construction.* Thousand Oaks, CA: Sage.

45. Ludema, J. D., Cooperrider, D. L., & Barrett, F. J. (2001). Appreciative inquiry: The power of the unconditional positive question. In P. Reason & H. Bradbury (Eds.), *Handbook of action research.* Thousand Oaks, CA: Sage, p. 191.

46. Ludema, J. D., Wilmot, T. B., & Srivastva, S. (1997). Organizational hope: Reaffirming the constructive task of social and organizational inquiry. *Human Relations, 50*(8), 1015–1052.

47. See Snyder, C. R., Rand, K. L., & Sigmon, D. R. (2000). Hope theory: A member of the positive psychology family. In C. R. Snyder & S. J. Lopez (Eds.), *Handbook of positive psychology.* Oxford, UK: Oxford University Press. Also see Luthans, F. (2002). Positive organizational behavior: Developing and managing psychological strengths. *Adacemy of Management Executive, 16*(1), 57–75.

48. See Whitney, D., & Trosten-Bloom, A. (2003). *The power of appreciative inquiry: A practical guide to positive change.* San Francisco: Berrett-Koehler, pp. 197–216.

CHAPTER 2

1. Cheryl Richardson can be contacted at cricha7455@aol.com.

CHAPTER 3

1. Srivastva, S., & Fry, R. E. (Eds.). (1992). *Executive and organizational continuity: Managing the paradoxes of stability and change.* San Francisco: Jossey-Bass.
2. Ford, J. D., & Ford, L. W. (1994). Logics of identity, contradiction, and attraction in change, *Academy of Management Review,* 19(4), 756–785.
3. Fredrickson, B. L. (2003). Positive emotions and upward spirals in organizational settings: Perspectives from the broaden-and-build theory. In K. S. Cameron, J. E. Dutton, & R. E. Quinn (Eds.), *Positive organization scholarship.* San Francisco: Berrett-Koehler.
4. Whitney, D., & Cooperrider, D. L. (2000). The appreciative inquiry summit: An emerging methodology for whole-system positive change. *OD Practitioner,* 31(1), 15.
5. Weisbord, M. R., & Janoff, S. (1995). *Future search: An action guide to finding common ground in organizations and communities.* San Francisco: Berrett-Koehler.
6. Whitney, D., & Cooperrider, D. L. (2000). The appreciative inquiry summit: An emerging methodology for whole-system positive change, *OD Practitioner,* 31(1), 20.
7. Ludema, J. D. (2001). Appreciative storytelling: A narrative approach to organization development and change. In R. Fry, F. Barrett, J. Seiling, & J. D. Whitney (Eds.), *Appreciative inquiry and organizational transformation: Reports from the field.* Westport, CN: Quorum Books.

CHAPTER 4

1. For more information on how to introduce appreciative inquiry, see Whitney, D., & Trosten-Bloom, A. (2003). *The power of appreciative inquiry.* San Francisco: Berrett-Koehler.
2. Some people call this the steering committee, the sponsorship group, or something similar, but the concept is the same. It is a small group of leaders who will provide oversight, direction, and resources for the summit.

3. Hunter Douglas Window Fashions Division's five-year journey with appreciative inquiry is described in detail in Whitney, D., & Trosten-Bloom, A. (2003). *The power of appreciative inquiry.* San Francisco: Berrett-Koehler.

4. Some people call this the core group, the design team, or something similar, but the concept is the same. It is a broadly representative group of people who do everything that is needed to make the summit happen. As described in Chapter 5, this includes defining the summit task, identifying the summit participants, determining the summit format, creating the summit design, preparing the summit communication strategy, and arranging the summit logistics.

CHAPTER 5

1. Whitney, D., & Cooperrider, D. L. (2000). The appreciative inquiry summit: An emerging methodology for whole-system positive change, *OD Practitioner,* 31(1), 16.

2. Cooperrider, D. L., & Whitney, D. (1999). *Appreciative inquiry: A positive revolution in change.* San Francisco: Berrett-Koehler.

3. Mohr, B. J., & Magruder Watkins, J. (2002). *The essentials of appreciative inquiry: A roadmap for creating positive futures.* Williston, VT: Pegasus Communications.

4. Keith Cox can be contacted at keith.cox@tirawaconsulting.com or 333-723-2222.

5. Ravi Pradhan can be contacted at rpkaruna@comcast.net or 410-480-4949.

CHAPTER 6

1. Cooperrider, D. L., Whitney, D., and Stavros, J. (2003). *The appreciative inquiry handbook.* Cleveland: Lakeshore.

2. Whitney, D., Cooperrider, D. L., Trosten-Bloom, A., and Kaplin, B. S. (2000). *Encyclopedia of positive questions* (Vol. 1). Cleveland: Lakeshore.

3. Whitney, D., and Trosten-Bloom, A. (2003) *The power of appreciative inquiry.* San Francisco: Berrett-Koehler.

4. Johansen, R., Martin, A., and Sibbet, D. (1991). *Leading business teams: How teams can use technology and process tools to enhance performance* (Addison-Wesley Series on Organization Development). Reading, MA: Addison-Wesley.

CHAPTER 7

1. Cooperrider, D. L., Stavros, J., & Whitney, D. (2003). *The Appreciative Inquiry Handbook*. Cleveland: Lakeshore Communications.
2. Cooperrider, D. L., Stavros, J., & Whitney, D. (2003). *The Appreciative Inquiry Handbook*. Cleveland: Lakeshore Communications.
3. Ludema, J. D., Cooperrider, D. L., & Barrett, F. J. (2001). Appreciative inquiry: The power of the unconditional positive question. In P. Reason & H. Bradbury (Eds.), *Handbook of action research*. Thousand Oaks, CA: Sage, p. 191.
4. Cooperrider, D. L., & Whitney, D. (1999). *Appreciative inquiry: A positive revolution in change*. San Francisco: Berrett-Koehler.
5. Cooperrider, D. L. (1990). Positive image, positive action: The affirmative basis of organizing. In S. Srivastva & D. L. Cooperrider (Eds.), *Appreciative management and leadership: The power of positive thought and action in organizations*. San Francisco: Jossey-Bass.
6. Ludema, J. D., Cooperrider, D. L., & Barrett, F. J. (2001). Appreciative inquiry: The power of the unconditional positive question. In P. Reason & H. Bradbury (Eds.), *Handbook of action research*. Thousand Oaks, CA: Sage, p. 191.
7. Srivastva, S., & Fry, R. E. (Eds.). (1992). *Executive and organizational continuity: Managing the paradoxes of stability and change*. San Francisco: Jossey-Bass.

CHAPTER 8

1. Polak, F. (1973). *The image of the future* (translated and abridged by E. Boulding). San Francisco: Jossey-Bass.
2. Polak, F. (1973). *The image of the future* (translated and abridged by E. Boulding). San Francisco: Jossey-Bass, p. 19.
3. Schwartz, R. (1986). The internal dialogue: On the asymmetry between positive and negative coping thoughts. *Cognitive Therapy and Research*, 10, 591–605.
4. Weisbord, M. R., & Janoff, S. (1995). *Future search: An action guide to finding common ground in organizations and communities*. San Francisco: Berrett-Koehler, p. 90.
5. Opportunity mapping is a variation on Marv Weisbord and Sandra Janoff's use of the "mind map" methodology. The purpose

of the opportunity map is to identify specific opportunities for organizational change and innovation. It is future focused and designed to generate energy for action. See Weisbord, M. R., & Janoff, S. (1995). *Future search: An action guide to finding common ground in organizations and communities.* San Francisco: Berrett-Koehler, p. 80.

6. Eileen Conlon can be contacted at colon@gwi.net or at (207) 641-8678.

7. See Magruder Watkins, J., & Mohr, B. J. (2001). *Appreciative inquiry: Change at the speed of imagination.* San Francisco: Jossey-Bass/Pfeiffer, p. 135.

CHAPTER 9

1. Ilene Wasserman can be contacted at IWASS@aol.com, 610-667-5305, or www.icwconsulting.com.

2. Boulding, K. E. (1966). *The image.* Ann Arbor: University of Michigan Press, p. 14.

3. Hock, D. (1999). *Birth of the chaordic age.* San Francisco: Berrett-Koehler.

4. Waterman, R. H. (1979). *Structure is not organization.* McKinsey Staff Paper.

5. Galbraith, J. R. (1995). *Designing organizations: An executive briefing on strategy, structure, and process.* San Francisco: Jossey-Bass.

6. Nadler, D. A., & Tushman, M. L. (1997). *Competing by design: The power of organizational architecture.* Oxford, UK: Oxford University Press.

7. Weisbord, M. R. (1978). *Organizational diagnosis: A workbook of theory and practice.* Reading, MA: Addison-Wesley.

8. For more examples and for further instructions on how to write provocative propositions, see Cooperrider, D. L., Stavros, J., & Whitney, D. (2003). *The appreciative inquiry handbook.* Cleveland: Lakeshore Communications.

CHAPTER 10

1. Owen, H. (1997). *Open space technology: A user's guide* (2nd ed.). San Francisco: Berrett-Koehler.

2. Gina Hinrichs coined the phrase "practical tactical planning" to reflect planning that moves you toward your objective (tactical) in

practice, not just on paper (practical). Gina now works as an independent consultant. She can be contacted at hinrichs@geneseo.net.

3. Barrett, F. J. (1998). Creativity and improvisation in jazz and organizations: Implications for organizational learning. *Organization Science*, 9(5), 605–622.

4. Presented at the First International Conference on Appreciative Inquiry, Baltimore, September 2001.

CHAPTER 11

1. Whitney, D. & Trosten-Bloom, A. (2003). *The power of appreciative inquiry: A practical guide to positive change*. San Francisco: Berrett-Koehler, p. 51.

2. Cooperrider, D. L. 1990. Positive image, positive action: The affirmative basis of organizing. In S. Srivastva & D. L. Cooperrider (Eds.), *Appreciative management and leadership: The power of positive thought and action in organizations* San Francisco: Jossey-Bass.

3. Gergen, K. J. (1999). *An invitation to social construction*. Thousand Oaks, CA: Sage.

4. von Bertalanffy, L. (1956). *General systems theory. General Systems: Yearbook of the Society for the Advancement of General Systems Theory*, 1, 1–10.

5. Sampson, C., Abu-Nimer, M., Liebler, C. & Whitney, D. (Eds.). (2003). *Positive approaches to peacebuilding: A resource for innovators*. Washington, D.C.: Post Publications.

CHAPTER 12

1. Bilamoria, D., & Cooperrider, D. L. (1991). *The Romanian orphans program: Challenges and responses of the collaborative alliance*. Paper presented at the annual conference of the Association for Research on Non-Profit Organizations and Voluntary Action, Chicago.

2. Mike Mantel can be contacted at mmantel@worldvision.org or at (219) 988-4622.

3. For more on second- and third-wave AI at World Vision, see Mantel, M. J., & Ludema, J. D. (2000). From local conversations to global change: Experiencing the worldwide ripple effect of Appreciative Inquiry. *Organization Development Journal*, 18(2), 42–53. Republished in Cooperrider, D. L., Sorensen, P. F.,

Whitney, D., & Yaeger, T. F. (Eds.). (2002). *Appreciative inquiry: Rethinking human organization toward a positive theory of change.* Champaign, IL: Stipes.

CHAPTER 13

1. Bob Roberts can be contacted at roberts.bob@attbi.com
2. Barrett, F. J. (1995). Creating appreciative learning cultures. *Organizational Dynamics, 24*(1), 36–49.
3. Drucker, P. F. (2002). *The effective executive.* New York: Harper Business.
4. Schiller, M. (2001). The road to appreciative leadership. In M. Schiller, B. Mah Holland, & D. Riley (Eds.), *Appreciative leaders.* Taos, NM: Taos Institute.
5. Whitney, D., & Trosten-Bloom, A. *Theory I: The gifts of appreciative leadership.* Unpublished manuscript. (For more information the authors can be reached at www.positivechange.org.)
6. McGregor, D. (1961). *The human side of enterprise.* New York: McGraw-Hill.
7. Ouchi, W. G. (1981). *Theory Z: How American management can meet the Japanese challenge.* Reading, MA: Addison-Wesley.
8. Cooperrider, D. L. (2001). Foreword. In M. Schiller, B. Mah Holland, & D. Riley (Eds.), *Appreciative leaders* (pp. x–xii). Taos, NM: Taos Institute.
9. Visit the BAWB website at appreciativeinquiry.cwru.edu/bawb.cfm.
10. BAWB Interview Guide, 2003, obtainable on the BAWB website.

OTHER BOOKS ON APPRECIATIVE INQUIRY BY THE AUTHORS

Partnering to Build and Measure Organizational Capacity: Lessons from NGOs Around the World.
Scott Johnson and James D. Ludema
CRC Publications, 1997

The Power of Appreciative Inquiry: A Practical Guide to Positive Change
Diana Whitney and Amanda Trosten-Bloom
Berrett-Koehler, 2003

Appreciative Inquiry: A Positive Revolution in Change
David L. Cooperrider and Diana Whitney
Berrett-Koehler, 1999 (booklet)

Appreciative Inquiry Handbook
David L. Cooperrider, Jackie Stavros, and Diana Whitney
Lakeshore Communications, 2003 (book and CD)

Encyclopedia of Positive Questions, Volume One
Diana Whitney, David Cooperrider, Amanda Trosten-Bloom, and Brian Kaplin
Lakeshore Communications, 2002

Appreciative Inquiry and Organizational Transformation: Reports from the Field
Ronald Fry, Frank Barrett, Jane Seiling, and Diana Whitney (Eds.)
Quorum Books, 2002

Appreciative Inquiry: An Emerging Direction for Organization Development
David L. Cooperrider, Peter F. Sorensen, Therese F. Yaeger, and Diana Whitney (Eds.)
Stipes, 2001

Appreciative Inquiry: Rethinking Human Organization Towards a Positive
Theory of Change
David L. Cooperrider, Peter F. Sorensen, Therese F.
Yaeger, and Diana Whitney (Eds.)
Stipes, 2000

Appreciative Inquiry: Change at the Speed of Imagination
Jane Magruder Watkins and Bernard J. Mohr
Jossey-Bass Pfeiffer, 2001

The Essentials of Appreciative Inquiry: A Roadmap for Creating Positive Futures
Bernard J. Mohr and Jane Magruder Watkins
Pegasus Communications, 2002

INDEX

ABOUT THE AUTHORS

James D. Ludema is an associate professor in the Ph.D. program in Organization Development at Benedictine University, a principal in the Corporation for Positive Change, and a founding owner of Appreciative Inquiry Consulting, a global firm that includes the world's leading thinkers and practitioners of appreciative inquiry. Previously, Jim was senior lecturer and executive director of the Social Innovations in Global Management (SIGMA) program at the Weatherhead School of Management, Case Western Reserve University.

For more than a decade, Jim has been an innovator and thought leader in the field of appreciative inquiry, teaching the methodology in the doctoral program at Benedictine University, offering public workshops and keynote addresses, and serving as a lead organizer of the first (2001) and second (2004) international conferences on AI. He has written numerous articles on AI, including "Appreciative Inquiry: The Power of the Unconditional Positive Question" (with David Cooperrider and Frank Barrett) and "Appreciative Future Search: Involving the Whole System in Positive Organization Change" (with Connie Fuller and Tom Griffin).

Jim is an internationally recognized organizational consultant. His practice focuses on the use of appreciative inquiry for large-scale corporate change initiatives, including strategy development, leadership development, core business redesign, culture change, customer service, and mergers and acquisitions. He has worked in North America, Europe, Asia, Africa, and Latin America with organizations in the corporate, nonprofit, and government sectors, including BP, McDonald's, John Deere, Ameritech, U.S. Cellular, Northern Telecom, Square D Company, Essef Corporation, Bell & Howell, Kaiser Permanente, World Vision, the City of Minneapolis, and many local and international nongovernmental organizations (NGOs).

Jim lives in Geneva, Illinois. He can be reached at jludema@ben.edu.

 **Diana Whitney** is president of the Corporation for Positive Change and a Distinguished Consulting Faculty at Saybrook Graduate School and Research Center. She is a founder and director of the Taos Institute, a founder of Appreciative Inquiry Consulting, and a founding consultant to the United Religions Initiative.

Diana is an internationally recognized consultant, keynote speaker, and thought leader on subjects related to appreciative inquiry, positive change, appreciative leadership, and spirituality at work. Her consulting practice focuses on the use of appreciative inquiry for corporate culture change, strategic planning, large-scale organization transformation, mergers, alliance and partnership building, leadership development, and service excellence. She teaches, speaks, and consults throughout the Americas, Europe, and Asia.

She has authored and edited nine books on appreciative inquiry, including the highly acclaimed guide *The Power of Appreciative Inquiry,* with Amanda Trosten-Bloom, and the *Appreciative Inquiry Handbook,* with David Cooperrider and Jackie Stavros.

Diana lives in Taos, New Mexico. She can be reached at diana@positivechange.org.

 **Bernard J. Mohr** is president/managing partner of the Synapse Group, Inc. (an international consultancy founded in 1979 , based in Portland, Maine) and a founding partner of Appreciative Inquiry Consulting, LLC.

Bernard's key interest lies at the intersection of society and the workplace. As the result of a conviction that the nature of our society is strongly influenced by the nature of our organizations, he is committed to organizational arrangements that not only enable mission effectiveness and economic sustainability but also foster meaning, community, and dignity—by involving the people actually doing the work in the design of their roles, goals, and structures. He has thirty-five years of experience supporting global corporations, government agencies, schools, and not-for-profits with accelerated processes for business transformation, evaluation, organization design, knowledge management, and strategic planning—through the integration of Socio-Technical Systems theory, Open Space Technology, and other large-scale processes with appreciative inquiry.

He is co-author (with Jane Watkins) of *Appreciative Inquiry: Change at the Speed of Imagination* (Jossey-Bass, 2001) and *Essentials of Appreciative Inquiry* (Pegasus Communications, 2002) and of numerous articles, such as "Appreciative Inquiry: Igniting Transformative Dialogue" (in *The Systems Thinker,* February 2001).

An international practitioner, author, and pioneer in appreciative inquiry, he developed North America's first Advanced Workshop in Appreciative Inquiry and the first Field Practicum in Appreciative Inquiry, and he originated the highly successful First International Conference on Appreciative Inquiry. A longtime member of the Socio-Technical Systems Roundtable, he is also an invited associate of the Taos Institute and a senior faculty member at NTL Institute (where for many years he served as senior faculty on the staff of the Facilitating and Managing Complex Systems Change program).

He can be reached at BernardJMohr@aiConsulting.com.

 **Thomas J. Griffin** is Director of Organization & Leadership Development for U.S. Cellular, currently the eighth largest wireless telecommunications company in the United States, headquartered in Chicago. Tom has previously held a variety of organization and leadership development positions for SBC/Ameritech and Texas Instruments. He has extensive experience in organization and leadership development, quality improvement, and adult learning. He is a member of the OD Network, the OD Institute, and the Academy of Management.

Tom's areas of interest and expertise include appreciative inquiry, large-group intervention methodology, whole systems change, group dynamics, leadership development, and quality improvement.

His publications include "Appreciative Future Search: Involving the Whole System in Positive Organization Change" (*Organization Development Journal*, 2000) and "Appreciative Leaders: In the Eye of the Beholder" (interview with Jim "Gus" Gustafson, vice president and general manager, MECHdata, Inc.) (available at taosinstitute.net).

Tom lives in Algonquin, Illinois, with his wife, Mary. He can be reached at tom.griffin@uscellular.com.

Berrett-Koehler Publishers

Berrett-Koehler is an independent publisher of books and other publications at the leading edge of new thinking and innovative practice on work, business, management, leadership, stewardship, career development, human resources, entrepreneurship, and global sustainability.

Since the company's founding in 1992, we have been committed to creating a world that works for all by publishing books that help us to integrate our values with our work and work lives, and to create more humane and effective organizations.

We have chosen to focus on the areas of work, business, and organizations, because these are central elements in many people's lives today. Furthermore, the work world is going through tumultuous changes, from the decline of job security to the rise of new structures for organizing people and work. We believe that change is needed at all levels—individual, organizational, community, and global—and our publications address each of these levels.

To find out about our new books,
special offers,
free excerpts,
and much more,
subscribe to our free monthly eNewsletter at

www.bkconnection.com

Please see next pages for other books
from Berrett-Koehler Publishers

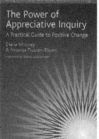

The Power of Appreciative Inquiry

Diana Whitney and Amanda Trosten-Bloom

The Power of Appreciative Inquiry is a comprehensive and practical guide to using Appreciative Inquiry for strategic large-scale change. Written by pioneers in the field, the book provides detailed examples along with practical guidance for using AI in an organizational setting.

Paperback original, 264 Pages
ISBN 1-57675-226-7 • Item #52267-415 $27.95

Change Is Everybody's Business

Pat McLagan

Change Is Everybody's Business challenges readers to realize the power they have to make things happen—to support, stymie, or redirect change. Pat McLagan draws on her 30 years of experience consulting on change projects worldwide to outline the beliefs, character traits, and actions that will enable anyone to welcome change and take advantage of it rather than fear and resist it. She shows readers precisely what they need to know to become more conscious participants in determining their own destiny at work—and in life.

Paperback original • ISBN 1-57675-190-2 • Item #51902-415 $16.95

Open Space Technology
A User's Guide

Harrison Owen

Open Space Technology: A User's Guide is just what the name implies: a hands-on, detailed description of facilitating Open Space Technology—a remarkably successful meeting strategy that has been used all over the world. OST enables self-organizing groups of all sizes to deal with hugely complex issues in a very short period of time. This practical, step-by-step user's guide—written by the originator of the method—details what needs to be done before, during, and after an Open Space event.

Hardcover, 175 pages • ISBN 1-57675-024-8
Item #50248-415 $24.95

Berrett-Koehler Publishers
PO Box 565, Williston, VT 05495-9900
Call toll-free! **800-929-2929** 7 am-9 pm Eastern Standard Time
Or fax your order to 802-864-7627
For fastest service order online: **www.bkconnection.com**

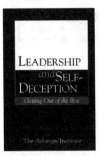

Leadership and Self-Deception
Getting Out of the Box

The Arbinger Institute

Leadership and Self-Deception reveals that there are only two ways for leaders to be: the source of leadership problems or the source of leadership success. The authors identify self-deception as the underlying cause of leadership failure, and show how any leader become a consistent catalyst of success.

Hardcover, 175 pages • 1-57675-094-9 • Item #50949-415 $22.00
Paperback • 1-57675-174-0 • Item #51740-415 $14.95

Empowerment Takes More Than a Minute
Second Edition

Ken Blanchard, John Carlos, and Alan Randolph

Empowerment Takes More Than a Minute shows managers how to achieve true, lasting results in their organizations. The authors explain how to empower the workforce by moving from a command-and-control mindset to a supportive, responsibility-centered environment in which all employees have the opportunity and responsibility to do their best.

Paperback, 145 pages • ISBN 1-57675-153-8
Item #51538-415 $12.95

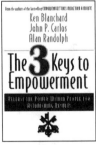

The 3 Keys to Empowerment
Release the Power Within People for Astonishing Results

Ken Blanchard, John Carlos, and Alan Randolph

This user-friendly action guide examines and expands on the three keys to empowerment originally presented in *Empowerment Takes More Than a Minute*—sharing information with everyone, creating autonomy through boundaries, and replacing the hierarchy with teams. It provides thought-provoking questions, clear advice, effective activities, and action tools for creating a culture of empowerment.

Paperback, 289 pages • ISBN 1-57675-160-0
Item #51600-415 $12.95
Hardcover • ISBN 1-57675-060-4 • Item #50604-415 $20.00

Berrett-Koehler Publishers
PO Box 565, Williston, VT 05495-9900
Call toll-free! **800-929-2929** 7 am-9 pm Eastern Standard Time
Or fax your order to 802-864-7627
For fastest service order online: **www.bkconnection.com**